Romanticism and Film

Franz Liszt and Audio-Visual Explanation

Will Kitchen

BLOOMSBURY ACADEMIC
NEW YORK • LONDON • OXFORD • NEW DELHI • SYDNEY

BLOOMSBURY ACADEMIC
Bloomsbury Publishing Inc
1385 Broadway, New York, NY 10018, USA
29 Earlsfort Terrace, Dublin 2, Ireland

BLOOMSBURY, BLOOMSBURY ACADEMIC and the Diana logo
are trademarks of Bloomsbury Publishing Plc

First published in the United States of America 2021
This paperback edition published in 2022

Copyright © Will Kitchen, 2021

Cover design by Eleanor Rose

Cover image: Wanderer above the Sea of Fog, circa 1817. Found in the
Collection of Kunsthalle, Hamburg. Artist Friedrich, Caspar David (1774–1840).
Photo © Fine Art Images / Heritage Images / Getty Images

All rights reserved. No part of this publication may be reproduced or
transmitted in any form or by any means, electronic or mechanical,
including photocopying, recording, or any information storage or retrieval
system, without prior permission in writing from the publishers.

Bloomsbury Publishing Inc does not have any control over, or responsibility for,
any third-party websites referred to or in this book. All internet addresses given
in this book were correct at the time of going to press. The author and publisher
regret any inconvenience caused if addresses have changed or sites have ceased
to exist, but can accept no responsibility for any such changes.

Library of Congress Cataloging-in-Publication Data

Names: Kitchen, Will, author.
Title: Romanticism and film: Franz Liszt and audio-visual explanation / Will Kitchen.
Description: New York: Bloomsbury Academic, 2020. |
Includes bibliographical references and index.
Identifiers: LCCN 2020029918 (print) | LCCN 2020029919 (ebook) |
ISBN 9781501361364 (hardback) | ISBN 9781501370953 (paperback) |
ISBN 9781501361357 (epub) | ISBN 9781501361340 (pdf)
Subjects: LCSH: Liszt, Franz, 1811-1886–Criticism and interpretation. |
Motion pictures–Aesthetics. | Motion pictures and music. | Romanticism.
Classification: LCC ML410.L7 K55 2020 (print) | LCC ML410.L7 (ebook) | DDC 780.92–dc23
LC record available at https://lccn.loc.gov/2020029918
LC ebook record available at https://lccn.loc.gov/2020029919

ISBN: HB: 978-1-5013-6136-4
PB: 978-1-5013-7095-3
ePDF: 978-1-5013-6134-0
eBook: 978-1-5013-6135-7

Typeset by Deanta Global Publishing Services, Chennai, India

To find out more about our authors and books visit www.bloomsbury.com
and sign up for our newsletters.

Contents

List of illustrations	vi
Introduction	1
1 Culture and transcendence: Three explanations of Romanticism	21
2 The archaeology of film music: Wagner, Liszt and the symphonic poem	41
3 Audio-visual explanations of Franz Liszt and his music: Cultural image and schematic types	79
4 'Nothing untrue, simply convenient': *Song Without End* (1960) and the Hollywood composer biopic	123
5 'Piss off, Brahms!': *Lisztomania* (1975) and Ken Russell in 1975	165
Conclusion	215
Appendix A: Music and language	223
Appendix B: Wagnerian terminology and film	229
Bibliography	234
Index	248

Illustrations

1	*Die Hunnenschlacht* by Wilhelm von Kaulbach (1850)	74
2	*The Black Cat* (1934)	95
3	*Lola Montès* (1955)	99
4	*A Song to Remember* (1945)	108
5	*Lisztomania* (1975)	115
6	*The Mephisto Waltz* (1971)	120
7	*Song Without End* (1960)	125
8	*Song Without End* (1960)	143
9	*Song Without End* (1960)	148
10	*Song Without End* (1960)	153
11	*Lisztomania* (1975)	167
12	*Tommy* (1975)	180
13	*Tommy* (1975)	182
14	*Tommy* (1975)	191
15	*Lisztomania* (1975)	194
16	*Lisztomania* (1975)	199
17	*Lisztomania* (1975)	201
18	*Lisztomania* (1975)	202

Introduction

Undoubtedly there is something of the dream factory in the world of Romantic virtuosity.

—Jim Samson[1]

Romanticism and audio-visual explanation

In 1835, Heinrich Heine, the Romantic poet who coined the term 'Lisztomania', wrote a prose fragment called 'Florentine Nights'. The protagonist relates an encounter with the virtuoso Niccolò Paganini (1782–1840), who appears, in the subjective view of the narrator, to alter in appearance while performing. His costume changes, his surroundings blur and shift, and the entire field of vision is restructured according to changes in the musical performance.[2] This episode, based on Heine's own experiences, articulates several important trends in Romantic aesthetics: the increasing importance of the visual in musical experience – music being received, contextualized and given meaning by a visual dimension – the subsequent impact on debates surrounding artistic meaning; and the cultural functions of important schematic concepts such as virtuosity, individuality and genius.

The visualizing potential of Romantic music allows Heine to describe Paganini as being like a 'dog' one moment and an 'automaton' the next; he becomes a 'vampire', a 'gladiator', a 'monk', and the conjuror of a musical 'magic-lantern play'.[3] Heine employs a multitude of such images and ideas to explain the fascinating virtuoso to the reader. A central idea is explained, or 'made sense' of, by the evocation of secondary ideas which create complex chains of signification. The author also employs such ideas to make sense of this Romantic

---

[1] Jim Samson, *Virtuosity and the Musical Work: The Transcendental Studies of Liszt* (Cambridge: Cambridge University Press, 2003), 78.
[2] Heinrich Heine, 'Florentine Nights', 1835, in *The Prose Writings of Heinrich Heine*, 179–242 (London: Walter Scott, 1887).
[3] Heine, 'Florentine Nights', 201–5.

phenomenon in a way that, consequent with the subject itself, reconciles contradiction and invites a kind of intuitive understanding. The narrator finds the experience overwhelming, transcending the distinction between musical sound and visual impression, giving both the experience and the genius at its centre a profound sense of value: 'the melody . . . extended into a colossal space which, not the bodily eye, but only the eye of the spirit could seize'.[4] The liminality of this musical experience is focused on the performer's body itself – a location of irreconcilable desire and difference: 'He was the man-planet about which the universe moved'.[5] There is something in this cinematic concept of audio-visual explanation – 'cinematic' both in the sense of combining sound with vision and in the seemingly immediate and intuitive clarity of understanding common to much film experience – which may be central to Romanticism itself.

This book unites and examines the themes identified in Heine's account: from the relationship between sound and vision which forms a key connection between Romantic aesthetics and film, through the representational functions of concepts such as genius and virtuosity, to the idea of intuitive explanatory processes. The Hungarian pianist and composer Franz Liszt (1811–86) will be our guiding object of study. An immediate successor to Paganini's cultural iconography, Liszt's name accommodates not only his music, along with what we will call his 'cultural image', but also the Romantic era he well represents in European aesthetic philosophy.

Of course, each of these elements has a particular relationship with film. The key connection between them is illustrated by Heine's representation of Paganini, demonstrating the complex processes of audio-visual explanation which developed during Romanticism and can still illuminate how we understand film experience today. To state neatly the logic that relates these subjects: where Romantic music can encourage intuitive visual understanding of historical musical experience, and films can encourage intuitive musical understanding of visual historical experience, film music discourse, in turn, can encourage intuitive historical understanding of musical visual experience. Using Franz Liszt as our guide, we will examine the logic(s) of this overarching Romantic intuitive explanatory principle – the audio-visual ways that things come to make sense, and the forces that guide that process.

---

[4] Heine, 'Florentine Nights', 206–7.
[5] Heine, 'Florentine Nights', 207.

The significance of Romanticism and Franz Liszt to Film Studies

Like Film Studies as a whole, film music studies underwent a revisionist programme following the high tide of theory in the 1970s. The impact of those metacritical debates that came in the wake of poststructuralism, cultural studies and cognitive psychology has been summarized by Rick Altman:

> Today we are beginning to understand the need for nothing less than an entire redefinition of film history, based on new objects and new projects. The only way to wage such a revolution is to inspect the widest possible range of objects, with a willingness to question their very names and identities, along with the contexts within which we have learned to understand them.[6]

For Altman, the twenty-first-century boom in film sound studies specifically does not possess a sufficiently theorized foundation, one that relates this field to a wider history of music and vision.[7] The only way to progress in meaningful ways, whether studying film sound, history or wider theoretical matters, has been to continue the process of challenging received opinions. This book will undertake a fragment of that revisionism by exploring the discursive roots of the complex historical relationship between sound and vision that lies at the core of film itself. The nominally 'Romantic' aspect of this privileged relationship is well exemplified by the common belief that the 'music dramas' of the German composer Richard Wagner (1813–83) were in some sense a proto-cinematic phenomenon. This discursive comparison between Wagner and cinema comprises one of the most significant points of contact between Romanticism and film, although it is far from exhaustive.

As a historical phenomenon, film emerged during the onset of what is often termed 'Modernism' in Western art, the technological and aesthetic development of cinema itself being one of the most significant contributors to that development. The emergent series of artists, works, styles and themes that are often subsumed under the idea of artistic modernism at the beginning of the twentieth century are commonly understood to be the successors of an earlier series, one that can be said to comprise 'Romanticism'. (Exactly what we mean by this term will be continually developed throughout this book.) This idea raises

---

[6] Rick Altman, *Silent Film Sound* (New York: Columbia University Press, 2004), 5.
[7] Altman, *Silent Film Sound*, 8.

the complex issue of whether film has its 'roots' in Romanticism, and what those roots might be.

As suggested, one methodological approach to this issue examines cinema's heritage in earlier practices of sensory illusion – a concept founded upon a historical dialectic of scientific rationalism and mystical sensationalism corresponding not only with the classical theoretical division between photographic revelation and entertaining attraction (exemplified by the approaches to film adopted by Siegfried Kracauer and Tom Gunning) but also with the more formal distinction between related Enlightenment and Romantic doctrines. Tom Gunning, for his part, hypothesized an expansive pre-history of cinema along these lines in his essay 'Flickers' (2004).[8] Relevant and important as these issues are, such approaches have the potential to overlook (as Gunning does) the specificity of the important contributions made to these debates by Romanticism in particular. Nevertheless, the relationship between Romanticism and film must be sought by exploring the broader philosophical conflicts between clarity and obscurity, intuitive (irrational) audio-visual understanding and (rational) explanation, freedom and ideology, and light and darkness.

The international institutionalization of cinema as an art form, entertainment industry, and object of criticism and analysis during the early decades of the twentieth century created various requirements and opportunities to situate, contextualize and value this development as a historical phenomenon. Cinema was confronted with various accusations of possessing a low cultural status. This was felt, for example, in film's supposed lack of autonomous aesthetic value, its 'merely' mechanical reproduction of reality, providing 'mere' entertainment for mass audiences, possessing a parasitic power to leech-off other established art forms such as literature and theatre, and, as Gunning notes, sometimes causing moral social outcries which raised the question of whether the medium of film itself was not 'evil' in some sense.[9]

To combat such claims, the champions of film needed, among other things, a respectable historical precedent. Filmmakers, theorists and various other contributors to filmic discourse pragmatically appropriated existing discursive objects to contextualize film as a respectable cultural phenomenon, one that did not supposedly appropriate from and degrade older forms of art, but rather had

---

[8] Tom Gunning, 'Flickers: On Cinema's Power for Evil', in *Bad: Infamy, Darkness, Evil, and Slime on Screen*, ed. Murray Pomerance, 21–37 (Albany: State University of New York Press, 2004).

[9] Gunning, 'Flickers', 22–4.

the potential to surpass or fulfil them in some way. Richard Wagner was one obvious choice to fill this role, as exemplified by the rhetoric of Sergei Eisenstein:

> The cinema is that genuine and ultimate synthesis of all artistic manifestations that fell to pieces after the peak of Greek culture, which Diderot sought vainly in opera, Wagner in music-drama, Scriabin in his color-concerti, and so on.[10]

But as Gunning and Eisenstein demonstrate, Wagner's music dramas themselves form only a part of a longer tradition of 'multimedia ambition' within Western aesthetics. This tradition has particular relevance to Romanticism, if we take this term to imply a certain combination of ideas about form, content, genius and society. It is this combination that will serve as our departure point, and we will explore the implications which follow from maintaining an awareness of film's historical position as a possible 'consequence' of Romantic aesthetics. This position follows from the recent film-related writings of the French philosopher Jacques Rancière, who, in works such as *Film Fables* (2001), expanded the terrain of film theory across a wider domain of nineteenth-century European philosophy.[11] We can now investigate the relationship between Romanticism and film from a perspective which, although still recognizing the key relevance of Wagner, adopts a more inclusive attitude and rigorous fidelity to the complex philosophical content of Romanticism as a discursive construct today. Despite often being contextualized as the quintessential form of artistic modernity, the dream realized by cinema is perhaps, in a very meaningful sense, Romantic.

In order to explore this subject and save our analysis from the potential for complete philosophical abstraction (for this is a distinct possibility when dealing with Romanticism), we need to select a theme – one which will enable us to progress from theoretical and historical discussions to the concrete textual analysis of films from a variety of production and reception contexts. Rhetorically speaking, we need a Romantic 'hero' to guide us.

Richard Wagner has worked very well in the past. There is no doubt that the Wagner comparison has at least been of vital significance to the development of cinema's critical discourse, even if it does not satisfy as an explanatory principle for the numerous and diverse practices of film and film music today. In recent years, a number of critics have rejected the totalizing conclusions drawn from the simple equation of Wagner's *Gesamtkunstwerk* ('total work of art') and

---

[10] Sergei Eisenstein, 'Achievement', 1939, in *Film Form: Essays in Film Theory*, 179–94 (San Diego, New York and London: Harcourt, Inc., 1949), 181.
[11] Jacques Rancière, *Film Fables*, 2001 (London: Bloomsbury, 2016), 6, 9–11.

the synchronized recorded soundtrack.[12] Given the scholarly expansion over the previous decades into areas that advance well beyond the simple equation of classical Hollywood style and the typical nineteenth-century Romantic melodrama or opera, it is worth asking the following: What can we hope to learn now by introducing another Romantic figure, Franz Liszt, as an alternative focus of theoretical activity? More explicitly, how can Liszt enrich our understanding of the broader connection between Romanticism and film beyond a musical context? And why, of all Romantic individuals, should we choose Liszt?

First, in recent years, Liszt studies has transformed into a rich and varied academic field. The cultural legacy of Wagner has long dominated film music history at Liszt's expense. In the early twentieth century, when commentators such as Theodor Adorno, Samuel 'Roxy' Rothapfel and Max Steiner were establishing Wagner's position as the 'father' of film music (see Chapter 2), Liszt would have to wait several decades until a revival of scholarly attention brought a fuller understanding of his significance to music history. Only later, with the work of Alan Walker in the 1980s, and the bicentenary of Liszt's birth in 2011, would Liszt's name find regular inclusion in studies addressing the cultural avant-garde. In 2009, Liszt scholar Michael Saffle wrote: 'Liszt is at long last coming into his own [as a subject of serious and varied academic study] . . . this process has been a lengthy and arduous one, and it is not over yet'.[13] Liszt is now credited with anticipating many developments more usually associated with the New Viennese School, Bartók, Scriabin, Ravel and Debussy, in addition to a previously underestimated influence on Wagner himself. It took a long time for the wider academic community to acknowledge the conclusion reached long ago by composers such as Copland, Bartók and Ravel: that Liszt, for all his scholarly disreputability, was 'the father of modern music'.[14]

Furthermore, by looking beyond Wagner while maintaining a focus on nineteenth-century European music, we can use Liszt to help us discern that broader relevance for Romantic aesthetics suggested by Rancière. As Lawrence Kramer notes, scholars are increasingly acknowledging that Liszt 'seems to have forced on his era the general question of the relationship of visuality to music'.[15]

---

[12] See Jeongwon Joe, 'Introduction: Why Wagner and Cinema? Tolkien was Wrong', in *Wagner and Cinema*, ed. Jeongwon Joe and Sander L. Gilman, 3–8 (Bloomington and Indianapolis: Indiana University Press, 2010).

[13] Michael Saffle, *Franz Liszt: A Research and Information Guide*, 3rd edn (New York and London: Routledge, 2009), 9.

[14] Cited in Alan Walker, *Franz Liszt: The Final Years, 1861–1886* (London: Faber and Faber, 1997), 17.

[15] Lawrence Kramer, *Musical Meaning: Toward a Critical History* (Berkeley: University of California Press, 2002), 74.

Liszt's innovative and challenging compositions, scandalous and magnetic public persona, transcendental virtuoso performance practices, inclusive European cosmopolitanism and progressive philosophical world view combine to make him one of the most fascinating, multifaceted and properly 'Romantic' of all historical individuals. The nineteenth-century piano – that musical instrument he made his own and pushed to the limits of its potential – becomes a symbol of his liminal cultural identity. It is uniquely able to encourage the problematizing of a host of symbolic boundaries, each with profound aesthetic and political implications, separating public and private, original and reproduction, past and present, and sound and vision. Between each of these conceptual dualities lies both Liszt and film itself.

If the concept of pre-cinema encompasses multimedia synthesis or audio-vision in its historical development as an aesthetic category, then it is time to seriously consider the role played by Romantic individuals other than Wagner in shaping the world into which film emerged at the end of the nineteenth century.

Explanation and archaeological analysis

One of the central premises of this book is that a particular tendency in Romantic aesthetics, one which can be identified as 'audio-visual explanation', presents a new discursive means of understanding film itself. One significant perspective that developed within twentieth-century philosophy – itself as much a product of Romanticism as it was a reaction against it – turned analysis away from attempts to determine the fidelity of any representation to 'truth' and towards questioning the relations between representations, the ways they are constituted, the functions they perform, and the uses to which they are they put. This shift of interest away from positivism combined with the rise of ideological criticism to stress the currency of a new kind of question: How and why are things explained to people in the ways that they are?

Ironically, it is worth explaining here the intended meaning of 'explanation', and in such a way that it subsumes audio-visual phenomena. We must not only possess a methodology which will allow us to understand how films 'explain' Liszt to us using Romanticism and vice versa but also understand how audio-visual explanation can, of itself, be called a Romantic phenomenon. To prepare the ground for this understanding, the following explanation of explanation combines insights provided by the little-known cultural theorist Morse Peckham, terminology associated with the work of Pierre Bourdieu, such as 'field' and 'habitus', and the theory of 'critical rationalism' developed by Karl Popper and Hans Albert.[16]

It seems clear that the subjective processes of understanding or making sense of any phenomena (defined in accordance with constructivist schematic cognition, as outlined in Chapter 3) form a complex field of localized power relations between individuals. These relations are determined by an ultimately irreducible dialogue between (a) rules that regulate appropriate actions and participants within a given field, (b) rules that regulate appropriate transference of actions and participants between fields, and (c) an individual participant's competency in recognizing and negotiating the identities and rules of such fields in relation to personal disposition. Such relations, determined through this dialogue between field, doxa and habitus, can form *explanations* – interpersonal impositions upon the processes of making sense.

Explanation is here understood not as a linguistic frame for the scientific statement of causation, but rather as an ideological social process that attempts to organize the relationship between a subject and an *explicandum* – a thing that is explained. The explicandum is not the explanation itself, but rather is the text, statement, audio-visual representation or non-textual behavioural action which becomes the object negotiated by the hermeneutic circle (see Chapter 3). An explanation might also be characterized as an intervention in the hermeneutic circle from 'outside', or a kind of corrective determined by interpersonal power relations. When Heine describes Paganini as being like a robot or an animal, he is, quite literally, 'explaining' Paganini to the reader – the reader finds that Heine has guided how they now understand what they recognize to be the subject of this statement, resulting from both parties making judgements regarding the meaning, intelligibility and acceptability of such concrete statements within a particular (in this case) literary context.

There are several more aspects to consider here. Although this social approach to the concept of explanation is largely distinct from theories of scientific causal explanation, one idea raised by Carl Hempel may be useful to retain. In 'Studies in the Logic of Explanation' (1948), Hempel and his co-author

---

[16] Morse Peckham, *Explanation and Power: The Control of Human Behavior* (New York: The Seabury Press, 1979). 'Habitus' names an embodied 'disposition' which enables individual social practice within intersecting 'fields' of cultural activity. On 'critical rationalism', see Karl Popper, *Conjectures and Refutations: The Growth of Scientific Knowledge*, 1963 (London and New York: Routledge, 2002); and Hans Albert, *Treatise on Critical Reason*, 1968 (Princeton: Princeton University Press, 1985).

Paul Oppenheim divide causal explanations into two parts.[17] The *explanandum* is the concrete statement of explanation (text, representation and action) that explains an explicandum, and the *explanans* is a class of additional statements appended to the explanandum which are necessary for the understanding and acceptance of an explanation. The explanans can be further divided into two groups: those which state 'antecedent conditions' and those which state general scientific laws.[18] Hempel suggests that, in terms of scientific causal explanation, these 'two sets of statements, if *adequately and completely formulated*, explain the phenomenon under consideration'.[19] The obvious question then arises regarding what constitutes adequacy, and Hempel suggests several conditions of adequacy which are applicable to causal scientific explanations only.[20] Yet with regards to completeness, it seems obvious that no explanation, even a causal scientific explanation, can, in principle, account for all antecedent conditions.

Antecedent conditions would appear to be exclusionary statements regulating what is and what is not appropriate content or context for any given explanation. We might say that, at their most basic level, explanans comprise the explanatory frame necessary for the understanding and acceptance of an explanation, the prerequisites necessary for any judgement in terms of 'adequacy' and 'completeness', and are therefore arbitrary and ideological in function.

One brief comparison might clarify this atypical definition of explanans. Sheldon Wolin writes in *Politics and Vision* (1960; 2004) that all political theories contain an implicit 'political metaphysic', or a certain system of unquestioned assumptions about time and space which are arbitrarily constructed after witnessing and interpreting a society from a certain social perspective.[21] This

---

[17] Carl G. Hempel and Paul Oppenheim, 'Studies in the Logic of Explanation', 1948, in *Theories of Explanation*, ed. Joseph C. Pitt, 9–50 (New York and Oxford: Oxford University Press, 1988).

[18] Hempel and Oppenheim, 'Studies in the Logic of Explanation', 9–10. To borrow one of Hempel and Oppenheim's examples, in explaining the optical illusion that an oar appears bent when it is half under water requires not only the statement of a scientific law of light behaviour but also the statement of several antecedent conditions. These may include a statement that the hypothetical oar is actually a straight object, that the observer is positioned above the waterline and is observing from a certain angle, that the oar might appear to be moving under the water due to further light disturbances caused by the movement of the water, but holding that that particular phenomena is not the one that is being explained by the current statement, and so forth. Hempel and Oppenheim suggest that even social, political, historical, linguistic and behavioural explanations can contain explanans of general laws and antecedent conditions (13–14); yet the appeal to general laws here is potentially less stable than in the sciences and more open to the influence of social judgements and power relations. Nevertheless, the intention remains for explanatory statements in these fields to subsume a phenomenon under a certain law of regularity, however it is determined.

[19] Hempel and Oppenheim, 'Studies in the Logic of Explanation', 10.

[20] Hempel and Oppenheim, 'Studies in the Logic of Explanation', 11–12.

[21] Sheldon S. Wolin, *Politics and Vision: Continuity and Innovation in Western Political Thought*, 2nd edn (Princeton: Princeton University Press, 2016), 16–18.

idea creates a double meaning for the term 'political vision', since nothing can be 'seen' except from a certain arbitrary point in time and space. Consequently, an explanation that is similarly stated from an arbitrary perspective is likewise constituted by a 'metaphysic' of assumptions that frames the explanation as both intelligible and relevant to the situation in question. The term 'explanans' can be used to name those secondary aspects of time, space and even society that it is apparently necessary to take for granted in order to render an explanation intelligible and relevant to its explicandum.

We might suggest that an explanation's 'meaning' will always follow from an interpretation that is reducible to neither the character of the explanandum nor the explicandum, and neither what its creator intended to explain nor the rules of the field in which the relation is recognized. Both the intention and the reception of an explanation is secondary to its status as an explanation – as an interpersonal imposition upon making sense – as Heine writing about something, and someone else reading and understanding it. This definition follows from, yet is also distinct from, Peckham's proposition that an explanation is essentially a direction for normative behavioural response – an instruction from someone to someone else, instructing them to respond to an explicandum in a certain way.[22] The essential point is that social explanations are primarily ideological, as opposed to causal, predictive or testable. To paraphrase Jacques Rancière, who begins *The Ignorant Schoolmaster* (1987) with a similar point, before all else, in the act of explaining something to someone, we express a judgement that they cannot understand it for themselves.[23]

All this occurs before we even reach a position of judgement regarding explanations, and consider what effect such judgements have on the world. The behaviours which follow explanations form the raw materials for constructing, maintaining and altering the identities and rules of specific fields of activity. Therefore, the power relations affected by social explanations can be said to always result from implicit judgements about good and bad, right and wrong, and appropriate and inappropriate responses to explanatory statements. These judgements similarly implicate not only the attitudes and methods of individuals but also, by extension, the individuals themselves. These ideological functions of

---

[22] Peckham, *Explanation and Power*, 86. The distinction between Peckham's definition and the one presented earlier concerns the inclusion in the latter of hypothetical processes of 'making sense', including schematic cognition. As a behaviourist, Peckham would perhaps have objected that such 'internal' concepts are inadmissible because they are unobservable.

[23] Jacques Rancière, *The Ignorant Schoolmaster: Five Lessons in Intellectual Emancipation* (Stanford: Stanford University Press, 1987), 6.

explanations are also strengthened through the potential for what we might call the 'erasure' of explanatory processes – their 'mythologization', in Roland Barthes's sense of the term, or 'phantasmagoria', to borrow from Theodor Adorno (see Chapter 2). This could take place in the following way: a hypothetical 'successful' explanation shifts the object of response from the explanandum (the explanatory statement) to the explicandum (the thing explained); the explanandum ceases to be the object of what Peckham calls judgements of 'personal' and 'procedural' appropriateness, along with its corresponding explanans. Judgements of personal and procedural appropriateness bear on whether the 'right' person is judged to be acting in the 'right' way appropriate to the situation.[24] In this hypothetical scenario, the explanans (statements of antecedent conditions and laws) are then taken for granted.

To give one brief example, when Heine describes Paganini's mesmerizing virtuoso performance, this representation invites the contemplation of many diverse and complex explanans: that the music Paganini is playing is actually valued as 'good' music, considering the profound effect it has in creating the vivid visual impressions which so impress the narrator; that the narrator's reported emotional and intellectual behaviour is an authentic and 'valid' response to the performance, in-line with contemporary Romantic reception practices, and not the product of a kind of 'madness' or misunderstanding on his part; that the specifically audio-visual quality of the description is rendered appropriate by the cultural 'aura' of Romanticism with which the work of both Paganini and Heine is suffused; and so on.

Each of these explanans, implying a particular valuation of the elements it contains, is the result of an interpretive conjecture on the part of the reader. Their range and contents will vary depending upon personal disposition, including competencies and interests. This means that the totalized 'content' of a representation is ultimately unknowable; any statement concerning its content is therefore only a conjecture that is only either easier or more difficult to defend. All three hypothetical elements – the representation, the statement and the criticism – are kinds of explanation.

The acceptance of an explanation, whether in the form of a text, representation or action, accompanies an erasure of its secondary, often ideologically weighted, explanans. Explanations not only regulate what is acceptable content for any state of affairs but also arrange that content in certain ways, and these arrangements

---

[24] Peckham, *Explanation and Power*, 45–7.

are not always questioned critically. On this point, we can now introduce ideas from Popper's critical rationalism to suggest that explanations which are well defended, frequently used or not subjected to criticism sufficient to refute them become metaphorically entrenched as traditions, habits, norms, rhetorical commonplaces or schemas. It is in this sense that explanations may become *intuitive* – the product of an 'unconscious' or 'non-rational' cognitive process, encouraging the uncritical acceptance of their explanans. While such normative explanations do not exclude the potential for innovation – the refutation of explanations or the creation of new rules and fields through emergent behaviour – they may remain constituted by those activities present within a given field: individual disposition (habitus) in conflict with rules and acceptable relations within and between fields (doxa). The comparison with Popper also highlights, as we will see, a critical imperative to 'improve' explanations.

Looking towards a practical methodology, the question then arises: How can we define or recognize the 'acceptance' of an explanation, as well as the arrangement of affairs that it legitimates according to explanans? And how can we use such ideas to frame a useful analysis of, in this case, Romanticism, both in filmic discourse and in representation, in addition to situating these ideas as a theoretical prerequisite for the analysis of film discourse and representation itself? These difficult methodological questions can be approached in several ways, and the next section will outline one functional answer in terms of what will be called 'risky archaeological analysis'.

The next step is to recognize that the aforementioned explanation of the term explanation corresponds with certain aspects of the archaeological analysis of 'discursive formations' suggested by Michel Foucault in *The Archaeology of Knowledge* (1969).[25] To avoid methodological confusion, what is enlisted here from Foucault's archaeology is simply the idea that when analysing any statement or field of discourse, the pertinent questions concern the conditions for its existence, its limits, points of relation to other statements or discourses, and in considering what is excluded. Above all, analysis should not expect to find totalities or the certainty of a closed text; multiplicity and rupture, relations and transformation, and 'compatibility and incompatibility' are the necessary expectations of such analysis.[26] What remains is an archaeological attempt to understand why a statement 'could not be other than it was', and what relations

---

[25] Michel Foucault, *The Archaeology of Knowledge*, 1969 (London and New York: Routledge, 2010), 34–43.
[26] Foucault, *The Archaeology of Knowledge*, 30–2, 41, 49, 69.

determine its potential for contributing to other fields of discourse.[27] The term 'archaeology' might imply that the objects of study are dead and buried, perfectly preserved instances of explanation 'caught in the act' like Pompeian figures, but that would be to miss Foucault's point. Explanatory processes shape not only how such objects are buried but also how they are unearthed and shaped into statements, becoming 'history' or 'facts'.

By highlighting these points, we avoid Foucault's self-confessed puritan approach to synchronic analysis – a disinclination to investigate the diachronic field of 'the history of ideas' or the development of authorial 'œuvres'.[28] In doing so, we also guard against the danger that Foucault's methodology may seem to invite shallow and inconclusive analysis. It is arguably easier to find rupture than unity in our objects of study, and to simply conclude that things are inconclusive. The methodological fear of subjective interpretation runs up against the impossibility of complete objectivity, and the consequence for worthwhile analysis is the need to make new, interesting and risky conjectures which we can subject to tests, as Popper might have said. We must therefore question the value of analysis which doesn't take risks. The pertinent aspect of Foucault's archaeology examines not the relics that are unearthed, but the layers of sediment in which they are discovered; expanding this metaphor, we might say that we begin to take risks when we conjecture about the characteristics of such sediment that stretches away from the artefact in question, lying mostly underground and out of sight. This conjectural character of risky archaeological analysis raises obvious methodological questions which will be answered in the next section, and they will also be framed in relation to the aims of individual chapters.[29]

To summarize, participants in discourse make choices for the inclusion and exclusion of elements, statements and explanatory schemes from varying fields of discourse based upon judgements of appropriateness. These judgements are determined by both the history and rules of that discourse as they encounter it and the need to ensure how things are understood by others. (Ironically, the earlier citations of Peckham, Bourdieu, Popper and Foucault are themselves examples of such choices.) As the processes of making sense enter the field of social explanation, the power relations between different

---

[27] Foucault, *The Archaeology of Knowledge*, 32.
[28] Foucault, *The Archaeology of Knowledge*, 154–6.
[29] This phrase is a reference to Popper's ideas on the conjectural character of human knowledge generally; see Popper, *Conjectures and Refutations*, 36–9.

players (habitus) active within any given field, organized by traditions (doxa), begin to compete with judgements of appropriateness, utilizing texts, statements, actions and representations, audio-visual or otherwise, as tools. If the capacity to be judged is the criterion for observable behaviour in others, as Peckham suggests, and if explanation is usefully understood as an interpersonal imposition on the processes of making sense, then *such tools are kinds of explanation*: texts, statements, actions and representations that not only attempt to elicit a kind of response that can be judged but also order that response in various ways.

This is what is meant by saying that film is a kind of audio-visual explanation. These tools, their functions and 'meanings', are the artefacts studied by risky archaeology: a method that conjectures about the explanans that are unaccounted for in any explanandum, and recognizes that, as the Heine example demonstrates, their intuitive and audio-visual aspects are often co-dependent, and, as we will see in Chapter 1, may also be said to have their roots in Romantic aesthetics itself.

Risky archaeology: Approaching the analysis of discourse and representation as explanation

Bearing in mind the conjectural character of risky archaeological analysis, how can we best approach the relationship between Romanticism and film by enlisting Liszt as an element of film and of film music discourse and representation? The initial problems are obvious. According to one perspective – another characteristic trend in twentieth-century philosophy – anything can be a sign, and all signs are potentially polysemous; consequently, the identification of any meaning at all is already the product of a judgement defended by explanatory forces.[30] Yet some sense of dominant reading is fundamental to any analysis seeking to avoid 'anything goes' relativism – hence that favourite phrase of philosophical hermeneutics: 'some interpretations are better than others'.[31]

Acknowledging the basic premise of such positions also clarifies what is meant by taking risks in archaeological analysis: that the analysis, as well as the perception, interpretation and explanation of anything at all, requires the

---

[30] Peckham, *Explanation and Power*, 16, 90–9.
[31] John D. Caputo, *Hermeneutics: Facts and Interpretation in the Age of Information* (London: Pelican Books, 2018), 12–13.

combined selection and repression of data that reaches us from the thing-in-itself. (In Chapter 3, we will explain the relationship between perception/cognition, philosophical hermeneutics and Kantian Idealism in more depth.) We have to interpret such 'facts' in order to save our responses from arbitrariness, or if we are to have anything to do with the thing at all. Borrowing one of Popper's favourite aphorisms, we might say that the better interpretations are those which can withstand the most rigorous tests while also explaining the most content in new and interesting ways.

Turning more specifically to the field of Film Studies, some commentators, beginning in the 1980s, defended the notion of dominant readings in the wake of poststructuralism while bearing in mind certain of these methodological problems. In *Narration in the Fiction Film* (1985), for instance, David Bordwell employs concepts from cognitive psychology to investigate a process of schematic reading which enables the identification of 'most likely' reading positions; but this 'most likely' will remain only one among many from a field which can never be fully known.[32] Historical materialist approaches similarly prioritize an interplay between textual analysis, historical context, and a more artificially compartmentalized, non-totalizing and irreducible understanding of audiences' multiple interpretive activities.[33] Yet all these elements are themselves necessarily based upon the discursive explanatory frameworks known and available for use at any given time, and their emergence, selection and employment are also the results of individual disposition on the part of historical individuals situated within irreducible cultural contexts.

In order to write any kind of analysis, therefore, we have to stand our ground somewhere and subject our statements to criticism. While explanatory processes always force particular readings, and can therefore be studied archaeologically, this cannot occur without risk of refutation according to judgements of appropriateness. We select our tools and build the best interpretations we can, then we criticize them. Film interpretation and film analysis share the same dialogue between defence and attack that, as we will see throughout this book, characterizes both interpretation and a significant element of Romanticism itself. Each act of perception, then interpretation and then explanation gives an object a new life, and this is also a cyclical process. What must be preserved in the analysis of texts is this sense of life, or three-dimensionality,

---

[32] David Bordwell, *Narration in the Fiction Film* (Madison: University of Wisconsin Press, 1985), 30–1.
[33] Janet Staiger, *Interpreting Films: Studies in the Historical Reception of American Cinema* (Princeton: Princeton University Press, 1992), 79–97.

for the artefacts being studied. They must not be limited to any totalizing or exclusionary statement. This is obviously impossible to prevent completely, but the danger can be borne in mind. As Bordwell makes clear, the schematic reading of representations can expose a text's potential for producing meaning while bearing in mind the ultimate unknowability of the full field of production and reception. What can emerge are specific reading potentialities around lexia which draw into focus the explanatory tools that aid attempts to make sense of them. Risky archaeological analysis answers the methodological problem that emerges when we begin to ask: How far can we 'read into' representations using such tools?

As suggested, there is one kind of risk we can take that has an explicitly ideological dimension. This consists in hypothesizing the erasure of explanans in intuitive audio-visual explanations, and then in adopting a critical imperative to conjecture as to their nature and expose them. The following chapters attempt this kind of exposure in different ways, but in most instances, they will revolve around the question of value. We will often ask the following: What does an explanation appear to value? What kind of judgements does it want us to take for granted? As noted already, we might call the potential result of these inquiries *the excavation of erased explanans*.

Turning briefly to this question of methodology in the analysis of film music, David Neumeyer has similarly suggested a need to adopt a variety of methodological approaches, achieving a 'profitable middle ground' between audio-visual interpretation, phenomenology, socio-historical context, reception, production history, star studies and other approaches.[34] Although Film Studies has long recognized the role that the conjunction of image and sound plays in forming meaning and affect, music itself can potentially evoke a large assortment of culturally, historically and individually specific associations. Music will trigger subjective responses, and we can only identify the most likely possibilities according to existing knowledge. An individual film and its contexts of reception can provide clues to build an appropriate awareness of the kind of knowledge an audience might employ to make sense of it. Textual analysis of a film featuring Wagner's 'Ride of the Valkyries', for example, can be credited with a cultural literacy that includes associations with Nazism, the Holocaust,

---

[34] David Neumeyer, 'Film Theory and Music Theory: On the Intersection of Two Traditions', in *Music in the Mirror: Reflections on the History of Music Theory and Literature for the 21st Century*, ed. Andreas Giger and Thomas J. Mathiesen, 275–94 (Lincoln: University of Nebraska Press, 2002), 292–3.

Vietnam, war in general and even simply helicopters, all perhaps justified by those schematic relations judged to be appropriate in association with this music in specific reception contexts.

Chapter structure

When people think of Franz Liszt, one particular instrument is likely to immediately come to mind. Yet as scholars, musicians and enthusiasts have long endeavoured to stress, Liszt was far more than a piano virtuoso. Although the virtuoso piano performance remains of vital importance, it is worth considering the wider relevance of its symbolic content. It is useful to bear in mind its importance, not only to Liszt's music and aesthetic philosophy more generally but also to the interconnecting ideas mobilized throughout this book: the Romantic concern with intuitive audio-visual aesthetics and the explanatory function of placing the unique and talented individual, the 'genius', at the heart of its effect – the paradoxical controlling condition of its 'free' intuitive understanding. The following chapter structure reflects a progression from Romantic 'freedom' down through Liszt's, the 'genius', attempt to author that freedom around 'poetic ideas'; the grounding and explaining of Romanticism in the image of Liszt at the piano itself; and, finally, to the concrete and complex realization of such ideas in selected film texts.

The central chapters present a chronological series of investigations charting the relevance of Romanticism to Film Studies, ranging from its philosophical roots in the late eighteenth century to selected film texts in the post-classical era of cinema.

Chapter 1 looks back to the time of German Idealism to construct a fictive relationship between Romanticism and film by making risky conjectures about the 'nature' of Romanticism itself, and by extrapolating from this relationship a rich philosophical and historical background for the concept of audio-visual explanation introduced earlier.

Chapter 2 advances to the decades of pre-, early and classical Hollywood cinema, addressing Richard Wagner's position in the history of film music discourse by introducing the alternative case of Liszt's symphonic poems and attempting to understand why it 'could not be other than it was'. Why did Wagner's name and ideas come to prominence, and what did such prominence exclude?

Chapter 3 will analyse the meeting point between nineteenth-century Romanticism and filmic 'explanations' of the past, framing an examination of representations of Liszt and his music in film while also illuminating the study of Romantic tropes and schemas more generally in reference to the concept of audio-visual explanation. Beginning with the premise that the idea of 'Liszt' exists as a cultural image that makes contact with certain schematic types in various representations, illustrative case studies will be used to examine how filmic representations attempt to order certain responses – or explain the 'meaning' of Liszt's cultural image – in reference to specific secondary explanatory schematic types.

In Chapters 4 and 5, the schematic reading of audio-visual explanations will expand through the mid- to late twentieth century onto a broader canvas of textual and contextual analysis. The schematic types identified in Chapter 2 will be considered within broader fields of creation and reception by an in-depth analysis of two case studies from differing socio-historical, production and reception contexts: *Song Without End* (1960) and *Lisztomania* (1975). Textual analysis will deepen the overarching methodology beyond the development and consistencies of key representational schemas to the specificities of individual contexts, and will be offered in conjunction with considerations of genre, stardom, auteurism and industrial analysis, providing, if not the illusionary authority of a totalizing study, then a sense of three-dimensionality to the texts under consideration. This will not treat the films as closed texts, but will rather see how their meaning can be opened up to a host of disparate but related nodes by way of unearthing certain audio-visual explanations through the risky archaeology of representational schemas.

Finally, having already introduced the critical imperative that follows from the recognition of the erasure of explanans, we may be moved to question the critical value of any analyses focused on the representation of Romanticism, and a single composer and piano virtuoso. Although studies of film representations commonly expose the explanatory processes that shape important concepts such as gender, sexuality and race, other less 'important' topics also come under the influence of schemas and their associated concepts: types and stereotypes. The study of filmic representations of composers and their music can provide significant insight into the explanatory processes of Othering that inform related, more 'important', types. Classical music plays a key role in establishing, maintaining and restructuring ideological social distinctions. As Pierre Bourdieu put it: 'nothing more clearly affirms one's "class", nothing more infallibly classifies, than tastes in music'.[35] Classical music's potent symbolic resources are partly a result of its capacity to evoke, as Michael Long suggested, a paradoxical combination of being-in-the-past and being-eternal, no-longer-ness and 'longevity, incorruptibility and universal value'.[36] This powerful mythological potential is drawn from a resource whose terrain is virtually unmapped. By the conclusion, we will come to understand that Romanticism cannot escape the political, just as it cannot escape the aesthetic and film cannot escape all three. Perhaps, as Rancière suggests, all four are, in a sense, one and the same.

---

[35] Pierre Bourdieu, *Distinction: A Social Critique of the Judgement of Taste*, 1979 (New York and London: Routledge, 2003), 18.
[36] Michael Long, *Beautiful Monsters: Imagining the Classic in Musical Media* (Berkeley: University of California Press, 2008), 26–7.

1

Culture and transcendence
Three explanations of Romanticism

Introduction

When we read the word 'Romanticism', it might initially evoke a number of names. In a literary context, these names might include a handful of poets who lived in the late eighteenth and early nineteenth centuries, including Wordsworth, Coleridge, Goethe and Schiller – names which might be roughly divided into English and German traditions. In a musical context, this word might evoke the names of certain composers who lived between the late work of Beethoven and Schoenberg's turn to atonality, or between Schubert and the mature works of Mahler or Richard Strauss. For philosophers, names such as Novalis and Hölderlin will suggest themselves; for painters, Delacroix, Friedrich and Turner.

From the variety of these names, the styles they represent and the historical periods in which their bearers lived, it is clear that no unified and incontestable definition of the word 'Romanticism' can be presented. This word can mean many things, and is perhaps best understood as a colligatory construct, an explanatory tool, an example of what Michel Foucault termed a 'discursive formation', or what Morse Peckham called a 'disjunctive category' – a category created by differences developed within institutional practices whose members do not all share the same thing in common.[1]

This chapter undertakes a rather deep dive into the backwaters of film and philosophy. It attempts to outline a detailed, fictive and pragmatic explanation of Romanticism that permits us to discuss its relationship with film. This

---

[1] Foucault, *The Archaeology of Knowledge*, 34–43; Morse Peckham, 'Cultural Transcendence: The Task of the Romantics', 1981, in *Romanticism and Ideology*, 3–22 (Hanover and London: Wesleyan University Press, 1995), passim.

relationship, of course, has the potential to be traced and developed in many different ways, enabling different kinds of analysis. For the purposes of the current study, we will utilize three explanatory paradigms: cultural transcendence, the aesthetic regime and philosophical aesthetics. Together these concepts will enable a correspondence between theories of ideological social explanation and audio-visual aesthetics, while permitting these categories to be of use in analysing the relationship between Romanticism and film. Subsequent chapters will proceed from this basis by inviting Franz Liszt, as a figure representative of Romanticism, to take centre stage in an exploration of various selected points of contact between these subjects.

What is Romanticism?

Romanticism is commonly explained as a historical reaction against Enlightenment doctrines of empiricism, positivism, manifest truth and an ordered universe – an outburst of irrationalism which found among its catalysts the political theory of Jean-Jacques Rousseau, the Terror of the French Revolution, the music of Beethoven and the anti-foundationalism of post-Kantian German Idealism.[2] ('Anti-foundationalism' can be defined here as a renunciation of the claim that knowledge can be authorized by appealing to its source or origin, and rather crediting an appeal to a critical discussion of the state of existing knowledge in light of its historical and fictive character in reference to an objective criterion of truth that acts as a partially knowable regulative principle.) But taken at its broadest meaning, Romanticism characterizes something less definable about the so-called long nineteenth century – a historical period bookended by the Enlightenment, the French Revolution and German Idealism at the one end and by artistic modernism, the Second World War and cinema at the other.

Romanticism does not name a historical period, a style or a cohesive set of aesthetic theories, yet it is colloquially treated as one or all of these. The term potentially activates a number of schemas associated with a period in European history between the late 1700s and the early 1900s, the result of a series of

---

[2] For typical overviews, see Carmen Casaliggi and Porscha Fermanis, *Romanticism: A Literary and Cultural History* (London and New York: Routledge, 2016), 1–46, 113–69; Manfred Frank, *The Philosophical Foundations of Early German Romanticism* (Albany: State University of New York Press, 2004), 23–37; Isiah Berlin, *The Roots of Romanticism*, 1965, ed. Henry Hardy (London: Pimlico, 2000), 21–4, 46–7, 52–4; Jürgen Habermas, *The Philosophical Discourse of Modernity*, 1985 (Cambridge: Polity Press, 1998), 1–50.

emergent philosophical and aesthetic positions, individuals, artworks and behaviours forming part of wider social, economic and political transformations. In addition, Romanticism's reaction against the empiricist and positivist attitudes of the Enlightenment situates it, as we will see, as a noteworthy historical precursor to certain trends in twentieth-century philosophy, including critical rationalism, philosophical hermeneutics and critical theory.

Like the ideas often subsumed by the term 'postmodernism', Romanticism accommodates various contradictions. Aspects of classicism and the Enlightenment often survive within its schematic framework, despite being concepts that Romanticism supposedly defined itself in the process of overthrowing. Also, like postmodernism, Romanticism is not a distinct break with an earlier period, but is an accumulation of disparate responses to prevailing social standards as they have been recorded across the histories of a number of cultural fields. This idea does, however, crystallize something that lies near the heart of Romanticism: the idea of genius, or innovative response – the idea that something is encountered, judged to be imperfect by someone special and responded to in a new way. By the end of this chapter, we will recognize the relevance of this Romantic image of genius to both film and audio-visual explanation.

Throughout its brief history, Film Studies has appropriated many of its most significant concepts and theories from the more respectable domain of literature. As we might expect, Romanticism has a strong critical heritage in literary criticism, where scholars such as M. H. Abrams, Northrop Frye and Frank Kermode created a robust theoretical field for a specific English literary tradition which became canonized in English universities during the mid-twentieth century. Yet the simple equation of Romanticism with concepts such as 'expression', 'imagination' and 'feeling', enabled by analysing the work of poets such as Coleridge, Wordsworth and Byron, creates a limited and misleading scope for application. A primarily 'literary' explanation of the relationship between Romanticism and film, based on such ideas, might quickly find itself reduced, by way of analogy between the practices and aesthetics of film and melodrama, to a familiar historical correlation between the style, performance and musical traditions of nineteenth-century theatre and their later Hollywood counterparts, and might miss many of the more interesting and significant elements to be explored throughout this book.

The field of literary criticism is also partly responsible for Romanticism being burdened with several decidedly negative ideological associations. In a tradition dating back to Goethe and Kant, several critics, including T. E. Hulme and Irving Babbitt, attacked Romanticism for its supposed aesthetic and ethical failings. An emphasis on nationalism, extreme emotion, subjective intuition, anti-rationality, ideologically mystifying sublimity and a valuation of individual genius at the expense of tradition and community has, in addition, long tainted the cultural images of figures such as Wagner, Herder, Hegel and Nietzsche as they fall within the retrospective historical shadow of the Third Reich.

As we will see throughout this book, it is often illuminating to bear in mind these complex associations, and perhaps even to give a certain amount of credence to a rhetorical position that treats the simultaneous development of both National Socialism and film as being among the many 'consequences' of Romanticism itself. By the end of this chapter, we will have seen how the near-simultaneous emergence of fascism and cinema in modern European history (give or take a decade) exposes the connection between the three explanatory paradigms we have chosen to explore.

It is therefore not literature but philosophical aesthetics more generally (understood to contain an intrinsic political or ideological dimension) which provides the necessary tools for the current study of Romanticism and film in terms of audio-visual explanation. The writings of Kant, Schelling, Schiller, Novalis and Schlegel, in particular, present an invaluable resource for understanding the philosophical context of Romanticism as a consequence of German Idealism. We must be open to this history of European philosophical aesthetics if we wish to understand how and why the word 'Romanticism', as a fluid discursive formation, can accommodate and enrich the analysis of cultural products as diverse as the work of Liszt and Hölderlin, Friedrich and Wagner, in addition to Nazism, rock music and cinema itself.

Romantic agency: Cultural transcendence

According to Morse Peckham, the term 'Romanticism' is perhaps best used to identify the cultural legacy of certain behaviours exhibited by a number of historical individuals who contributed to a changed perspective on Western cultural values.[3] Peckham explains Romanticism by coining the term 'cultural

---

[3] Morse Peckham, 'Introduction', in *Romanticism and Ideology*, xiii–xx (Hanover and London: Wesleyan University Press, 1995), xiii.

transcendence', or social deviancy and innovation as a distinct behavioural pattern:

> This arises from the [Romantic individual's] judgement of explanatory collapse (the failure of ideologies), alienation from the culture and society's institutions, cultural vandalism, social withdrawal, reducing the interaction rate to a minimum, randomising behaviour, selecting a promising emergent innovation, collecting a little group of supporters and propagandising the cultural emergent.[4]

These behaviours result in a critical and constructive interaction among various schemas of cultural value. The typical array of key Romantic phrases, tropes and ideas – including subjective introspection, revolution, progress, solitude, freedom, irrationalism, madness and a fascination with nature, antiquity, death and extreme emotional states – developed because they were fruitful concepts for accommodating the oppositional activity of cultural transcendence. This term subsumes freedom, dynamism, movement, dissatisfaction with things as they are and, as we will see further, an incessant desire for the unification of what the German Idealists called the 'subjective' and the 'objective'. It gives Romanticism the character of an infinite striving.

Rhetorically speaking, the Romantic individual is a utopian; they feel at home nowhere save in that ideal that their imagination can almost grasp. They act to transform their world while guided by an ideal. In Romantic art, the classical emphasis on final achievement changes to this sense of perpetual striving – from pleasure to constant dissatisfaction and from unity to fragmentation and back again. As we will see when we analyse the relationship between the audio-visual explanation and the Romantic genius figure, this last is a shift which, due to the influence of the aesthetic category of the sublime, corresponds problematically to that other perpetually differed split between community and individual.

The dissatisfaction with one's environment and an incessant striving for ideals is the critical imperative that forms the essence of Romanticism's political progressiveness. (This is also the reason why it cannot be compared anachronistically, although it certainly can incompletely, to later philosophical positions such as critical rationalism, philosophical hermeneutics and critical rationalism.) For Peckham, the typical Romantic fascination with death, madness or antiquity develops a continually transformational imperative, 'not to question the value of life is to accept unhesitatingly the platitudes of one's culture

---

[4] Peckham, 'Introduction', xix; see also Peckham, *Explanation and Power*, 272–82.

... [its] ideology'.[5] If the Romantic individual is one who stands apart from society, or things as we find them, in order to criticize them through the power of the imagination, then this paradoxically places the unique individual – the 'genius' – at the heart of culture itself. Kant's description of the concept of genius in the *Critique of Judgement* (1790) exemplifies the role it was initially allocated in Romantic aesthetics.[6] The artistic genius is the one who 'gives the rule to art' in nature's stead.[7] The recipient of a gift from nature, the genius operates through untutored originality; they are unable to communicate their gift to others, and are also themselves blind to the motives which inspire their work. After Kant, the concept of individual genius takes pride of place in Romantic aesthetics, replacing, as Hans-Georg Gadamer explained, the previously privileged concept of the judgement of taste and appropriating with it an implied knowledge of the means to realize an ideal community.[8]

Due in no small part to Romanticism, individuality, subjectivity and antisocial behaviours – the questioning of the status quo – came to the fore as significant schematic elements of cultural value throughout the nineteenth century. This history is partly responsible for the conflicts and tensions surrounding the genius figure as a cultural type. Situated as society's other, the genius possesses a unique perspective, enabling them to shape their subject – whether it be music, politics, literature or science – in ways that reveal truths otherwise inaccessible to the community. But in the creation of great works, the genius often articulates the creative process as a struggle, or even a quasi-religious experience. The suffering caused by cultural transcendence is then articulated as something valuable. (This is often a problematic value allocation that, as we will see in Chapter 3, demands a kind of ideological negotiation within explanatory cultural representations.) In a more complex formulation, the genius myth resides in a contradiction between Romantic artistic idealism and the always-insufficient ability of an individual artist to realize those ideals.

Either way, the Romantic genius, as a cultural type, is placed in a position which is, if not philosophically paradoxical, then at least politically unstable: expected to stand apart from society while their cultural transcendence guides that society to a better future. With the development of modernity, the critical

---

[5] Peckham, 'Cultural Transcendence', 12.
[6] Immanuel Kant, *Critique of Judgement*, 1790 (Indianapolis and Cambridge: Hackett Publishing Company, 1987), §46–50, 174–89.
[7] Kant, *Critique of Judgement*, §46, 174.
[8] Hans-Georg Gadamer, *Truth and Method*, 1960 (London and New York: Continuum International Publishing Group, 2012), 31–52.

imperative of the genius becomes a newly problematic notion with regard to its wider social function. We will see here how far this problem extends into the field of audio-visual explanation, along with other Romantic schemas. But Peckham's notion of cultural transcendence can form only one part of the story of Romanticism. As its principle of agency, cultural transcendence is the content of Romanticism, and not its form, or the movement, and not the vehicle. We might understand this form or vehicle to be a broad programme of multimedia aesthetics, something that can be clarified, while maintaining an understanding of its crucial ideological dimension, by turning to Jacques Rancière's concept of the aesthetic regime.

Romantic aesthetics: Multimedia and the aesthetic regime

'The aesthetic regime' is the latest development in a series of three historical periodizations explored by Jacques Rancière in his recent philosophical works.[9] It overtakes and develops alongside the classical or 'representative' regime around the time of the German Idealists, and is concurrent with the emergence of Romanticism. The rise of the aesthetic regime throughout the nineteenth century was characterized, in part, by new discourses surrounding the supposed autonomy of different means of artistic expression. A paradox is established in modern aesthetics, whereby not only different media develop increasingly autonomous cultures of value and practice but also individual works simultaneously become populated with various means of expression appropriated from their neighbours. A belief in an equivalence of translation between media becomes a bankrupt notion at the very moment that their 'materials' become 'mixed' to a new degree.[10] Art's autonomy is won at the cost of its dissolution as a distinct field of practice and recognition. In the aesthetic regime, the notion of appropriate form is abolished, leading to a condition where *'everything speaks'*[11] – a phrase borrowed from Novalis.

According to Rancière's argument, cinema becomes the logical development of this Romantic poetics.[12] Some of the effects that classical film theory

---

[9] Jacques Rancière, *The Politics of Aesthetics*, 2000, ed. Gabriel Rockhill (London: Bloomsbury, 2017), 15–25; *Film Fables*, 8–9; *The Future of the Image*, 2003 (London and New York: Verso, 2009), 39, 42; *The Emancipated Spectator*, 2008 (London and New York: Verso, 2011), 60–1.
[10] Rancière, *The Future of the Image*, 42.
[11] Rancière, *The Politics of Aesthetics*, 18; Rancière, *Film Fables*, 8–9; emphasis in original.
[12] Rancière, *Film Fables*, 7–11, 160–79; Rancière, *The Future of the Image*, 5.

considered 'unique' to the medium of cinema can supposedly be found in the philosophy, art and literature characteristic of this aesthetic regime. More theoretically, by combining the camera's objective capturing of reality with the filmmaker's subjective manipulation of the produced image, film itself strives after the union of the objective and the subjective in the 'absolute' outlined in the final chapter of F. W. J. Schelling's *System of Transcendental Idealism* (1800)[13] – one of the founding texts of Romantic aesthetics. Throughout his writings, Rancière is more interested in exploring, from a Marxist perspective, the tensions which develop between the co-present logics of different regimes in certain films – tensions which create ruptures in the sensory allocations of form and function to certain filmic elements, rendering sensible an allegorical rupture in the various forms and functions of social life. It is interesting to note that this enunciation of a political dimension to aesthetic form appears to encourage the reading of a certain 'Romantic' theme within analogous discussions by Theodor Adorno, who writes in his *Aesthetic Theory* (1970):

> The liberation of form, which genuinely new art desires, holds enciphered within it above all the liberation of society, for form – the social nexus of everything particular – represents the social relation in the artwork; this is why liberated form is anathema to the status quo.[14]

As with the Romantic behavioural drive encapsulated by Peckham's term cultural transcendence, formlessness, or boundarylessness, in aesthetic form is articulated as an inherently 'progressive' idea with the potential to destabilize and call into question the currently accepted conditions of social arrangement.

Despite adopting a different approach to the relationship between Romanticism and film to the one pursued in this book, Ranicère's work has the value of combining an awareness of the political dimension to aesthetic experience with a reiteration of the importance of *multimedia synthesis* to Romantic aesthetics more generally. From the conflation of art and philosophy pursued within the *Athenäum* and the New Mythology (see further) to the photographic descriptions in Flaubert's novels; from the cathedral-like novels of Victor Hugo to the partial formlessness of Liszt's symphonic poems; from Wagner's *Gesamtkunstwerk*, to the birth of the seventh art of cinema – the one that appropriates and then either fulfils or corrupts the value of its constituent

---

[13] F. W. J. Schelling, *System of Transcendental Idealism*, 1800 (Charlottesville: The University Press of Virginia, 2001), 219–36.

[14] Theodor Adorno, *Aesthetic Theory*, 1970 (London: Bloomsbury, 2017), 345.

parts; the long nineteenth century is suffused by a notion of art without borders. Romantic art becomes a multisensory domain, at once both emotive and cognitive, without rules, limitations or expectations. Ultimately, what we find in this discursive field is an opportunity to think about film – that epitome of art under technological modernism – as quintessentially Romantic.

In this way, Rancière's work on the aesthetic regime compliments Peckham's theory of cultural transcendence, expanding an explanation of Romanticism as a contemporary phenomenon. Where Peckham stresses the modern relevance of the traditional notion of genius and mutability of action, Rancière reopens the question of expressivity and mutability of form.

Another area of particular significance concerns the relationship between music and language. The Romantic era was also a time when music was more explicitly reconsidered for its potential to function as a means of communication. Although the new multimedia imperative in Romanticism developed from practices which extended back beyond the nineteenth century, it was buttressed by a corresponding development in musical philosophy, namely, the idea that music post-Beethoven had found the means to express things – to express in the abstract – to express as a qualitatively different form of knowledge. Music is reconsidered as 'language' at this time because of its very combination of being unbound by reference to an external world (mimesis), its potential for intense emotional impact and non-categorical yet supposedly 'universal' cognition, and its status as the product of genius. The various contributions to the philosophy of language made by Romantics such as Schlegel, Novalis and Herder, in addition to the musical innovations of composers such as Beethoven, created the right conditions for a reconsideration of the boundaries between sound and vision as vehicles for the communication of truth.[15] As in Rancière's formulation, the old explanatory function of mimesis and representation is overtaken by autonomous expressivity and innovative connectivity free from rule-bound epistemological determination. The cultural transcendence exhibited by Romantic composers such as Beethoven, Liszt and Wagner are particularly forceful examples. Even today, their works are often called musical 'expressions' of 'truths' deemed important for whole societies, whole nations, or – at the most sublime abstraction of this rhetoric – the whole of mankind itself. Yet these 'truths' remain the creations of individuals (Romantic geniuses), and, as we will soon

---

[15] Andrew Bowie, *From Romanticism to Critical Theory: The Philosophy of German Literary Theory* (London and New York: Routledge, 1997), 56–75; see appendix A.

come to understand, they are the results of intuitive audio-visual explanations. Romanticism delineates the value of these truths as well as their possibility for impacting upon society.

As we can see, it is essential to retain the duality of the Kantian notion of genius, as the one who gives the rule to art, alongside the principle of rule-free cognition in aesthetic experience, as well as the ideological dimension of this relationship. Furthermore, it is this very relationship that lies at the heart, not only of Franz Liszt's entire aesthetic programme but also what we have called audio-visual explanation more generally, subsuming the currently employed discursive understanding of the nature and effects of film itself. If film's Romanticism can be understood as being in its potential for what Schiller called 'aesthetic education', then the ideological power of explanation inherent in that understanding must be explored in all its nuances. It is to that element that we turn next.

Romantic explanation: Philosophical aesthetics and sublime genius

The works of the German Idealists contributed to a Romantic conception of art as a vehicle for moral social development. Post-Kantian philosophical Romanticism sought to unify a divided modern world through reconciliation between a desired ideal community and an ideal of individual imagination that was required for its development. It sought an answer along the lines of a natural, ethical intuition in which 'every individual expresses and signifies the whole'.[16] The maturation of Romanticism itself can be hypothetically situated at this moment in European aesthetics, although, as the writings of Peckham and Rancière make clear, the concept cannot be easily reduced to the cultural or philosophical output of this or any other, time and place.

The background knowledge required to form a proper understanding of this time and place is complex enough to begin with. The turn towards philosophical idealism in the late eighteenth century meant that the modern subject, who had found in empiricism and positivism ever more powerful explanatory means to

---

[16] Dieter Sturma, 'Politics and the New Mythology: The Turn to Late Romanticism', in *The Cambridge Companion to German Idealism*, ed. Karl Ameriks, 2nd edn, 314–35 (Cambridge: Cambridge University Press, 2017), 329.

understand the conditions of reality in both its natural and social contexts, began to reflect more drastically upon its own capacity for knowledge itself. In other words, as Hegel declared in his *Lectures on the Philosophy of History* (1822–30), the modern subject faces the discovery that 'man stands on his head, that is, on thought, and reality is constructed in terms of it'.[17] Kant's influential concept of transcendental idealism, developed in the *Critique of Pure Reason* (1781), hypothesized a fundamental epistemological gap, and suggested that the world that appears to our senses is incomplete somehow – mediated by deterministic *a priori* elements of cognition which provide the minimum conditions for experience itself.[18] The result was an unbridgeable gulf between 'subjective' and 'objective', or sensory appearance and things-in-themselves, and this division became a keystone of subsequent philosophical thought in Europe. German Idealist and Romantic philosophers worked from this hypothesis that declared objective reality not directly and completely accessible through the senses, and sought ways to bring the two, objective and subjective, together. Among the pressing questions that Kantian philosophy raised for the Romantics were the following: How do we have access to truth? Given that we cannot know to what extent the modern subject is free from religious and natural determinism, by what principles should we live? How can the conditions of a good life be explained to ourselves? Reconciliation was required between the objective public world and the subjective world of emancipated modern subjectivity. Striving after truth in the 'absolute' unity of subjective and objective was the order of the day, and art seemed to be the right tool for the job.

Kant's *Critique of Judgement*, Schiller's *On The Aesthetic Education of Man* (1795) and Schelling's *System of Transcendental Idealism* well represent a contemporary faith in art to provide the cognitive basis for a more moral society following the questioning of positivist and empiricist doctrines after the Enlightenment and the Terror of the French Revolution.[19] Due to the constitution of modern subjectivity, the ineffability of art, which was stronger in some media than others, seemed to increase its 'explanatory' power. This moment marked the development of the modern meaning of 'art' itself, as something more than the result of technical proficiency. Although Hegel was pessimistic about the

---

[17] Georg Wilhelm Friedrich Hegel, *Lectures on the Philosophy of History*, 1822–30 (Aalten: Wordbridge, 2011), 401.

[18] Immanuel Kant, *Critique of Pure Reason*, 1781 (Indianapolis and Cambridge: Hackett Publishing Company, 1996), A42 B59, 94.

[19] Kant, *Critique of Judgement*, Introduction VI, 26–8; Friedrich Schiller, *On the Aesthetic Education of Man*, 1795 (London: Penguin, 2016); Schelling, *System of Transcendental Idealism*, 218–36.

philosophical value of modern art, others were less so.[20] Schelling expressed the view that art has a cognitive potential to reveal a qualitatively different kind of truth about the world, or knowledge of the absolute, which was beyond the power of philosophy or science.[21] He rejected the unknowability of the Kantian thing-in-itself, and suggested that objective and subjective come together in art. For Schelling, 'the work of art's basic character is an "unconscious infinity"' – meaning that there is always more meaning in a work of art than can be found.[22] What is revealed to us in the work of art cannot be equated with what we experience as a sensual object. This is what makes art superior to science as a means of philosophical activity, since the latter involves inherently conscious activities which isolate the object by reducing it to properties of time and space, missing, in the process, the union of subjective and objective. Art, in contrast, remains open, maintaining the space for the possibility of such a unity. This move, effectively placing art in the service of a perpetually deferred ideal, returns us to that familiar concept of Romantic striving.

Armed with this new-found power, art could supposedly become the new philosophy, a new religion headed by 'artist-priests', and adopt the unifying function which was traditionally accomplished by religious faith before the Enlightenment, and ultimately bring about the 'aesthetic education' of mankind. In the famous fragment 'The Oldest Program for a System of German Idealism' (c1795), the Romantics heralded the development of a 'New Mythology' which would hold the potential to communicate with people at all social levels and to unite a divided mankind by educating them to a better moral condition.[23] All this was, of course, in accord with the Romantic reversal of representative aesthetics described by Rancière in his formulation of the aesthetic regime. Instead of mimesis, the principle of Romantic art was now expression – the ability not to copy the world as it appeared to the senses (for the self-evident truth of such representations had become questionable along with the doctrines of empiricism and positivism), but rather to reveal its hidden truth in a new way, accomplishing in the process its own kind of autonomous philosophy that, since it required no specialist knowledge, could also, in theory, be practised by everyone.

---

[20] Georg Wilhelm Friedrich Hegel, *Introductory Lectures on Aesthetics*, 1822–29 (London: Penguin Books, 2004), 12.
[21] Schelling, *System of Transcendental Idealism*, 218–36.
[22] Schelling, *System of Transcendental Idealism*, 225.
[23] Friedrich Hölderlin, et al., 'The Oldest Program for a System of German Idealism', c1795, in *Essays and Letters*, 341–2 (London: Penguin, 2009), passim.

But in a more practical sense, if a new sense of community was to be forged through aesthetic participation, then someone had to create artworks that would enable the desired unification of modernity's dirempted subjectivity. Someone, in other words, had to take the reins of the absolute and control the ways that human life would make sense to everyone else. Franz Liszt himself is a prime example, for his own opinions corresponded with the Kantian/Hegelian view of 'genius' as one who was endowed with particular gifts – one who would 'march' and his public would 'follow'.[24] Living in a culture of philosophical aesthetics shaped by Kant, Hegel and Schiller, and due to the more specific influences of Alphonse Lamartine and the Saint-Simonians, Liszt saw the Romantic artist as one who should strive to become, quite literally, an 'artist-priest' – a mediator between God and man, a bridge between the sublime and the everyday that all artists could supposedly become.[25] Schiller had described something very similar when he penned a moral rallying-cry for artists everywhere:

> Live with your century, but do not be its creature; serve our contemporaries, but give them what they need, not what they praise. Without having shared their guilt, share with them with noble resignation their punishments . . . take on their suffering . . . your own nobility will awake their own . . . . The gravity of your principles will scare them off, but they will be able to bear them in play . . . Chase from their pleasures all caprice, frivolity and coarseness . . . wherever you find them surround them with refined, great, inspirational forms, encircle them with symbols of excellence, until appearance conquers reality, and art nature.[26]

The shaping of such an ideal community through cultural transcendence – the path to *Bildung* as the desired result of an ethical aesthetic education – was now, with Romanticism, in the hands of certain people who were supposedly better suited to the task than others.

At the same time the concept of the sublime resurfaced in Romantic aesthetics. It brought together the twin mythologized, authoritative and irresistible powers of nature and the artistic genius. The sublime began with Longinus as a concept in rhetoric (in its Aristotelian sense as the art of persuasion) and developed, through Addison and Burke, associations with a perceptual encounter with

---

[24] Hegel, *Introductory Lectures on Aesthetics*, 31; see Kant, *Critique of Judgement*, §49, 186–7; Ralph P. Locke, *Music, Musicians and the Saint-Simonians* (Chicago: University of Chicago Press, 1986), 44.
[25] Andrew Haringer, 'Liszt and the Legacy of Lamartine', in *Liszt's Legacies*, ed. Michael Saffle and James Deaville, 72–91 (Stuyvesant: Pendragon Press, 2014), 73; Locke, *Music, Musicians and the Saint-Simonians*, 101.
[26] Schiller, *On the Aesthetic Education of Man*, 32.

threatening natural powers. By the time Kant theorized the sublime in the *Critique of Judgement*, the term had come to name a certain state of mind elicited upon the encountering of an object which causes the mind to overburden its faculties of comprehension.[27] The object is credited with a cognitively problematic and paralysing kind of significance caused by an over- or under-determination of meaning.[28] In the sublime moment, a mixture of pain and satisfaction is found in the part-comprehension of unimaginable totalities, such as the night sky or God. We credit our imagination with being able to grasp the ungraspable, if only incompletely, and we find that 'there is nothing we cannot read into it'.[29]

The cultural images of Romantic composers such as Beethoven, Paganini, Liszt and Wagner in particular combine these three etymological roots of the sublime in rhetoric, nature and cognition. Quasi-natural 'force of nature' associations joined with a seemingly unprecedented power to 'convince' people through the ineffable affective power of their music, which was, of course, acknowledged to be a product of genius. This is 'convincing' in the abstract – the mobilization of social energy to no particular end in itself, or the eliciting of Romantic emotion, ready perhaps to be directed towards 'mass' cultural transcendence (a utopian contradiction).

The sublime provides a name for a kind of highly affective moment of 'making sense' of something; it is 'intuitive' in the sense that it bypasses rational thinking, and as such becomes particularly significant to much of what was valued in Romantic art. But at its most problematic, the sublime legitimates a state of existence which is not understood by those who experience it, conferring upon it, and those who wield it, a sense of unquestionable value.

For an example, we might return to Heine's 'Florentine Nights' and that description of an audio-visual performance by Paganini. While on stage – playing music that undercuts the concept of reason by Romantic ineffability – the virtuoso becomes an exemplar of the Romantic genius type whose charismatic authority, or, in Heine's rhetoric, through the reporting of their sheer existence, mutates into a mystifying sublimity:

> In the midst of this space hovered a shining sphere, upon which, gigantic and sublimely haughty, stood a man who played the violin. Was that sphere the sun?

---

[27] Kant, *Critique of Judgement*, §23–8, 97–123.
[28] See Thomas Weiskel, *The Romantic Sublime: Studies in the Structure and Psychology of Transcendence* (Baltimore and London: The John Hopkins University Press, 1976), 26.
[29] Weiskel, *The Romantic Sublime*, 26–7.

I do not know. But in the man's features I recognised Paganini, only ideally lovely, divinely glorious, with a reconciling smile.[30]

Only a few pages before, Heine had described Paganini with the assistance of other, contradictory schematic types: as a demonic figure draped in chains, with a face displaying a 'lusty-goat nature', conjuring melodies like the songs of 'fallen angels'.[31] But this momentary negative understanding has swiftly been either forgotten or reconciled.

Either way, this potential of the genius figure placed the Romantic artist in a powerful position, one that would, as the century progressed, become viewed with mistrust. From its very inception, the Romantic prioritization of individual freedom and feeling was suspected of leading to authoritarianism, as Kant himself was among the first to realize. As early as 1786, he warned against the 'natural consequence' of this doctrine:

> If reason will not subject itself to the law it gives itself, it will have to bow under the yoke of laws which others impose upon it . . . the inevitable consequence of declared lawlessness in thinking (an emancipation from restriction of reason) is that freedom to think is finally lost.[32]

Even today, the cultural schemas of the artist and genius types commonly accommodate a sense of irrationality, alienage, danger and unpredictability which may find its root in the Romantic notion of the genius type as one who can, if not overcome, then perhaps redefine the boundaries between good and bad, acceptable and unacceptable, and subjective and objective – change the ways that things in the world intuitively make sense to people. This is, in other words, a mythologizing (Barthes) or sublime erasure (phantasmagoria [Adorno]) of explanatory processes. Sublimity – a characteristic not of an object but of its reception – has the potential to become the ultimate suspension of the critical faculties. One recognition that a theory of social explanation appears to warrant is that selective forgetting – or a willingness to play with what is deemed relevant to understanding a situation – may be a necessary condition of explanation itself, and as Rancière's philosophy more broadly can also help us to understand, the aesthetic meets the political at the boundary between what is deemed legitimate for inclusion in a situation and what is not.

---

[30] Heine, 'Florentine Nights', 207.
[31] Heine, 'Florentine Nights', 204.
[32] Cited in Lucien Goldmann, *Immanuel Kant*, 1967 (London: Verso, 2011), 120.

In accord with the role played by explanans in all explanations (as we saw in the introduction), audio-visual explanations, such as films, are subject to complex social determinations regarding what is legitimate content and context for their 'truth'. But, as Romanticism implies from the very history of its concept, although that 'truth' can be questioned, there are grave dangers lurking behind that critical imperative. A sense of both the author's naivety as to the material conditions of history (when read from a critical ideological perspective) and one of uncanny prescience may combine when we read today these lines from the end of Schelling's *System of Transcendental Idealism*:

> A new mythology is itself to arise, which shall be the creation, not of some individual author, but of a new race, personifying, as it were, one single poet – that is a problem whose solution can be looked for only in the future destinies of the world, and in the course of history to come.[33]

By the end of this book, we may say we have found it and recognized in it the conflation of Hegelian historicism, a discursive appeal to the spirit of a *volk* and the mythologized individual will of the genius – the supposed 'single poet' or artist-priest who speaks with one voice on behalf of society as a whole – in the works of Wagner, Hitler and Hollywood, respectively.

Conclusion: Film as Romantic explanation

There are crucial distinctions between the explanation of Romanticism constructed earlier and the many typical formulations of the concept. The dynamic of Romanticism is understood here not as a transcendental affirmation of a subjectivity proclaiming its sublime grasp of any absolute truth found in objective nature, but rather as an all-embracing critical imperative which turns both inner and social life towards principles of dialogue and openness. As with Kantian transcendental idealism, critical rationalism, philosophical hermeneutics and critical theory, a belief in an objective truth is justified not as a reason to claim knowledge of such truth as a privilege gained through the agency of a subject as a limited socio-historical individual, but rather as a joyful confession that truth cannot ever be reduced to such a privilege, but remains standing over us as a judge of our own eternal efforts to grasp it. In addition,

---

[33] Schelling, *System of Transcendental Idealism*, 233.

and as we have hinted already, this explanation of Romanticism appears to invite several further parallels with the philosophical concerns of other twentieth-century philosophical positions. To paraphrase the argument forwarded by Max Horkheimer at the end of *Eclipse of Reason* (1947), the path to social emancipation and freedom depends upon giving priority to a critical encounter between a Romantic objective criterion of truth and the various explanations of reality provided by the dominant historical traditions.[34] Perhaps there is a certain equation to be found between Romanticism, as a perpetually traumatized openness to the new, and the 'self-critique of reason' which Horkheimer called for as an essential task – essential in order to ensure the moral survival of a modernity which was itself traumatized by both the Holocaust and the cultural enthronement of those sublime audio-visual explanations of reality which were starting to be provided by the Hollywood dream factory. Romanticism today occupies this complex and contested ground between openness to the New, as a category of social ordering and epistemology, and the powerful explanatory conditions inherent to the interaction between that category (as embodied in the figure of the genius) and history itself. Romanticism can be demarcated as a historical period, rhetorically and incompletely, by tracing the dark shadow cast by the Third Reich back over the German Idealists – from the birth of cinema under Edison and Lumière to the sublime comet of 1811 which heralded the birth of the genius Franz Liszt; from Adorno to Hegel; and from one 'end of art' to another.

The earlier explanation of Romanticism, while situating this concept as one with an enriched applicability to film, also raises a number of significant questions: What relevance does the Romantic concept of genius have to film as a product of cooperative effort? Given the emancipation of the autonomous artwork from authorial intention in the aesthetic regime, and the development of an interpretive logic that allows 'everything' to 'speak', as Rancière claims, what effect might this have on the efficacy and function of audio-visual explanation as an ideological process? What does the aforementioned explanation of Romanticism mean for a hermeneutics of film? What is the relationship between this last question and what is normally meant by the term 'Romantic hermeneutics', for example, the work of Novalis, Schlegel and Schleiermacher? And what is the relevance of the previously explained method of risky archaeological analysis to this new

---

[34] Max Horkheimer, *Eclipse of Reason*, 1947 (London: Bloomsbury, 2013), 123.

set of questions, and its relationship to the central schema of Popper's critical rationalism: interpretation as conjecture and test?

What these questions call into view is the need to re-address the relationship between Romanticism and those other philosophical positions mentioned earlier (which, at first glance, seem antithetical to what the term has historically stood for), and in such a way that enlightens our conceptualization of film as a kind of audio-visual explanation. We might begin by considering these useful summary passages written by Elizabeth Millán-Zaibert:

> Schlegel's position is that we can never begin with the certain knowledge of ... [first principles]; instead we must begin with what we have – a history of what has been thought by other philosophers before . . . . Philosophy is historical, but is not therefore reduced to history, because it concerns the analysis and investigation of ideas, opinions, and thoughts; philosophy is best understood via a historical critique of these ideas, opinions, and thoughts . . . . When history is incorporated into the very method of philosophy itself, we can access a given contribution of a philosopher not only by *classifying* her arguments as valid or invalid, sound or unsound [as the more systemic philosophical projects of earlier 'non-Romantic' German Idealists might imply], but also by *comparing* the merits of the contribution to other contributions made by other philosophers from different periods.[35]

It seems that there is not so much of a leap to be made between this idea of Romanticism – explained according to concepts of anti-foundationalism, historical comparison and a 'striving' imperative based upon comparative criticism – and certain other ideas more familiar to contemporary European aesthetic and political philosophy. Armed with various audio-visual explanations of things in the world, and similar visions of possible worlds, conjured by the imagination of the genius, Romanticism has provided us with a key to understand and compare such explanations in new ways. This connection could perhaps be illuminated by envisioning a combination (too large a task to be accomplished in one book) of the concept of audio-visual explanation developed thus far and certain general principles shared by critical rationalism, philosophical hermeneutics, critical theory and the particular tributary of post-Althusserian Marxism represented by Rancière – namely, openness to the category of the New

---

[35] Elizabeth Millán-Zaibert, 'Introduction: "What is Early German Romanticism?"', in Manfred Frank, *The Philosophical Foundations of Early German Romanticism*, 1–21 (Albany: State University of New York Press, 2004), 10–14.

and a refusal to leave traditions unquestioned. As should already be clear, the audio-visual explanations provided by film involve this medium in the earlier discussion, no matter how complex it might become.

Given this scope of application, the Romantic concept of intuitive audio-visual explanation that the current selection of analytical tools has made possible also has the potential to overrun the bounds of the current study. Consequently, in subsequent chapters, the figure of Franz Liszt will become a beneficial 'limiting device', ultimately returning this argument from theoretical and philosophical abstraction back down to the textual analysis of films themselves. After having explored the relationship between Romanticism and film on a number of different analytical 'levels' in the following chapters – theory/philosophy, discourse, representation and textual analysis – we will return to the potential for additional theoretical/philosophical research in the conclusion. By then, we will have begun to see, in our journey through the decades, not only how Romanticism can be used to explain elements of film discourse and textual representation, and vice versa, but also how a Romanticized conception of interpretation itself can enrich our understanding of cultural representations as explanations more generally, and schematic cognition as a means of innovating new possibilities for understanding.

2

The archaeology of film music

Wagner, Liszt and the symphonic poem

The scope of the symphonic poem is almost infinite.

—R. W. S. Mendl[1]

Introduction

Film music didn't appear from nowhere. Peter Franklin's assertion that 'film music is older than film' strikes us today as received wisdom.[2] In the first decades of cinema, and later, when the sound film spread as an institutionalized phenomenon in the early 1930s, a particular question was asked: What part should music play in this new technological hybrid of an artistic medium? The practice of choosing existing music to fit new films was in evidence as early as 1895, but following the introduction of sound, the development and standardization of film music practice cemented the dominant narrative and vococentric tendencies in Hollywood film production.[3] Film music in Europe, too, continued to follow the three established principles of 'synchronisation, subjugation and continuity' and the same three modalities of 'compilation, improvisation and original score'.[4] Techniques such as 'kidding' (matching diegetic events with tangentially related popular tunes) disappeared because they

---

[1] R. W. S. Mendl, 'The Art of the Symphonic Poem', in *The Musical Quarterly* 18, no. 3 (1932): 461.
[2] Peter Franklin, *Seeing Through Music: Gender and Modernism in Classic Hollywood Film Scores* (Oxford: Oxford University Press, 2011), 3.
[3] Scott D. Paulin, 'Richard Wagner and the Fantasy of Cinematic Unity: The Idea of the *Gesamtkunstwerk* and the History and Theory of Film Music', in *Music and Cinema*, ed. James Buhler, Caryl Flinn and David Neumeyer, 58–84 (Hanover: Wesleyan University Press, 2000), 65; James Buhler and Hannah Lewis, 'Evolving Practices for Film Music and Sound: 1925–1935', in *The Cambridge Companion to Film Music*, ed. Mervyn Cooke and Fiona Ford, 7–28 (Cambridge: Cambridge University Press, 2016), 28.
[4] Buhler and Lewis, 'Evolving Practices for Film Music and Sound: 1925–1935', 10.

broke the increasingly important illusion that a film was a self-contained world. Aside from such changes, things appeared to go on much as they had done in the silent era, only now music was tied to the images more rigorously and more finally than was possible before. In this sense, the sound film presented a whole audio-visual text, unified and bonded. Yet, paradoxically, the fragmentation that appeared to be inherent to silent film music also became more pronounced, as the now 'discontinuous' score, as Royal S. Brown defined it, was counterpointed with newly significant dialogue.[5] For such reasons, the historical discourse of film music, like other fields within Film Studies, has had to deal with a moving target – both unstable and disreputable, and parasitic and hybridized.[6]

There is a marked self-reflexive tendency with regard to this historical situation of classical Hollywood musical style. In the wartime thriller *Above Suspicion* (1943), for example, a live performance of Liszt's Piano Concerto No. 1 (1830–56), accompanies an assassin killing a German officer, blurring, if not the implied source, then the functions of diegetic and non-diegetic music. In a later scene, a reconstruction of the murder with piano accompaniment centres around the mood created by the music – 'morbid' as one character describes it. The dramatic Romantic sound is explicitly linked to conventions of narrative cinema by the constructed evocation, in both cases, of the very diegetic event of proairetic suspense that it accompanies – the assassin, the gun and the victim. Here, Romantic musical sound becomes a powerful presence, both serving its narrative function and also announcing itself – catching itself in the act – as a fundamental albeit anachronistic pillar of cinematic convention.

This chapter is concerned with the names of two Romantic composers, Richard Wagner and Franz Liszt, and their relationships with film. In different ways, they experimented with the relationship between music and vision, music and extra-musical, but their names themselves are important beyond their works. One name, as we will see, is commonly cited as a forebear of, and key inspiration for, the dominant musical practices of classical Hollywood cinema, and even certain aspects of the apparatus of film spectatorship itself. The other was developing an integrated audio-visual aesthetic approach while suffering from a long-standing critical and academic neglect that lasted throughout the crucial period of theoretical development for film and film music discourse.

---

[5] Royal S. Brown, *Overtones and Undertones: Reading Film Music* (Berkeley: University of California Press, 1994), 94.
[6] See Guido Heldt, 'Film-Music Theory', in *The Cambridge Companion to Film Music*, ed. Mervyn Cooke and Fiona Ford, 97–113 (Cambridge: Cambridge University Press, 2016), 101

In this chapter, we will attempt to understand why Wagner's name attained the position it did in film and film music discourse, and then forward the alternative case of Liszt and his symphonic poem project to throw new light on the complex legacy of Romanticism in film.

Film music and Romanticism

To answer the questions pertaining to music's new role in film, practitioners and critics looked to existing models, and, following the lead of the scores themselves, tended to focus on musical Romanticism.[7] (In this context, Romanticism is understood as a historical period in Western music bracketed by the figure of Beethoven at its commencement and those of composers such as Mahler, Schoenberg and Richard Strauss at its dissolution.)

The nominally 'Romantic' sound of the classical Hollywood score was a consequence of a variety of social, economic and aesthetic determinants. A rising interest in atonality and anti-Romantic sound in early twentieth-century music, exemplified by the New Viennese School and Soviet-era composers, also led to a conceptualization of the dominant strain of Hollywood film music as an anachronistic holdover of nineteenth-century aesthetics, or what Peter Franklin called 'modernism's musical other'.[8] In addition to its ready availability for many large movie theatres in the silent era, the Romantic orchestra provided a suitable model for the Hollywood score due, as K. J. Donnelly noted, to its 'significant emotional effect and the regular enormity of its sound'.[9] Claudia Gorbman, too, suggested that the familiar sound of the Romantic orchestra provided 'quick and efficient signification' to mass audiences.[10] Franklin went further in suggesting that 'cinematic narrative [itself] might, in some sense, have been born out of late-Romantic music', as part of a broader cross-fertilization among aesthetic forms

---

[7] Academics as diverse as Caryl Flinn, Royal S. Brown, Richard Taruskin and Matthew Bribitzer-Stull appear to concur on the legitimacy of a kind of Romantic 'arrested development' characterizing the Hollywood aesthetic that extends beyond the tropes and registers of the musical score. See Caryl Flinn, *Strains of Utopia: Gender, Nostalgia, and Hollywood Film Music* (Princeton: Princeton University Press, 2006), 7, 91; Brown, *Overtones and Undertones*, 117–18; Richard Taruskin, *The Oxford History of Western Music*, 6 vols. (Oxford: Oxford University Press, 2005), 3: *Music in the Early Twentieth Century*, 549; Matthew Bribitzer-Stull, *Understanding the Leitmotif: From Wagner to Hollywood Film Music* (Cambridge: Cambridge University Press, 2015), 280.
[8] Franklin, *Seeing Through Music*, 36; also Taruskin, *Music in the Early Twentieth Century*, 551.
[9] K. J. Donnelly, *The Spectre of Sound: Music in Film and Television* (London: BFI, 2005), 167.
[10] Claudia Gorbman, *Unheard Melodies: Narrative Film Music* (Bloomington and Indianapolis: Indiana University Press, 1987), 4.

such as the novel, concert hall music and cinema, which developed between them new methods of subjective expression for mass audiences:

> What we glimpse here is a broad intertextual field in which symphonic music, opera, and popular dramatic genres like melodrama form a constellation in which the mechanisms of late-Romantic musical meaning seem not only displayed but also revealed as focusing and driving something of the whole character of the mass entertainment 'art' experience of the early twentieth century and beyond.[11]

Nevertheless, as the century progressed, film music discourse displayed a tendency to situate opera, specifically, as the relevant model and forbear of the synchronized recorded soundtrack. This might have been inevitable considering two particular developments. First, by 1900, most compilation film scores took their material from opera.[12] This enabled cheap and quick musical accompaniment from a diverse stockpile that was familiar, pleasant to hear, and with easily grasped associative and symbolic potential. Second, the retrospectively formed connections between opera and film were based on a perception of a fundamental similarity in their combination of music with performed narrative and the resultant emotional effect. As Richard Taruskin noted, 'it turned out that a movie soundtrack could be remarkably like an opera in its function, if not precisely in its means'.[13] Ernst Bloch suggested in 1913 that theatrical musical practices, removed from the need to entice customers into theatres by a sideshow rallying-call approach, now functioned 'solely in conjunction with the moving images. The result bore a *natural resemblance* to ... opera'.[14] As we will see, this 'natural resemblance', which actually developed according to a variety of institutional and economic needs, became strongest with regard to the 'music dramas' of Richard Wagner.

Wagner and cinema

The comparison between Wagner and cinema has a long history in industrial, critical and academic discourses, often serving an explicitly evaluative explanatory

---

[11] Peter Franklin, *Reclaiming Late-Romantic Music: Singing Devils and Distant Sounds* (Berkeley: University of California Press, 2014), 135, 127–8.
[12] Altman, *Silent Film Sound*, 251.
[13] Taruskin, *Music in the Early Twentieth Century*, 549.
[14] Ernst Bloch, 'On Music in the Cinema', 1913, in *Literary Essays*, 156–9 (Stanford: Stanford University Press, 1998), 157.

function. The discontinuous historical development of film technology in the nineteenth century encouraged a variety of mythic explanations of the origins of cinema, and the Wagnerian *Gesamtkunstwerk* is a significant example of this tendency. Later in the chapter we will see how Wagner's name and ideas were appropriated to serve three practical and discursive positions: positive, compositional and negative.

The flexibility of Wagner as a discursive construct was partly a result of the fact that film became entangled in the issues surrounding Wagner as an agent of cultural change at the turn of the century. In 1904, the musicologist Arthur Elson wrote: 'It seemed as if . . . [Wagner] summed up in his works the whole range of musical possibilities.'[15] Like Beethoven's Ninth Symphony (1824) before him, Wagner's music dramas appeared the gravitational centre of contemporary musical thought. Musicologist Carl Dahlhaus wrote:

> There is no mistaking the mark Wagner left on his time, yet its nature is hard to define since it manifested itself . . . in vague but powerful currents of feeling. . . . We could, with only a tinge of exaggeration, speak of the 'cultural re-evaluation' of the end of the century as being born from the spirit of . . . Wagner's music.[16]

Whether exaggerated or not, this articulation of a vague potential for influence created opportunities for developing a functional *resemblance* between Wagner and cinema in film and film music discourses. Early cinema impresarios such as Samuel 'Roxy' Rothapfel proclaimed the Wagnerian ancestry of innovative thematic musical accompaniment practices soon to become dominant in American cinemas.[17] Roxy's claim to Wagnerian ancestry has been augmented by many other prominent figures, including the composers Max Steiner, Dmitri Tiomkin, Miklós Rózsa, Joseph Carl Breil and Gottfried Huppertz, who all credited Wagner with providing the ideal model for film composition.[18] Wagnerian concepts such as 'unending melody' and the leitmotif became

---

[15] Cited in Leon Botstein, 'Wagner and Our Century', in *Music at the Turn of the Century: A 19th Century Music Reader*, ed. Joseph Kerman, 167–80 (Berkeley: University of California Press, 1990), 167.

[16] Carl Dahlhaus, *Between Romanticism and Modernism*, 1974 (Berkeley: University of California Press, 1980), 10–11.

[17] Rick Altman, 'Early Film Themes: Roxy, Adorno and the Problem of Cultural Capital', in *Beyond the Soundtrack: Representing Music in Cinema*, ed. Daniel Goldmark, Lawrence Kramer and Richard Leppert, 205–24 (Berkeley: University of California Press, 2007), 212.

[18] Bribitzer-Stull, *Understanding the Leitmotif*, 273; Flinn, *Strains of Utopia*, 13, David Bordwell, 'The Classical Hollywood Style, 1917–60', in David Bordwell, Janet Staiger and Kristen Thompson, *The Classical Hollywood Cinema: Film Style and Mode of Production to 1960*, 3–84 (London and New York: Routledge and Kegan Paul, 1985), 34.

commonplace in film music publications throughout the 1910s and the 1920s, including citations in Ernö Rapée's famous guides for cinema musicians.[19]

In retrospect, Wagner's own innovations in performance practices also resemble later cinema experiences. Some of the ideas explored by film theorists such as Christian Metz and Jean-Louis Baudry – in terms of the apparatus of spectatorship creating a dreamlike space where the supposed unity of selfhood is altered – appear to have, if not their origin, then at least a significant precursor in Wagner's work. The invisible orchestra, front-facing seats and darkened auditorium of Wagner's Bayreuth *Festspeilhaus*, all appear to prefigure the immersive, darkened and self-forgetful apparatus of cinema. This resemblance has since been maintained in both academic and industrial contexts by token mentions and broad comparisons by prominent figures such as David Bordwell and Howard Shore.[20] The comparison between Wagner and cinema survives through a host of such resemblances, each serving particular explanatory functions.

Once they were established as a more than technological attraction, early film productions made efforts to conceal the mechanical apparatus that had once been the core of its novelty. Calls for continuous music throughout the length of a film fostered the notion of a film as an integrated whole, displaying an operatic aspiration for sensory continuity and craft. This new formulation altered the perception of the soundtrack's role and value. As Rick Altman pointed out, in the 1910s, music was increasingly subordinated to an increasingly generalized 'whole film' signification: 'no longer dominant, music would henceforth be required by trade press arbiters to serve three complementary masters: *the general nature of the picture*, the film's narrative, and its central characters' – and the former tended to dominate.[21] Film composers therefore had the task of grasping the 'general character' of a film project (although this was not always clear during production) and then composing or compiling 'appropriate music'.[22] Contemporary commentators such as Clarence E. Sinn propagated this approach among composers: 'try and find *the predominant theme* . . . don't pay too much attention to little details and accessories of a picture unless they have an important bearing on the scene or the story'.[23] Altman states that these widespread views

---

[19] Flinn, *Strains of Utopia*, 14–15; Joe, 'Why Wagner and Cinema', 4.
[20] Bordwell concludes that the classical Hollywood score shares the Wagnerian opera's partial self-consciousness and partial communicativeness while dispensing with large-scale temporal construction in favour of 'moment-by-moment heightening of the story'; Bordwell, 'The Classical Hollywood Style, 1917–60', 33–5; see Joe, 'Why Wagner and Cinema?', 6.
[21] Altman, *Silent Film Sound*, 243.
[22] Altman, *Silent Film Sound*, 244.
[23] Cited in Altman, *Silent Film Sound*, 244.

'provided a new standard against which all film accompaniment' was measured.[24] It was not until the mid-1930s that, as Caryl Flinn writes, 'these practices and techniques settled into a more or less stable set of conventions', drawing their terminology, if not exactly the precise compositional practices, freely from Wagnerian aesthetics, appropriating the leitmotif, 'unending melody' and the *Gesamtkunstwerk* concepts.[25]

Needless to say, modern film music scholarship has treated the emergence of these three concepts in film music practice and criticism as a consequence of a broader recontextualization of Romanticism in film music generally in both institutional terms (auteurism in composition) and stylistic terms (orchestral sound). As we will see, some argue that these Wagnerian ideas are only labels – problematic, badly-defined and imposed upon a fundamentally different 'medium'. As this chapter progresses, we will also see how these appropriated ideas approach, to a remarkable degree, those which Franz Liszt, Wagner's great Romantic contemporary, was mobilizing in his symphonic poem project.

Wagnerian aesthetics and cinema's symbolic capital

Like the concept of the auteur, the attractiveness of Wagnerian aesthetics to film and film music discourses rested on its potential to endow film with greater cultural value. As noted earlier, for film composers, the invocation of Romanticism generally, and Wagner specifically, was a means of raising the legitimacy of their profession. Music was regarded as so unimportant that it was uncommon for film composers to be credited before 1932.[26] By citing Wagner in their music, press statements and documents of various kinds, both specific composers and film music generally acquired what Pierre Bourdieu called 'symbolic capital': the accumulation of prestige and honorific status as a means to personal social value. In a similar way, early film theorists occasionally turned to classical music to validate film itself. Hugo Münsterberg, Siegfried Kracauer and Béla Balázs, among others, valued film according to principles of quasi-musical unity, adopting familiar and honorific musical terminology, including 'leitmotif', to describe the supposedly unique functions and abilities of film as a

---

[24] Altman, *Silent Film Sound*, 246.
[25] See Appendix B; Flinn, *Strains of Utopia*, 17–18.
[26] Clifford McCarty, *Film Composers in America: A Filmography, 1911–1970*, 2nd edn (Oxford: Oxford University Press, 2000), 9.

medium.[27] As part of a broader array of early aestheticizing tendencies, Wagner's name and ideas were evoked as part of this *positive discourse* concerning film's legitimacy as an art form.

Scott D. Paulin and Rick Altman questioned this 'natural' association between Wagner and cinema which developed in the discourses of film and film music in the early twentieth century; they recognized that Wagner's name had become a 'fetish object', serving various economic and cultural functions.[28] Paulin concludes that Wagnerian aesthetics played a 'talismanic role' in discourse by endowing its subject with a degree of symbolic capital appropriated from classical music, and, further, by 'denying the fundamental disunity' of the classical Hollywood product, warding-off accusations 'of film's material heterogeneity, discontinuity, mass production . . . mechanical reproduction' and multiple authoring.[29] This process centred around the adoption, adaptation and dissemination of those three particular Wagnerian concepts – leitmotif, 'unending melody' and the *Gesamtkunstwerk* – within a particular strain of *compositional practice* commonly associated with composers such as Max Steiner and Erich Wolfgang Korngold.

All three Wagnerian terms were adopted with transformational effect by film music discourse, often rendering problematic whatever theoretical consistency they might have accrued. 'Leitmotif' is here understood as a particular lineage of the common practice of 'reminiscence motifs' (a recurring associative musical idea), only one endowed with an explicitly Wagnerian heritage and talismanic function. The identification of leitmotif in a work implies a sense of organic unity or 'web' construction in large-scale musical form. Many so-called leitmotifs in film music are adequately described by the simple term 'motif'. 'Unending melody' in its original Wagnerian usage means the avoidance of cadences, ornament, transitional or formulaic material, which was, for Wagner, the same as 'unmusical' material.[30] The definition in early film music discourse that restricts the concept to a simple idea of continuous music was the result of a technological imperative; there was need for continuous music, or 'unending melody', to disguise the sounds of projecting machinery. Finally, the *Gesamstkunstwerk*, as we have seen, presented a suggestive and respectable model for proto-cinematic

---

[27] See Lydia Goehr, 'Film as Visual Music: Duplication, Dissonance and Displacement', in *Elective Affinities: Musical Essays on the History of Aesthetic Theory*, 204–56 (New York: Columbia University Press, 2008), 213.

[28] Paulin, 'Richard Wagner and the Fantasy of Cinematic Unity', 59; Altman, 'Early Film Themes', 212–19.

[29] Paulin, 'Richard Wagner and the Fantasy of Cinematic Unity', 77–9.

[30] Carl Dahlhaus, *Nineteenth Century Music*, 1980 (Berkeley: University of California Press, 1989), 199–200.

value, situating the so-called seventh art as the one that integrated all others. Despite their undeniably significant contributions to film music criticism and practice, a reliance on the terminology of Wagnerian aesthetics such as leitmotif, 'unending melody' and *Gesamtkunstwerk* as explanatory frameworks for film music is certainly reductionist.

Negative discourse: Wagner and Adorno

Significantly, Wagnerian terminology was employed to mobilize questions of cinematic value in both positive and negative senses. In addition to the talismanic and compositional functions that served to raise the value of cinema, those who sought to criticize certain aspects of cinema also turned to Wagner, citing him within a *negative discourse* regarding film's political legitimacy. Although this has been a less widespread approach, it has been adopted by a number of prominent Marxist theorists. Kracauer, for one, employed the *Gesamtkunstwerk* concept in 'The Cult of Distraction' (1926) to characterize the supposedly reactionary illusion of 'organic' unity created in the cinema-going experience.[31] But it was in several publications in the 1940s and the 1950s that Theodor Adorno, along with his co-writers Max Horkheimer and Hanns Eisler, solidified Wagner's negative relationship to film.

The Frankfurt School philosophers accused Wagner of being the progenitor of cinema's role in the abhorred culture industry. Specifically, Wagner and film shared a tendency towards 'phantasmagoria', or the harmful ideological illusion, outlined in Adorno's *In Search of Wagner* (1952), that the consumed product is self-producing.[32] Phantasmagoria is related both to Marx's concept of 'alienation' and the Romantic sublime, creating a state of wonder in a listener who becomes reassured, compliant and uncritical. From Adorno's perspective, Wagner's music was commodified to a greater extent than that of any previous composer, just like film would later become in Hollywood's most offensive kind of ideologically mystifying realist text. Aligning with a broader tendency to consider Romantic music as narcotic or drug-like, Adorno also positioned Wagner's music itself as

---

[31] Siegfried Kracauer, 'The Cult of Distraction: On Berlin's Picture Palaces', 1926, in *The Continental Philosophy of Film Reader*, ed. Joseph Westfall, 197–200 (London: Bloomsbury, 2018), passim.
[32] Theodor Adorno, *In Search of Wagner*, 1952 (London and New York: Verso, 1991), 149; Theodor Adorno and Max Horkheimer, *Dialectic of Enlightenment*, 1944 (London and New York: Verso, 1997), 124; Theodor Adorno and Hanns Eisler, *Composing for the Films*, 1947 (London: The Athlone Press, 1994), 4–6.

inducing a numb and unthinking state of awareness – a kind of proto-cinematic 'witchcraft'.[33] For the Frankfurt School philosophers, both Wagner's music dramas and his film music supposedly demand less critical attention from their audiences; commodified and simplified at levels of production and consumption, both tell the audience what to feel, facilitating a dangerous ideological mystification. Adorno inherited this cautionary position from late Nietzsche, who expressed similar concerns regarding the dangerously persuasive potential of Wagner's music in *The Case of Wagner* (1888), overturning the verdict of his more famous previous book *The Birth of Tragedy* (1872).[34]

Bayreuth's hidden orchestra, the newly darkened auditorium and the supposedly narcotic qualities of Wagner's music itself all achieve, for Adorno, questionable ideological effects on the viewing and listening subject. What Adorno achieved in relation to Wagner and film is similar, in a way, to many other examples from the history of Film Studies, when a theorist appropriates a concept from an older established discipline and puts it to new use, after it first being suitably modified to suit the study of film and the theorist's personal interests. Beyond this, perhaps Adorno's key significance lies in popularizing the idea that, as K. J. Donnelly puts it, 'film music constitutes a system of control' of one kind or another[35] – a system possessing a powerful and varied intuitive explanatory potential. As we will see, this is perhaps where the comparison between film and Romanticism has the most theoretical weight, and in such a way that by no means limits it to Wagnerian aesthetics.

Reconsidering Wagner in Film Music Studies

Modern academics tend to agree that traditional film music discourse, whether positive, compositional and negative, has perhaps been led 'too quickly and easily to Wagner'; Franklin, Altman, Matthew Bribitzer-Stull, Buhler and David Neumeyer, all concur that although much film music was undoubtedly influenced by his music dramas, 'that hardly makes a case for Wagner being the

---

[33] Theodor Adorno, *Minima Moralia*, 1951 (London and New York: Verso, 1987), 201.
[34] Friedrich Nietzsche, 'The Case of Wagner: A Musicians Problem', 1888, in *The Birth of Tragedy and The Case of Wagner*, 155–92 (New York: Vintage, 1967), passim; Friedrich Nietzsche, 'The Birth of Tragedy', 1872, in *The Birth of Tragedy and The Case of Wagner*, 17–151 (New York: Vintage, 1967), 126–30.
[35] Donnelly, *The Spectre of Sound*, 1, 4.

one who fathered the genre'.[36] The argument obscures something significant: it prolongs an uncertainty that relates film music to wider pre-cinematic cultural formations of music and visuality throughout the Romantic period which are not reducible to Wagnerian opera.

The recent development of a concept called 'cinematic listening' illustrates this point well. By the 1790s, European audiences were accustomed to finding their own images in supposedly absolute music.[37] In the Romantic period, this division between public expressions of absolutism and more private, often specifically visual, musical experiences became a widespread reception practice. Visualizing music was even actively encouraged by some (including Liszt, as we will see). Orchestral music in particular was potentially seen as well as heard, a phenomenon sometimes termed 'cinematic listening' – as explored by Peter Franklin, Ben Winters and Michael Long. Musical experiences were described with subjective 'proto-cinematic visualised narratives'.[38] The extract from Heine on the opening pages of this book neatly illustrates this phenomenon. Extensions of visual listening practices, such as 'sound-tracing' (mental visualizations or physical gestures as neurological responses to audible impressions), occasionally find expression in quasi-cinematic language. Cinematic descriptions continued into the twentieth century, sometimes featuring terms such as 'intercutting', 'shot', 'cut' and 'dialectic between continuity and fragmentation', evidencing direct appropriations from film discourse.[39]

Due to this newly significant relationship between music and visuality, the nineteenth century must still be considered the primary backdrop for the development of film music practice, particularly the classical Hollywood style, but with the additional requirement of studying other previously overlooked influences alongside Wagner. Peter Franklin, Katherine Preston and Michael Pisani, for example, have persuasively argued that Italian opera, musical theatre and symphonies 'are equally relevant' to this discussion.[40] Academic studies of

---

[36] Franklin, *Seeing Through Music*, 38; Altman, 'Early Film Themes', 205; Bribitzer-Stull, *Understanding the Leitmotif*, 264.
[37] Richard Will, *The Characteristic Symphony in the Age of Haydn and Beethoven* (Cambridge: Cambridge University Press, 2002), 16–17.
[38] Franklin, *Seeing Through Music*, 90; Ben Winters, *Music, Performance, and the Realities of Film: Shared Concert Experiences in Screen Fiction* (New York and London: Routledge, 2014), 119–46; Long, *Beautiful Monsters*, 50, 66–72, 111–12; Franklin also suggests that, in this sense, the classical film score can be considered a 'refracted and fragmented echo' of the nineteenth-century Romantic symphony; Franklin, *Seeing Through Music*, 88–95.
[39] Winters, *Music, Performance and the Realities of Film*, 134.
[40] Franklin, *Seeing Through Music*, 115; Katherine K. Preston, 'Introduction: From Nineteenth-Century Stage Melodrama to Twenty-First-Century Film Scoring', *Journal of Film Music* 5, nos. 1–2

music traditions in melodrama have also surfaced in recent decades, relating not only to the specific pairing of music with unsung dialogue but also to the evocative and emotional scores that are read to anticipate later Hollywood products. By the time of the transition to sound, the American cinema-going public would have been far more familiar with the musical conventions of melodrama than with Wagnerian opera; however, melodrama lacked the symbolic capital required by film composers and commentators to justify the value of their profession.

Alongside finding such alternatives to Wagner, the previously obscure concept of 'mood' has also become better understood. Composers and critics have often suggested two basic approaches to film scoring: (a) colouristic, mood or atmospheric and (b) linear, thematic or motivic; such binary models, although simplifying a highly variable terrain, were often employed in early musical criticism.[41] The motivic approach, as we have seen, often led to the citation of Wagner, yet as Robert Nelson pointed out in 1946, mood scoring (an approach that would not typically attempt to map a dense structure of leitmotifs or rigorously employ Mickymousing) was often a simpler task for composers and music departments when working under time constraints.[42] As the decades progressed, studies by Claudia Gorbman, Noël Carroll and K. J. Donnelly, to name only a few, explored beyond the motivic approach, addressing the importance of mood setting, atmosphere, synchronization and affect.[43] Mood has taken a central role in film music discourse, supposedly originating in 'the complex of all conative elements of the filmic system', as Gorbman put it, and returning again as a significant part of this total.[44]

Of course, this development is not entirely novel. It is well known that sheet music compilations for silent films were compiled according to situation and appropriate mood. As Jeff Smith summarized, the critical perspective that situated the action-event relationship as the primary determinant of classical Hollywood film scoring (exemplified by Mickymousing) was established, not as a historical

(2012): 7–14; Michael V. Pisani, 'When the Music Surges: Melodrama and the Nineteenth Century Theatrical Precedents for Film Music Style and Placement', in *The Oxford Handbook of Film Music Studies*, ed. David Neumeyer, 559–82 (Oxford: Oxford University Press, 2014), passim.

[41] William Darby and Jack Du Bois, *American Film Music: Major Composers, Techniques, Trends, 1915–1990* (Jefferson: McFarland and Company Inc., 1990), xv; Robert U. Nelson, 'Film Music: Color or Line?', in *Hollywood Quarterly* 2, no. 1 (1946): 57–65.

[42] Nelson, 'Film Music', 63.

[43] Gorbman, *Unheard Melodies*, 11; Noël Carroll, 'Notes on Movie Music', 1986, in *Theorising the Moving Image*, 139–45 (Cambridge: Cambridge University Press, 1996), passim; Donnelly, *The Spectre of Sound*, 94.

[44] Gorbman, *Unheard Melodies*, 30.

consequence of conditions relevant to earlier silent film, but on a problematic and ahistorical basis.[45] Attributes such as genre, characterization, setting and mood were of greater significance in shaping what people actually heard during a film than what the Wagner argument allowed for. Yet even this broader understanding, facilitated by looking beyond Wagner, is, of course, only another part of a complex socio-historical development with both aesthetic, individual and industrial aspects. Altman and Gorbman agree that the explanatory citations of opera, symphony and melodrama in film music discourse 'only answer the question in part'.[46] More than this, Altman criticizes the inadequate state of the literature which must serve as a foundation for the melodramatic approach, relying as it does upon non-canonized practices and works that have not benefited from the selective preservation of the institutions which regulate the materials that make up music history: 'Since there is relatively little scholarship on nineteenth century stage music (other than opera), students of silent film sound have sometimes been forced to base their claims on rather thin knowledge'.[47]

Despite the drawbacks of simply finding alternative Romantic musical traditions to serve as raw materials for the archaeology of film music, there is still something significant that connects these objects of study beyond the specificities of each particular tradition. As the discussion of Rancière's aesthetic regime in the previous chapter has prepared us to recognize, nineteenth-century opera, the symphony post-Beethoven, theatrical melodrama and the symphonic poem can all be grouped together as *Romantic multimedia forms*. Aside from Wagner, another principal player in these developments, and one whose role in the pre-history of film music is to be considered here in depth, was Franz Liszt.

Rediscovering Liszt in music history

In 1864, reeling from critical disapproval, Liszt wrote:

> It seems to me now, high time that I should be somewhat forgotten, or at least placed very much in the background.[48]

---

[45] Jeff Smith, 'Music', in *The Routledge Companion to Philosophy and Film*, ed. Paisley Livingston and Carl Plantinga, 184–94 (London and New York: Routledge, 2009), 187.
[46] Altman, *Silent Film Sound*, 10; Gorbman, *Unheard Melodies*, 35.
[47] Altman, *Silent Film Sound*, 10.
[48] Cited in Alan Walker, 'Liszt and the Twentieth Century', in *Franz Liszt: The Man and His Music*, ed. Alan Walker, 350–64 (London: Barrie and Jenkins, 1970), 357.

That is exactly what happened. After his retirement as a touring virtuoso in 1847, Liszt had become regarded as a mere 'sideshow to Wagner's centre, a cultural trill'.[49] This state of affairs persisted for decades. The late twentieth century saw a gradual revival of interest in Liszt and a revaluation of his significance to music history. From the work of Humphrey Searle in the 1960s through Alan Walker, Keith T. Johns and Leslie Howard in the 1980s and the 1990s to Dana Gooley and Michael Saffle in the 2000s, not only was Liszt's music being propagated and defended by new generations of musicians and academics but the ideas behind them were also better understood. Many of Liszt's most radical works went unperformed for decades, during which time his canonization faltered. In the late nineteenth century, aside from the stigma of virtuosity which partly prevented Liszt from being taken seriously as a composer during his highly creative Weimar period (1847–61), a surplus of critical attention was paid, as we have seen, to Wagner as an agent of cultural change. Around the time of the Bayreuth premiers of 1876, as Walker put it: 'Wagner's star waxed . . . [as Liszt's] own waned'.[50] Given the tumultuous upheavals in music history that followed, consequent with the emergence of cinema, Liszt's contemporary efforts to revitalize church music seemed, to critics, composers, philosophers and the public at large, far less relevant to the direction of European cultural history. As for the symphonic poems that Liszt created during his Weimar period, as Johns notes, these compositions 'have been very little studied, either by Liszt's biographers or by historians of musical style', being largely 'overshadowed' by Wagner's work.[51]

Putting our hypothesis simply: during the burgeoning institutionalization of cinema and early film music practices in the last decade of the nineteenth century, extending into the twentieth, Wagner, rather than Liszt, was on the minds of those who were majorly responsible for shaping the terminology, practices, critical and theoretical reception of film and its music.

As we have seen, Wagner provided the readily-graspable symbolic capital necessary to accomplish a number of institutionally determined tasks. This is by no means intended to downplay the significance of Wagner to the discourses of cinema and film music, only to demonstrate that his inclusion in those

---

[49] Susan Bernstein, *Virtuosity of the Nineteenth Century: Performing Music and Language in Heine, Liszt and Baudelaire* (Stanford: Stanford University Press, 1998), 82.
[50] Walker, *Franz Liszt: The Final Years*, 354.
[51] Keith T. Johns, *The Symphonic Poems of Franz Liszt* (Stuyvesant: Pendragon Press, 1997), 2, 10.

discourses, and the exclusion of other elements such as Liszt, was the result of discursive formations that fulfil certain needs for valuation, symbolic power and explanation. As Leon Botstein reminds us: 'The historical correctives emerging from the relatively recent revival and long overdue reconsideration of Liszt as an innovator and visionary have not diminished the enormity of Wagner's significance or aesthetic influence'.[52] By examining the music of Liszt in the context of film music history we can step further out from the shadow of Wagner that has long loomed over this subject.

Liszt and contemporary philosophy of music

In order to understand Liszt's symphonic poems, it is necessary to present a brief overview of the ideas in early nineteenth-century musical aesthetics which influenced their creation. It is an issue demanding an awareness of Hegel as much as Beethoven, and the placement of Liszt's symphonic poems within histories not only of musical practice but also, more significantly when tackling the subject of Romanticism, of philosophical aesthetics. As we saw in Chapter 1, the German Idealist and Romantic philosophers fostered a belief that music was superior to language as a means of expressing truth. Burgeoning in the nineteenth century was a widespread desire to weave an authored connection between music and extra-musical associations using this vague communicative capacity, one some expected to transcend the possibilities inherent to all previous forms of art. It was claimed that art had the capacity to go beyond philosophy and science as a means of understanding the world, and with Romanticism came a widespread belief that music, in particular, could communicate a kind of 'message' more effectively and truthfully than was allowed for by the supposed limitations of grammatical language. The music and ideas of the post-Beethoven progressives, Berlioz, Liszt and Wagner, can be attributed, in part, to this new-found belief in music's unprecedented and largely untapped philosophical, social and political power. Liszt's formulation of the symphonic poem was a creative response to this background, although he was more directly influenced by the lectures given by the composer and musicologist François-Joseph Fétis, in addition to the writings of Hegel and Herder.

---

[52] Botstein, 'Wagner and Our Century', 168.

Fétis believed that musical theory, rather than an increasingly refined understanding of an objective aesthetic 'truth', was a progressively inclusive series of perspectives in a state of flux.[53] Liszt attended Fétis's Parisian lectures during the 1830s, and was inspired to approach his music with a certain degree of experimentation. Hegel, for his part, influenced nineteenth-century aesthetics not through any consistent interpretation of his general philosophical system, but rather in a piecemeal fashion, from individual ideas and statements. This was how Liszt responded to Hegel, both in his important essay 'Berlioz and his Harold Symphony' (1855), and in his contemporary symphonic poems, and it is worth considering the several ways that the philosopher's influence can be recognized in Liszt's ideas.[54]

First, the sense of 'freedom' inherent in the symphonic poem (see further) allied with the Hegelian view, inherited from Kant, that the artist is one removed from society, 'endowed with wholly peculiar gifts', and whose creative mind should be allowed 'free play'.[55] The symphonic poem project would also seem to be an indirect reaction against the supposition, shared by Hegel and Kant, that the arts existed within an insoluble hierarchy; for while Hegel discouraged the combining of the arts, Liszt, along with Schelling, believed and put into practice the assumption that art forms were often improved when combined or considered in relation to others. Liszt believed in an inherent plasticity to art-matter. He once wrote that 'Raphael and Michelangelo make Mozart and Beethoven more easy for me to understand'; as Liszt scholar Alan Walker identified: 'Herein lay the germ of Liszt's theory of programme music'.[56] In addition, as Joanne Cormac has stressed, Hegel's distinction between epic, dramatic and lyric poetry also influenced the early development of the symphonic poems; Hegel's conception of the lyric form – associated with the expression of subjective moods and feelings, and interior reflection over exterior action – provided an aesthetic foundation for several of Liszt's first drafts.[57]

Finally, and perhaps most significantly, the influence of Hegel is apparent in Liszt's ideas concerning the role that music could play in social development. According to Hegel, spectators identify aspects of their own self within artworks

---

[53] Thomas Christensen, 'Fétis and Emerging Tonal Consciousness', in *Music Theory in the Age of Romanticism*, ed. Ian Bent, 37–56 (Cambridge: Cambridge University Press, 1996), 37.
[54] Franz Liszt, 'Berlioz and his Harold Symphony', 1855, in *The Romantic Era: Source Readings in Music History*, ed. Oliver Strunk, 106–33 (New York: W. W. Norton and Company, 1965), 119–21.
[55] Hegel, *Introductory Lectures on Aesthetics*, 31; see Kant, *Critique of Judgement*, § 46–50, 174–89.
[56] Alan Walker, *Franz Liszt: The Virtuoso Years, 1811–1847* (London: Faber and Faber, 1983), 266.
[57] Joanne Cormac, *Liszt and the Symphonic Poem* (Cambridge: Cambridge University Press, 2017), 16–20.

and then enter into 'refreshed' relationships with them; those newly reconfigured 'elements of understanding' enlighten the perspectives of other persons.[58] The spectator observes in an artwork a 'mirrored' representation of an abstract element of their own self; this element is then perceived in removal from the self and purged of its sublimated power through a re-contextualization in the 'controlled environment' of the work.[59] Art encourages a sympathetic mode of address in which the spectator's perception of the subject and surrounding context is altered through a subjective 'filter' – a process of identification that is suggested through contemplation of the artwork itself and 'the points of view which it involves'.[60] As we saw in Chapter 1, despite the individually divergent interests and terms they employed in forming their theories, philosophers such as Hegel, Schelling and Schiller fostered that general belief that art could enable an understanding of things beyond the subjective, and that by playing a key role in the pursuit of *Bildung*, or the aesthetic education of mankind, they could develop a better sense of moral community.

At this stage two questions arise: How do such concepts inform Liszt's symphonic poems? And what does this have to with film? The answers lie in examining the means by which Liszt attempted to present a new aesthetics of social communication rooted in that multimedia imperative we have already encountered in the discussion of Rancière's aesthetic regime. Liszt recognized that music did not possess a capacity to evoke specific thoughts in any sense that allowed it to communicate like a language. Being fundamentally lacking in this regard, music required a programme to counteract this deficiency, and to turn it into an effective means of social or philosophical communication. Liszt's conception of musical 'language' was, therefore, dependent on a creative multimedia synthesis.

Liszt, as well as Wagner, perhaps lay closer to Schelling than Hegel in believing that art had a valuable role in human life, that it could 'say' something philosophy couldn't and that the means to achieve this lay in combining the various arts together. However, in a historical sense, it was Herder rather than Schelling who most likely influenced Liszt in this regard. Although Schelling initially theorized about art's truth-value in a generalized sense, the ability of music, specifically, to express a kind of essential and sharable truth developed from Herder. Liszt was very familiar with this

[58] Hegel, *Introductory Lectures on Aesthetics*, 54–5.
[59] Hegel, *Introductory Lectures on Aesthetics*, 54.
[60] Hegel, *Introductory Lectures on Aesthetics*, 54–5.

German philosopher, who, during his lifetime, like Schiller and Goethe, was a celebrity in Weimar – that city in which Liszt served as a cultural figurehead during the development of his symphonic poem project – and, in his capacity as the city's *Kapellmeister*, he organized several festivals in the name of his fellow honoured citizens.

Herder considered sound to be the pure expression of the interiority of things in the world. Since 'everything that sounds in nature is music', music is, therefore, an expression of truth, or a revelation of aspects of being which are normally hidden from sight alone.[61] Following from this observation, some modern studies have agreed that sound can convey an understanding of interiority; a sound produced by, or appearing to correspond to, the visual or tactile existence of an object can suggest an element of that object's inner truth or essence.[62] Where sight is typically the perception of surface from a distance, sound's resonance can be suggestive of size, consistency, material and other elements which cannot be guaranteed by sight. As a consequence, sound provides a supposedly essential and unmediated expression of the 'interior' (the 'soul') of an object.[63] (Phenomenological film studies have extended the legacy of this Romantic discourse to explain film music's 'completing' effect – its compensating for a 'lack' in the 'primitive condition' of the cinematic image by providing a sense of interiority, or a 'body', compensating for the physical absence inherent to film images).[64]

Like Schelling and Liszt, and unlike Hegel, Herder believed that there was a contemporary need for music to unite with other arts, since music was once part of the same family as other means of expression, such as 'words and gestures', but had experienced a lengthy process of separation from them by means of 'reverence', or the spiritualized high-art values built around certain kinds of music, dependent upon a ritualized processes of production and consumption.[65] Liszt may have felt sympathy for Herder's belief in the fundamental cooperative capacity of musical and non-musical arts, and intended symphonic poems as a means of reuniting them in a new and radical way.

---

[61] Johann Gottfried von Herder, '[from] *Kalligone*', 1800, in *Musical Aesthetics: A Historical Reader, Volume II – The Nineteenth Century*, ed. Edward A. Lippman, 33–43 (Stuyvesant: Pendragon Press, 1988), passim.
[62] See Donald M. Lowe, *History of Bourgeois Perception* (Chicago: University of Chicago Press, 1982), 6.
[63] Lowe, *History of Bourgeois Perception*, 6.
[64] Lawrence Kramer, 'Classical Music, Virtual Bodies, Narrative Film', in *The Oxford Handbook of Film Music Studies*, ed. David Neumeyer, 351–65 (Oxford: Oxford University Press, 2014), 355–8.
[65] Herder, '[from] *Kalligone*', 39–40.

As a result of these combined influences – Hegel, Schelling, Herder and Fétis – Liszt saw the rise of programme music in the mid-nineteenth century as a necessary and inevitable evolutionary step. As he wrote in the Berlioz essay:

> there have always been combinations of music with literary and quasi-literary works; the present time seeks a union of the two which promises to become a more immediate one that any that have offered themselves thus far.[66]

Theorizing the symphonic poem

By 1854, in a climate shaped by the philosophical ideas outlined earlier, Liszt had come to believe that the time was right for 'a radical transformation in art', to be achieved by redefining the boundaries between music and other media, and between artists, society and God.[67] His exposure to the contemporary culture of philosophical aesthetics, shaped by ideas of 'aesthetic education' and progressive multimedia historical development, was also augmented by the social imperative for the Romantic artistic genius inherent to the idea of the 'artist-priest' developed by Alphonse Lamartine and the Saint-Simonian religious movement.[68]

1854 was also the year in which Liszt rebranded a series of orchestral compositions of various types, origins and purposes 'symphonic poems' (*sinfonische Dichtungen*). He would make several revisions and additions to the series as the years passed, and the final list consists of thirteen single-movement orchestral works which mostly take inspiration from a pre-existing work of literature, painting or historical event:

Ce Qu'on Entend sur la Montagne (1846–54)
Tasso, Lamento e Trionfo (1847–57)
Les Préludes (1844–54)
Orpheus (1853–4)
Prometheus (1850–9)
Mazeppa (1826–54)
Festklänge (1853–61)

---

[66] Liszt, 'Berlioz and his Harold Symphony', 128–30.
[67] Franz Liszt, 'About Beethoven's Music to Egmont', 1854, in *Dramaturgical Leaves, Essays About Musical Works for the Stage and Queries About the Stage, its Composers and Performers*, ed. Janita R. Hall-Swadley, 83–94 (Lanham: Rowman and Littlefield, 2014), passim.
[68] See Haringer, 'Liszt and the Legacy of Lamartine', 73; Locke, *Music, Musicians and the Saint-Simonians*, 101.

Héroïde Funèbre (1830–54)
Hungaria (1854)
Hamlet (1857–8)
Hunnenschlacht (1857)
Die Ideale (1856–7)
Von der Wiege bis zum Grabe (1882)

Like 'Romanticism' itself, an authoritative definition of the symphonic poem is impossible to present, since composers following Liszt have used the term for a variety of purposes, and Liszt's original conception was also subject to change. But, above all, freedom is key to the symphonic poem. For Liszt the new form was a Romantic celebration of the formlessness of the 'natural' world; music should have 'luxurious, unfettered growth'.[69] This sense of freedom could be achieved by partially dispensing with traditional forms and allowing each programme to shape the music in a unique way; this may include narrative, topics and traditional formal structures, but, more broadly, it involved a multimedia approach integrating music and other art forms which are more traditionally dependent upon vision. Liszt was profoundly interested by his understanding of a visual dimension to music. He often claimed to have some 'poetical image' in mind when he performed – constructing a mental picture of the music then finding a way to project it. He would point to a sunset and advise his pupils to 'play that!'[70] It was this sense of anti-formalism – a willingness to mix the senses of sound and vision – that made Liszt one of Eduard Hanslick's key antagonists.

The poetic idea

In addition to philosophical aesthetics, Liszt's symphonic poems also developed in response to general trends in nineteenth-century musical reception practices. As Walker explains: 'Liszt was well aware of the general public's fondness for attaching stories to instrumental music, from Bach to Chopin, in an attempt to explain the inexplicable'.[71] Yet this common process of 'explaining' non-programmatic music through the imposition of subjective narratives conflicted

---

[69] Liszt, 'Berlioz and his Harold Symphony', 113.
[70] Walker, *Franz Liszt: The Final Years*, 232, 247–9.
[71] Alan Walker, *Franz Liszt: The Weimar Years, 1848–1861* (London: Faber and Faber, 1989), 306. Aniruddh D. Patel explains this phenomenon from a position of cognitive psychology: 'It does seem plausible that a "narrative tendency" in music perception is related to our constant trafficking in coherent linguistic narratives, whereby sound structure is used to infer a sequence of logically

with Liszt's philosophy of music. Liszt believed that music's capacity for 'communication' was more actual, more malleable, than such casual reception practices implied. Yes, music should be allowed to function on its own terms, independent of any extra-musical content that might be foisted upon it by imaginative listeners, but rather, when handled correctly, both music and programme could work together to illuminate a designated 'poetic idea'.[72] The symphonic poem was Liszt's experiment to demonstrate this.

It is inaccurate to retain the idea that music was or could become, for Liszt, a 'language', exactly – a specific sign system either conventional or iconic in any supposedly universally applicable sense. Rather, it is closer to the mark to say that Liszt believed music could be treated in such a way that it could, as Carl Dahlhaus put it, 'say unmisconstruably what it is intended to say'.[73] This is something quite different. It depends upon that previously mentioned tenant of Romantic aesthetics holding that music's indefiniteness – its ability to surpass language as a means of philosophical expression – could be turned to specific expressive, often political, religious or nationalized educative (explanatory) purposes.

To understand Liszt's symphonic poems, it might be useful at this stage to distinguish between programme source, programme and poetic idea. The *programme source* is the pre-existing artwork or myth that inspired the music and the *programme* is the point of contact between the two, typically a written preface to the score. The *poetic idea,* on the other hand, is the thing they all share – the transcendental construct they evoke, embody or represent.

Liszt implies that a symphonic poem could be inspired by an existing work of art, such as a painting, and could express the same poetic idea as that painting while being independent of the specific programme source.[74] (It must be noted here that an explanation of Liszt's symphonic poems that centralizes the concept of poetic ideas presents only part of the story. Other concepts, including narrative, topics, register and mimesis are also significant, particularly in their relation to film music, as we will see).

---

connected events in the world, linked by cause and effect'; Aniruddh D. Patel, *Music, Language and the Brain* (Oxford: Oxford University Press, 2008), 324.

[72] Modern music histories which mention Liszt's symphonic poems, although rarely addressing the poetic idea concept in detail, usually understand that they were not meant to be descriptive but rather expressive of the 'general atmosphere' of a programme source, and that the music was 'a summary of and not a commentary on' that programme source. This usually suffices to distinguish them from many similar works by Beethoven, Mendelssohn and Berlioz. See Geoffrey Hindley, et al., *The Larousse Encyclopaedia of Music*, 6th edn (London: The Hamlyn Publishing Group Limited, 1983), 320.

[73] Dahlhaus, *Nineteenth Century Music*, 241.

[74] Walker, *Franz Liszt: The Weimar Years*, 358; Liszt, 'About Beethoven's Music to *Egmont*', 87.

As Liszt understood his self-appointed task, when considering programme sources:

> There was no need to choose between the many interpretations which these sublime monuments had provoked, nor to mould afresh . . . [these myths]. It was sufficient to translate into music those phases of feeling, which, under the repeatedly varied forms of the myth, together constitute its entirety, its soul; viz; boldness, suffering, endurance, and redemption.[75]

This 'soul' of the myth is, in other words, its poetic idea, and is usefully compared to Kant's notion of 'aesthetic ideas' as outlined in the *Critique of Judgement*:

> [Aesthetic ideas] strive towards something that lies beyond the bounds of experience, and hence try to approach an exhibition of rational concepts (intellectual ideas) [but] they are inner intuitions to which no concept can be completely adequate . . . something that prompts the imagination to spread over a multitude of kindred representations . . . . In a word, an aesthetic idea is a presentation of the imagination . . . [which is bound up] with such a multiplicity of partial representations that no expression that stands for a definite concept can be found for it.[76]

Both Liszt's poetic ideas and Kant's aesthetic ideas can be seen as a means to name the ideal 'objects' that lie 'behind' an artist's products, being also the 'spirit that animates . . . their works'.[77] These two names for the same kind of 'idea' are 'ideal' in the sense that they cannot be adequately expressed by language, concept or any other concrete or mentally graspable means.[78] In this sense, they can evoke the Romantic sublime.

Both Liszt's chosen programme and his music *pointed to* something – the elusive signified of various concrete signifiers. Liszt did not aim to guide his audiences to a precise, 'correct' interpretation, but rather in the general direction of the poetic idea. The poetic idea of *Tasso* (1847–57), for example, can be pointed to both by literary and musical means. Goethe's programme source takes one path, and Liszt's symphonic poem, with the initial assistance of a programme to indicate the poetic idea, takes another.

---

[75] Franz Liszt, [Preface to] *Prometheus*, 1950–59, in *Liszt: Symphonic Poems* (1.3), 1–2 (Upper Saddle River: Gregg Press, 1966), passim.
[76] Kant, *Critique of Judgement*, §49, 181–5.
[77] Kant, *Critique of Judgement*, §49, 184.
[78] Kant, *Critique of Judgement*, §49, 182.

Liszt wished to stress that music could do this – the act of pointing – as well as any other art that had already been culturally enthroned, like literature, painting, sculpture and perhaps more so. Carl Dahlhaus's comment captures the scandalous quality of this anti-formalist agenda: 'Liszt is like a usurper, grasping in the name of music what was poetry's property'.[79] Strictly speaking, Liszt sought not equality among the arts but to demonstrate the superiority of music as a means of expression; in terms of communicating this elusive element of understanding, music supposedly surpassed pictorial representation or language.

As noted earlier, to understand the poetic idea concept does not give us the whole story. Following Keith T. Johns's semiotic analysis of Liszt's symphonic poems in the 1990s, Liszt studies began to acknowledge that the symphonic poems operated on a more flexible principle than was previously allowed for regarding any hypothetical scale between poetic idea and narrative-like mimetic representation. Liszt scholars Michael Saffle and Dana Gooley maintain that Liszt's symphonic poems 'do tell stories', although in a variety of ways.[80] To employ Russian Formalist terminology, such ways almost always make the temporal sequence of events, the syuzhet, impossible to follow or impossible to transform into a fabula, or 'story', on a moment-by-moment basis. The music can create the impression that a fabula can be formed through the sequential development of motives, topics, registers and occasional mimetic moments, all often structured by a loose application of formal models. Regardless of the varieties evident in the music and programmes, in a way, Saffle is right to note that 'Liszt told the same story . . . over and over again . . . one of suffering followed by triumph';[81] this is the typically Lisztian fabula which can be subjectively identified in many of his works dependent upon conventional listening practices and personal interpretation competencies.

It seems reasonable to state that there would be no way of ascertaining the poetic idea of any of Liszt's symphonic poems if we were deprived of their programme information. Musical topics, registers, mimesis and even the conductor's physical gestures may give us clues, but nothing more. These elements make the 'pointing' more aggressive. We need something extra-

---

[79] Carl Dahlhaus, *Esthetics of Music*, 1967 (Cambridge: Cambridge University Press, 1982), 61.
[80] Michael Saffle, 'Orchestral Works', in *The Liszt Companion*, ed. Ben Arnold, 235–79 (Westport and London: Greenwood Press, 2002), 240; Dana Gooley, *The Virtuoso Liszt* (Cambridge: Cambridge University Press), 240–1
[81] Saffle, 'Orchestral Works', 240.

musical and authored in order to proceed. We need to know the direction that the pointing enacts.

For Liszt, the ultimate goal of the symphonic poem project was to ensure that music would no longer be challenged as a parasite of poetic value, but would rather find a way to express poetic value supposedly on its own terms. Liszt wrote:

> With the help of a programme . . . [the composer] indicates the direction of his ideas, the point of view from which he grasps a given subject. The function of the programme then becomes indispensable, and its entrance into the highest spheres of art appears justified.[82]

The development of this communicative capacity through innovative aesthetic experiments, based on the idealized ineffability of music, corresponded to the pursuit of *Bildung* during the Romantic period. Art and politics meet again in the tension between the supposed freedom inherent to the aesthetic field of experience and the inevitable explanatory function of all social representations. Liszt was a Romantic genius – an agent of cultural transcendence – who attempted to create a New Mythology using ground-breaking audio-visual means.

Beyond the poetic idea: Topics, registers and mimesis, the 'music of moments' and clarity

As we begin to look for ways to articulate connections between Liszt's symphonic poem concept and the classical Hollywood score, some initial issues requiring consideration are those not accommodated by the poetic idea explanation. For our purposes they can be compartmentalized as (i) topics, registers and mimesis, (ii) the 'Music of Moments' concept and (iii) clarity, although all three are all closely related.

i. Topics, registers and mimesis

One of Liszt's most significant contributions to the history of musical form was his incorporation of multiple movements into a single flowing whole. Musical topics, registers and mimesis played a key role in determining the structure of such pieces that were freed from a rigorous adherence to formal development.

---

[82] Liszt, 'Berlioz and his Harold Symphony', 127.

The segmentation of large-scale works previously determined by formal tradition was now employed primarily for aural, textural qualities in creating contrasts over time, and, as we have seen, often in relation to non-musical ideas. As Charles Rosen put it, Liszt demonstrated to subsequent composers how musical texture, sound and 'violence and delicacy of gesture' could become a primary means of organizing, moment-by-moment, large-scale musical structures.[83] Having now explored the philosophical background of Liszt's symphonic poems we must now seek to explain how these radical new works were not only multiplicities – fragmented works constituted and experienced on a moment-by-moment basis – but also subjected to processes that presented them as a unified and clarified whole, and how this condition relates them to film music.

First, by addressing the question of musical topics, registers and mimesis, we can identify one potential bridge between Liszt and, at least certain kinds of, film music. The study of musical topics and registers addresses the evocation of extra-musical meanings through connotation. Like schematic types (see Chapter 3), topics and registers can often be functionally reduced to specific type-labels such as 'the pastoral', 'the heroic' or 'the martial', accommodating generalized schemas of musical symbolism that feedback into a fragmented, culturally and historically determined 'languages' of intonation.[84] Registers can be understood along similar lines as conventional systems of classification 'based on words, syntax, form and sounds' or 'conventionalized lexical, syntactic and prosodic choices' which are 'commonly shared by a community'.[85] The concept of mimesis is exemplified by a more direct (denoted as opposed to connoted) and imitative reference to non-musical sounds.

In his study of Liszt's music, Jim Samson offers a description of how such functions interact with programmes and formal structures to suggest meaning. In each piece of programme music,

> a signal is sent out by the title, and that enables, indeed invites, a reading of the musical events in the light of a program. The topics . . . are focused by the programme, and formal functions . . . acquire metaphorical meanings (become plots) in relation to these topics.[86]

---

[83] Charles Rosen, *The Romantic Generation* (Cambridge: Harvard University Press, 1995), 541.
[84] See Patel, *Music, Language and the Brain*, 321.
[85] Long, *Beautiful Monsters*, 5, 12; see also Deborah Tannen and Cynthia Wallat, 'Interactive Frames and Knowledge Schemas in Interaction: Examples from a Medical Examination/Interview', 1987, in *The Discourse Reader*, ed. Adam Jaworski and Nikolas Coupland, 346–65 (London and New York: Routledge, 1999), 352.
[86] Samson, *Virtuosity and the Musical Work*, 191.

Liszt's employment of topics as a sequential compositional tool, determined by a larger programmatic sequence, is highly suggestive of film music, which, as James Buhler notes, regularly employs topics 'for efficient communication'.[87] Liszt's symphonic poems and many instances of film music share a conjunction of evocative musical topoi and a fragmented, overarching freedom from traditional musical forms. What the listener to Liszt's symphonic poems might experience is something *resembling* a classical Hollywood film score: lengthy, episodic and mood-focused topical music employing the typical European Romantic orchestra, implying the presence of some overarching idea not reducible to the music itself, and lacking the rigorous formal development of much nineteenth-century European orchestral music. If this description of a hypothetical impression is deemed feasible, then the comparison between Liszt and the classical Hollywood score might at least be made on the level of appearances.

ii. The 'music of moments' concept

By creating works that utilize a variety of formal syntheses, Liszt in his symphonic poems presented an array of unified single-movement orchestral works comprised of blended and contrasted musical episodes, each uniquely determined by the individual programme and incorporating topical devices, registers and mimesis. The poetic idea concept presents a totality that subsumes an expansive canvass of fragmented and contracting sequences, sections and moments. This gradual unfettering of music from the demands of traditional form might, in a hypothetical sense, lead us to our second issue: the concept of the 'music of moments', variously suggested by Carl Dahlhaus and George Gershwin.

In his essay 'The Composer and the Machine Age' (1933), Gershwin suggested that modernity's impact on music since the French Revolution was most clearly felt in new treatments of tempo and sound textures; the drive towards the mechanical, the reproductive, the fast and the commercial, that began to influence Western culture during the nineteenth century, impacted music on a micro rather than macro level, resulting in a concept Gershwin called 'Music of Moments': the moment-to-moment expression of the uniqueness of a temporal

---

[87] James Buhler, 'Ontological, Formal and Critical Theories of Film Music and Sound', in *The Oxford Handbook of Film Music Studies*, ed. David Neumeyer, 188–225 (Oxford: Oxford University Press, 2014), 212.

period.[88] This concept finds various outlets in the 'formless' symphonic poem, the Mickymousing film score and Schoenberg's proclamation that his music never repeats itself.[89] Here the prioritization of expressing the 'unique identity of one instant in the music', as Dahlhaus phrased it, becomes distantly related to the classical Hollywood score described by Gorbman, where, 'robbed of its musical structure ... [the music] modulates and changes colour, chameleonlike, in moment-to-moment difference to the narrative's images'.[90] As we are now in a position to recognize, Liszt, as well as Wagner, played his part in bringing about this development in the history of Western music.

iii. Clarity

As indicated earlier, in tandem with this drive towards a fragmentary, episodic and complex multiplicity was a unifying drive towards a simplified, clarified and unified whole, due to the unifying function of the programmatic title and associated poetic idea. As Jim Samson notes, Liszt's titles often only indicated 'a prevailing unity of mood or single semantic meaning'; acting as a point of orientation, they narrow the potential readings available for listeners.[91] This third point – the notion of a drive towards clarity – takes us, once again, towards film by engaging with a historical debate over efficient communication with mass audiences. As a noteworthy proponent of 'clarity' as an important explanatory concept in Film Studies, Noël Carroll argued that film music can be best explained not by its compensation for a perceived 'lack' (as the Herder/phenomenological argument suggests), but rather by its immediate legibility to mass audiences;[92] clear communication here outweighs the compensatory embodiment of the 'absent' cinematic image.

Liszt's symphonic poem project attempted to make orchestral music easier to engage with for the non-musically educated public. Compared to the Wagnerian tendency to endow large-scale orchestral music with a dense texture of associative development, Liszt's symphonic poems focused on clarity. As we saw, the supposed indefiniteness of music, although its primary source of

---

[88] George Gershwin, 'The Composer in the Machine Age', 1933, in *Modernism and Music: An Anthology of Sources*, ed. Daniel Albright, 386–9 (Chicago: University of Chicago Press, 2004), passim.
[89] Arnold Schoenberg, 'On Program Music, Tradition, and the Public – The First American Radio Broadcast: An Interview with William Lundell', 1933, in *A Schoenberg Reader: Documents of a Life*, ed. Joseph Auner, 247–50 (New Haven: Yale University Press, 2003), 250.
[90] Dahlhaus, *Between Romanticism and Modernism*, 73–4; Gorbman, *Unheard Melodies*, 1.
[91] Samson, *Virtuosity and the Musical Work*, 177, 187.
[92] Carroll, 'Notes on Movie Music', 144; see also Buhler, 'Ontological, Formal and Critical Theories of Film Music and Sound', 204.

emotional power and value in Romantic aesthetics, was also a barrier between the artistic ideal and audiences; Liszt believed that the musician traditionally 'speaks a mysterious language that can only be understood after special study'.[93] By introducing a programme, topics, registers and mimesis, a composer created music with which it was easier for audiences to engage. What was desired was effective communication, displaying music's ability to transcend language, but maintaining an ability to accomplish a kind of 'universal meaning' function easily accessible to musically uneducated audiences. The rhetoric of the time, employed by both Liszt and Wagner, would refer to this group as 'the people', or the *volk*.

Through a consideration of the various issues identified earlier, including cinematic listening, narrative and this last group consisting of topics, registers and mimesis, Music of Moments and clarity, we can see how Liszt's symphonic poems begin to *resemble* the film soundtrack. However, two questions remain to be answered: (a) if the symphonic poem is comparable to the classical Hollywood score, what significance can be gleaned from how this genre, or pseudo-genre, developed during the historical period between Liszt and film, in the works of Richard Strauss, for example? And (b) if we allow the validity of this resemblance between symphonic poems in general and certain kinds of film music – those 'classical' scores which at first glance might seem indebted to Wagnerian music dramas or other Romantic symphonic traditions – to what use can this resemblance be put?

The symphonic poem after Liszt

Do you happen to know the difference between programme music and real music? I don't!

—Richard Strauss[94]

Even during his lifetime, Liszt's ideas were not widely disseminated or understood. His difficult writing style was not successful in communicating a convincing defence of his aesthetic philosophy. He and his few advocates

---

[93] Franz Liszt, *An Artist's Journey: Lettres d'un Bachelier es Musique, 1835–41* (Chicago: University of Chicago Press, 1989), 34.
[94] Cited in Norman Del Mar, *Richard Strauss: A Critical Commentary on His Life and Works, Volume 1*, 1962 (London and Boston: Faber and Faber, 1986), 198.

emphasized the historical precedents for the symphonic poem, keen to demonstrate the legitimacy of Liszt's project by stressing, in historicist fashion, that the new form was not a radical break with tradition but rather the culmination of a tendency that had been long developing in European music.[95] In addition, contemporary advocates of more conservative musical aesthetics, openly hostile to Liszt's ideas, were also gaining strength. The influential critic Eduard Hanslick maintained that the intrusion of non-musical elements into symphonic forms was a corruption of music's unique potential for abstract expression; music should supposedly remain uncontaminated by other mediums.[96] George Bernard Shaw, another prominent music critic, was content to dismiss Liszt's work on similar grounds.[97]

This conservative vogue for formalism contributed to a partial blackening of the concept of symphonic poem in the period between c1850 and the early 1900s. A new generation of composers had come to the fore, upholding the conservative views of Brahms and Schumann, and the music of Liszt and his followers was relegated to comparative obscurity. The popularity of Bayreuth had split the progressive camp. Max Bruch, Hans Pfitzner and Max Reger shunned the symphonic poem to pursue Brahms's examples of symphonic form and chamber music. This neglect was compounded by a dearth of musical analysis of existing works due to a perceived lack of need: 'musicology and audiences were in agreement: musical picture books do not need to be analysed'.[98] The symphonic poem continued to encounter criticism from Paul Mies, Carl Nielsen and Paul Hindemith, who adopted Hanslick's concerns with fresh insights provided by contemporary science, anthropology and philosophy.[99] Bear in mind that this was the epoch into which cinema emerged.

---

[95] James Deaville, 'The Controversy Surrounding Liszt's Conception of Programme Music', in *Nineteenth Century Music: Selected Proceedings from the Tenth International Conference*, ed. Jim Samson and Bennett Zon, 98–124 (Farnham: Ashgate, 2002), 102, 111, 117.

[96] Eduard Hanslick, *On the Musically Beautiful*, 1854 (Indianapolis: Hackett Publishing Company, 1986), 10–11.

[97] George Bernard Shaw, *Shaw's Music: The Complete Musical Criticism of Bernard Shaw*, ed. Dan H. Laurence, 2nd edn (London: The Bodley Head, 1981), 2: 1890–3, 72–3, 213, 460.

[98] Walter Werbeck, 'Richard Strauss' Tone Poems', in *The Richard Strauss Companion*, ed. Mark-Daniel Schmid, 103–44 (Westport: Praeger Publishers, 2003), 121.

[99] Paul Mies, '[from] *Über die Tonmalerei*', 1912, in *Music in European Thought: 1851–1912*, ed. Bojan Bujić, 121–5 (Cambridge: Cambridge University Press, 1988), 122; Paul Hindemith, 'from *A Composers World*', 1950, in *Modernism and Music: An Anthology of Sources*, ed. Daniel Albright, 60–3 (Chicago: University of Chicago Press, 2004), passim; Carl Nielsen, 'from "Words, Music and Program Music"', 1925, in *Modernism and Music: An Anthology of Sources*, ed. Daniel Albright, 55–60 (Chicago: University of Chicago Press, 2004), 56.

Despite this resistance, a number of prominent composers were drawn to the genre. By the first decade of the twentieth century, a growing community was advocating Liszt's symphonic poems as the new ideal of musical composition. Yet they moved away from Liszt's model, and a lack of a distinctive theoretical foundation allowed composers to adapt the form to meet various creative impulses. The symphonic poem rode twin waves of folkloric nationalism and poetic/literary mythology into the twentieth century, gradually spreading across the musical output of Europe, Russia and the United States as part of a reappraisal of music's capacity to be compared and amalgamated with other arts, primarily painting, during the onset of modernism. Nationalism and mythology became the strongest branch in the Central and Eastern European tradition, typified by the work of Sibelius and Dvořák. Scriabin, Tchaikovsky and Rachmaninov mobilized diverse picturesque and literary resources in Russia, and natural and geographic elements predominated in the symphonic poems of Delius, Vaughan Williams and Bax. Their programmes are almost always non-narrative, and they take their primary purpose to be the creation of an impression, mood or 'musical picture'.

The legacy of the symphonic poem was insidious. According to Stephen Banfield, there was 'scarcely a composer of the period [from Elgar to Stravinsky] who did not create powerful programmatic or referential tokens in their symphonic music then supress or deny them'.[100] The stigma attached to programme music could burden any composer seeking the approval of the conservatories or wanting to appear to have broken with the past. Such was the case with Richard Strauss, who distanced himself from Liszt in the 1890s in an effort to assert an individual voice. The first years of the twentieth century saw not only the popularization of the symphonic poem as a musical form and the problematizing of a cultural stigma against representational associations in 'art' music but also, more generally, as Rick Altman reminds us, 'a historical high point for music expressly designed to evoke a visual image', not only in the concert hall but also in military bands, and street and stage music, all of which fed into the contemporary development of the sounds of cinema.[101]

---

[100] Stephen Banfield, 'Music, Text and Stage: The Tradition of Bourgeois Tonality to the Second World War', in *The Cambridge History of Twentieth-Century Music*, ed. Nicholas Cook and Anthony People, 90–122 (Cambridge: Cambridge University Press, 2004), 102–3.

[101] Altman, *Silent Film Sound*, 46.

Richard Strauss: Towards Mickymousing

In the 1890s, Richard Strauss was part of the progressive Lisztian tradition. While publicly distancing himself from his unfashionable forebearer, he privately admitted Liszt's influence on his 'tone poems' (his preferred term). Like Liszt before him, Strauss perceived a need for a 'new kind of instrumental music', and his tone poems encouraged the creation of new forms for 'every new subject'.[102] In certain tone poems, Strauss also sought to represent a central idea through large-scale, panoramic musical structures; in doing so, he fused Wagnerian leitmotif and Lisztian poetic idea approaches, often with the intention of expressing something in 'the most general and universal way possible'.[103] Tone poems such as *Tod und Verklärung* (1889), *Till Eulenspiels lustige Streiche* (1895) and *Ein Heldenleben* (1898) can appear to present a more narrativized, cause-and-effect logic than is apparent in Liszt's own works. Sometimes working from traditional formal frameworks, Strauss will present a succession of aural events that often directly resemble filmic Mickymousing, such as the finale of *Don Juan* (1888), with its mimetic illustration of the hero's death. Such works present an obvious comparison between Strauss and, for example, Max Steiner's highly fragmented and illustrative film scores, dense with musical mimesis.

Strauss pursued brevity and clarity in his tone poems – a more economical use of music. Ease of communication, however, was undermined by an elitist culture of musical reception that privileged the educated listener familiar with the 'high' cultural programme source. Despite the symbolic capital of the programme sources, another similarity between the symphonic poem and film music can be found in this critical perception as low-status mediums; Strauss's tone poems were regularly attacked by critics claiming that they were 'not really "real" music', and 'should not be taken seriously'.[104] The music's density, detail and invitation to moment-by-moment interpretation correspond to an example described by Paul Mies: 'listening to music with a knowledge of the programme involves a matching of music and programme moment by moment, if we are to understand the work'.[105] Such an ideal reading position situates the music and the extra-musical as equally constructive and interdependent elements in forming

---

[102] John Williamson, *Strauss: Also Sprach Zarathustra* (Cambridge: Cambridge University Press, 1993), 16.
[103] Williamson, *Strauss: Also Sprach Zarathustra*, 19.
[104] Werbeck, 'Richard Strauss' Tone Poems', 115.
[105] Mies, '[from] *Über die Tonmalerei*', 125.

a meaningful whole. The spectator is positioned between the two, and produces 'meaning' for the overall work based on personal interpretative competencies, while being assisted by narrativized musical topics, registers and mimesis.

By 1910, Strauss's tone poems were established in the repertoires of German orchestras, forming part of the musical background for composers such as Steiner and Korngold, who would soon move to California and set the standard for the classical Hollywood score. The specifically visual quality of the music's reception was early established for Strauss's contemporaries – even if it was seen as a handicap to its musical worth – in a synthesis of 'Liszt's daring structures and Wagner's sonorous textures'.[106] Eduard Hanslick wrote in 1893 that the 'realism' of Strauss's tone poems 'lacked only the final step': accompaniment by a visual representation of the scene or character being evoked by the music.[107] This final step, the one Hanslick feared, was, rhetorically, the step taken by cinema only a few years later.

Audio-visual performances practices as pre-cinema

As mentioned earlier, Liszt's symphonic poems, like film, are representative of the logic of Rancière's aesthetic regime, privileging the cooperation of different mediums and the erasure of the notion of appropriate form. Liszt considered music-making to be a collaborative activity, believing that 'great artists never worked in isolation – the input of many could be heard in a single composition'.[108] Interestingly, this was less apparent with Wagner, whose cultural image is so bound up with notions of egomania and authorial control that it hints at a small counterargument to Adorno's formulation of Wagner's paternal relationship with cinematic production.

Liszt's symphonic poems appear to be an effort to construct a collaborative and ahistorical community of artists, where multiple individuals' efforts contribute to the same artwork. This ideal has been called Liszt's utopian 'Republic of the Imagination'.[109] The symphonic poem *Mazeppa* (1826–54), for example, is the

---

[106] Werbeck, 'Richard Strauss' Tone Poems', 113.
[107] Cited in Mark-Daniel Schmid, 'The Early Reception of Richard Strauss' Tone Poems', in *The Richard Strauss Companion*, ed. Mark-Daniel Schmid (Westport: Praeger Publishers, 2003), 157.
[108] Anna Harwell Calenza, 'Liszt, Italy and the Republic of the Imagination', in *Franz Liszt and his World*, ed. Christopher H. Gibbs and Dana Gooley, 3–38 (Princeton: Princeton University Press, 2006), 9.
[109] Celenza, 'Liszt, Italy and the Republic of the Imagination', 6.

result of the labours of not only Liszt but Beethoven and Victor Hugo as well. We have already seen the anti-Hegelian root of this plasticity. By proclaiming a partial role in the production of symphonic poems, Liszt, once again, appears closer to the workings of the Hollywood 'dream factory'. The texts produced by Romantic virtuosity and Hollywood become the products of a mediating force, simultaneously actualizing and idealizing, with charisma, glamour and the stigma of aesthetic cheapness. This is where we also glimpse that idealized notion that both the film and symphonic poem could be included among the few cooperative art forms, like Erwin Panofsky's famous comparison between the film and a cathedral.[110] Long before Roland Barthes proclaimed 'The Death of the Author' (1967), Liszt's 'poetic ideas' were shattering the traditional, even Romantic, model that held a single author accountable for their work.[111]

Liszt attacked the boundary between music and visuality not only in his scandalous mannerisms of virtuoso performance (see Chapter 3), but also through radical experiments in multimedia performance practice. During the development of his symphonic poems, Liszt undertook several projects which explored the relationship between music and visuality, extending his authorship of their reception by organizing the mise-en-scène of performance spaces.

One kind of experiment involved removing musicians from the sight of the audience. For productions of his *Dante* Symphony (1856), for example, he stipulated that the organ, choir and harmonium should be 'placed out of sight, behind curtains' if possible; 'under these ideal conditions', Liszt wrote, the music seems to 'float disembodied above the auditorium'.[112] Matthew Wilson Smith is wrong, therefore, to state that Bayreuth's *Festspielhaus* 'marks a qualitative break with the past' in the orchestrated visual concealment of the means of production for musical sounds.[113] Liszt's audio-visual experiments predated Bayreuth, being possibly an extension of his recognition of the key role played by vision in shaping musical reception gained during his earlier virtuoso career. Bearing in mind that problematic ideological connection between Wagner and cinema explored by the Frankfurt School, it is interesting to note that, here, Adorno's phantasmagoria – the sublime erasure of the traces

---

[110] Erwin Panofsky, 'Style and Medium in the Motion Pictures', 1934, in *Film Theory and Criticism: Introductory Readings*, ed. Gerald Mast, Marshal Cohen and Leo Braudy, 4th edn, 233–48 (Oxford: Oxford University Press, 1992), 244.
[111] Roland Barthes, 'The Death of the Author', 1967, in *Image-Music-Text*, 142–8 (London: Fontana Press, 1977), passim.
[112] Cited in Walker, *Franz Liszt: The Weimar Years*, 312.
[113] Matthew Wilson Smith, *The Total Work of Art: From Bayreuth to Cyberspace* (London and New York: Routledge, 2007), 36.

of production – rebounds upon Liszt himself, who is also a phantom presence throughout *In Search of Wagner*.[114]

Some of Liszt's other experiments in audio-visuality appear today as striking instances of proto-cinema, distantly related to devices such as the kinetoscope, zoetrope and panorama, only from a musical-aesthetic rather than a scientific-technological perspective. A two-piano version of Liszt's *Hunnenschlacht* (1857) was once performed before an audience who sat facing the painting by Wilhelm Von Kaulbach that inspired the music.[115] This visual representation of a battle between the Romans and the Huns in 451 CE would have been appreciated by an audience who sat contemplating it while listening to Liszt's piano rendition. As the composer, Liszt wrote and performed this music not so much to provide a kind of 'silent film' accompaniment to the picture (because the picture, of course, didn't move), but rather because the music and the picture point towards the same poetic idea. The picture gives it a visual dimension, confined to a frame, while

Figure 1 *Die Hunnenschlacht* by Wilhelm von Kaulbach (1850)

---

[114] Adorno, *In Search of Wagner*, 78, 149.
[115] See Marsha L. Morton, '"From the Other Side": An Introduction', in *The Arts Entwined: Music and Painting in the Nineteenth Century*, ed. Marsha L. Morton and Peter L. Schmunk, 1–21 (London and New York: Routledge, 2000), 9.

the music gives it an audible dimension and duration. The two were presented together as an event of audio-visual multimedia aesthetic appreciation.

Liszt's *Dante* Symphony provides another interesting example. According to Alan Walker, Liszt had planned to accompany performances of this work with lantern slides featuring drawings made by the German artist Bonaventura Genelli.[116] It would appear that the slides were never made, but they would have depicted scenes from the symphony's programme source, Dante's *Divine Comedy* (1320). There are records that these multimedia ideas were being considered by Liszt as early as 1842, although the project was eventually abandoned. The sitting audience would, again, have listened to the hour-long Romantic symphony in a presumably darkened space while facing a screen showing a succession of images sharing the poetic idea identified with the music. We can only speculate as to what images would have been shown at what point in the music, what they would represent and what associational relationships might have been constructed by their counterpoint. These questions themselves result from a position that has already inscribed the proto-cinematic quality of such an audio-visual multimedia experience. What is perhaps most significant is that a Romantic fascination with music and visuality extended, with Liszt, in a different, but in retrospect no less 'cinematic', direction to that of Wagner. In terms of flat-screen or projected light experience, he may even have come nearer to film than did Wagner.

In *A History of Pre-Cinema* (2000), Stephen Herbert presents a definition of pre-cinema artefacts that requires them to display three features: (a) they must be 'time-based visual media', distinguished from visual media 'in which the entire work was visible at an instant'; in addition, pre-cinematic artefacts must attempt (b) the 'reproduction of reality', and (c) approach a 'large-screen cinema' experience.[117] Unsurprisingly, Herbert's definition prioritizes visuality at the expense of sound; yet even with this condition, we can see how Liszt's experiments meet several requirements. The temporal dimension of the music prevents the work from being consumed in a single instant, and the similarity with 'large-scale cinema experience' is clear from the earlier descriptions. And, if we accept a historicist position on the 'reproduction of reality' criteria, we might expect Liszt, as a Romantic composer, to consider his multimedia performances to offer a more 'real' representation of their subjects than any photograph could achieve.

---

[116] Walker, *Franz Liszt: The Weimar Years*, 50.
[117] Stephen Herbert, *A History of Pre-Cinema*, 2 vols. (London and New York: Routledge, 2000), 1, xi.

Conclusion

This chapter has contributed to an ongoing 'counter-Wagnerian' tendency in film music scholarship, exposing another neglected tributary of influence on film and film music from the domain of Romantic aesthetics. We have explored why Wagner came to prominence in film and film music discourses, and asked what such formations excluded.

At the beginning of the twentieth century, Wagner's music dramas offered the 'obvious' model for three conflicting but co-present channels of film music discourse: compositional practice, positive discourse and negative discourse. In the first instance, film music composers such as Korngold, Steiner, Rózsa and Tiomkin adopted, adapted and practised Wagnerian musical techniques, principally the leitmotif, in their compositions for film soundtracks. This operated in conjunction with the more generally Romantic instrumentation, topics and registers of the classical Hollywood orchestra which ensured a standardized Hollywood sound that often resembled the Wagnerian opera, despite any actual divergences. Second, in addition to those very same composers, critics and distributors created and capitalized on a positive discursive function of the Wagner connection by publicly encouraging the comparison to increase the symbolic capital of their professions and products. Third, the Wagnerian comparison was also appropriated within a critical tradition of Marxist discourse; cultural theorists such as Adorno, Eisler, Horkheimer and Kracauer repositioned Wagner as a 'negative' precedent for the supposedly politically illusory, distracting and phantasmagoric cultures of cinematic consumption.

In addition to the exploration of the discursive formations attendant on film music and Romanticism, this chapter has explored Liszt's symphonic poems and their multimedia imperative, evidencing a key aspect of the historical trajectory of Jacques Rancière's aesthetic regime and its relation to film. Obviously, the practice of finding alternatives to Wagner's cinematic paternity from other instances of Romantic art is not an original one. As we have seen, many academics have exposed the importance of other nineteenth-century musical forms such as melodrama, Italian opera and the symphony. This chapter has attempted to do something similar for Liszt, and introducing, with the expanded field of Romantic scholarship constructed in the previous chapter, a new and exciting theoretical tool with which to explore this field.

As mentioned earlier, Rancière agreed with the assertion that 'cinema as an artistic idea predated the cinema as a technical means', and presented, in *Film*

Fables, a means of discovering a pre-history of cinema in Romantic aesthetics specifically.[118] What we also glimpse here is the potential to connect the Lisztian poetic idea concept with cinema via Rancière's philosophy more generally. We might accomplish this by considering Rancière's own positioning of Kantian 'aesthetic ideas' within a history of the dialectical power of images in the modern world, their ability to embody the blending of mediums inherent to the aesthetic regime and their consequent power of political transformation – a history that is tantalizingly imagined throughout Rancière's philosophical works. This will be a task for future research. For now, the issue of boundary effacement that such a possibility raises will become increasingly important in subsequent chapters, as we explore the representational schemas that orbit, and contribute to, understandings of, Liszt and Romanticism itself.

---

[118] Rancière, *Film Fables*, 6–11.

3

Audio-visual explanations of Franz Liszt and his music

Cultural image and schematic types

There has never been a shortage of observers who wish to re-write Liszt's life according to a script of their own devising.

—Alan Walker[1]

We experience momentary flashes when we seem to have an intuitive grasp of the divine, when we can sense its presence within us, like a mystical insight, a supernatural understanding of the harmony of the universe
  What's a filmmaker to do with that?

—Franz Liszt and John C. Tibbetts[2]

Introduction

When something is represented in a film, that audio-visual explanandum establishes relationships with existing constructions of knowledge, or 'schemas', which determine not only what that thing is taken to be but also its association with the various explanans, concepts and ideas, which delineate and contextualize it. Taking Franz Liszt as an example, and using a combination of historical biographical material and illustrative film case studies, this chapter will examine several 'schematic types' commonly used to explain Liszt's 'cultural image'.

Having pursued the connection between Romanticism and film through the decades, it is now necessary to turn our attention from discourse to the medium

---

[1] Walker, *Franz Liszt: The Weimar Years*, 85.
[2] Cited in John C. Tibbetts, "'A Search Party of Orphans': Composers on Film', in *Liszt: A Chorus of Voices*, ed. Michael Saffle, John C. Tibbetts and Claire McKinney (Stuyvesant: Pendragon Press, 2012), 343.

itself, and to the task of examining the diverse audio-visual explanations of Romanticism provided by cinematic texts themselves. Subsequent chapters will present expanded case studies addressing in greater detail the issues introduced here. But in order to undertake this analysis, we must first attempt to explain, following the allusions to Romanticism, schematic cognition and philosophical hermeneutics made in earlier chapters, the unifying imperative that connects these topics. Through an analysis of Liszt and film, we will also enrich our understanding of how the idea of audio-visual explanation might, as we saw in Chapter 1, be considered Romantic in itself, and not just by virtue of its content and form.

Schema theory

We can begin by defining 'schema'. This is a common term in academic parlance, and there is conceivably little confusion over its meaning or the uses to which it is often put. The term was perhaps most notably appropriated and adapted for Film Studies by David Bordwell. However, due to the centrality of its role in the following analysis, and the employment of the twin concepts of cultural image and schematic type later, it is worth explaining the term clearly and demonstrating not only its appropriate application to the subjects below but also its Romantic heritage.

A *schema* is here understood to be a hypothetical mental construct of knowledge on a given subject which develops over time, and aids perception and cognition. This definition recognizes a certain congruity between schemas, types and images, and is derived from a wide-ranging etymological study, summarized further, involving contributions from Kantian transcendental idealism, philosophical hermeneutics and cognitive psychology. Although distinctions have been drawn between perception as low-level and cognition as high-level neural activities, it would appear that schema theory can apply to both levels, sometimes effecting the transition from one to the other.

Schema theory, as we intend to use it further, is rooted in the Kantian distinction between appearances and things-in-themselves, hypothesizing the cognitive mediation of a reality that is inaccessible in its entirety. In this sense, schema theory also corresponds with Karl Popper's philosophy of critical rationalism and the twentieth-century hermeneutic tradition associated with Martin Heidegger, Hans-Georg Gadamer and Paul Ricœur, according to which interpretation itself is understood to be a fundamental and unavoidable human activity. Their shared central assumption is one of epistemological constructivism: in order to understand something, we meet it halfway. Perception, cognition and understanding are all constructive processes of *making* sense that are dependent upon the state of existing data. This data comprises both the characteristics of the object as we perceive it and those of the schemas (including traditions, fore-structures or prejudices) that we ourselves bring to it from our own personal history. As one useful metaphor explains it, when we encounter an object, we step into its history like we would step into a flowing river.[3] To step into that flowing river twice in the same way is as impossible a task as grasping the Kantian thing-in-itself. Consequently, the ways we make sense of the object that is the 'source' of the river, as well as the river itself, and even our own steps through it, are only ever interested conjectures which are subject to test and revision.

The 'hermeneutic circle' names a continual constructive communication, testing activity or dialogue between schemas and objects, traditions and texts, and their parts and wholes, which takes place throughout the process of interpreting something. Philosophical hermeneutics attempts to come to terms with objects, actions and texts after the realization of their inevitable transcendence from what Ricœur calls their '*Sitz-im-Leben* [site-in-life]', or the lost point of origin where intentioned production is at one with reception.[4] This flight creates an ultimately irreducible polysemy, and the interpreted object becomes, like the Kantian thing-in-itself, forever out of reach in its entirety. To fill this gap – a gap analogous to that between subject and object – a dialogue of tests is created between an uncritical constructivist cognitive pre-understanding that is both highly conditioned and intuitive ('making sense'), and highly critical processes of social explanation.

Kant took an important step towards such developments when he began his *Critique of Pure Reason* with the assertion that all knowledge of the world is built from what we already know, and is filtered through a certain *a priori* cognitive framework; from this basis, Kant then introduced the concept of a 'schema' as a mediating element of understanding between phenomenon and mental 'categories' of data organization, making categorization itself possible.[5] The Kantian schema is an *a priori* understanding of a concept which cannot be

---

[3] Caputo, *Hermeneutics*, 107.
[4] Paul Ricœur, 'Phenomenology and Hermeneutics', 1975, in *From Text to Action*, 25–50 (London and New York: Continuum, 1992), 30.
[5] Kant, *Critique of Pure Reason*, A 1, B 1, 43; A 137, B 176, 209–10.

reduced to any specific concretization or instance of phenomena; it is 'the pure synthesis' expressed by a category that is fundamental to its identity.[6] In other words, a schema resembles the essence of its associated concept, being the 'rule' for its perception, recognition and understanding.

The epistemological implications of schematic cognition were subsequently explored in psychology, most notably by Henry Head, F. C. Bartlett, Otto Selz and Jean Piaget, whose contributions on 'body schema', 'active settings', 'anticipatory schema' and 'deforming and compensatory' effects explored the ways the mind fills-in gaps based on expectations when perceiving the world.[7] But while for Kant schemas are what remains 'while everything else changes', being what is fundamental to the categorization of any phenomena, these later psychological interpretations recognized their necessarily changeable, and therefore historical, character.[8]

In *Cognition and Reality* (1976), Ulrich Neisser developed an illuminating model of schematic cognition based on a cyclical three-stage hybrid of direct and indirect perception theories.[9] According to Neisser, an already existing mental schema first directs a person's expectations regarding their potential engagement with the world through their perceptual apparatus (historical knowledge of categorical systems); second, those expectations direct the person's actual engagement with the world through that apparatus (seeing things a certain way); finally, the engagement with the world itself directs the modification of the initially employed schemas (violation and correction). Like the hermeneutic circle, this adaptive, or 'trial-and-error', process creates both correctives and augmentations of schematic cognitive structures; objects and actions are made sense of through a cyclical process of schematic expectation, perceptual input, schematic violation and adaptation. This model also allows for the fact that schemas can be 'wrongly' employed, recognized and judged as such, and changed to work better in the future.

Later developments in the humanities expanded schematic operations to a cultural level by recognizing that these constructive processes apply not only to objects and actions but also, necessarily, to all kinds of texts and

---

[6] Kant, *Critique of Pure Reason*, A 142, B 181, 214.
[7] See F. C. Bartlett, *Remembering: A Study in Experiential and Social Psychology*, 1932 (Cambridge: Cambridge University Press, 1995), 198–202, 301–14; Jean Piaget, *The Psychology of Intelligence* (New York and London: Routledge, 2001), 40–3.
[8] Kant, *Critique of Pure Reason*, A 144, B 183, 216.
[9] Ulrich Neisser, *Cognition and Reality: Principles and Implications of Cognitive Psychology* (San Francisco: W.H. Freeman and Company, 1976), 20–4.

representations. By developing the explanatory power of 'cultural schemas', the psychological hypothesis of schema theory, already adapted from a Kantian philosophical foundation and Popperian critical imperative, dissolves into a host of corresponding theoretical tributaries including processes of language, symbolization, connotation, narrative and myth as F. C. Wallace demonstrated.[10] Expanding the central hypotheses of schema theory into the cultural field in this way has generated some fruitful theorizing about certain kinds of aesthetic explanation – in other words, the creation and reception of representations. (Representations that are judged to evoke typical and regular formations of connotive meaning; as we will see in the next section, this idea will be the basis of a distinction between cultural image and schematic types).

One of the more famous expansions of schema theory into the cultural field was accomplished by E. H. Gombrich in *Art and Illusion* (1959), where 'schema' was developed as a specifically historical concept in aesthetic representation.[11] Like cognitive psychologists, Gombrich understood that representational schemas must change over time to explain the changing characteristics of stylistic realism. In arriving at this conclusion, Gombrich followed Popper's critical rationalism, whereby scientific knowledge is enacted by a continual process of 'conjecture and refutation'; an existing construct of knowledge is held to be provisionally 'true' until new information refutes it.[12] Gombrich applied Popper's trial-and-error model of evolutionary epistemology to the history of artistic style and representation by substituting the terms 'conjecture and refutation' with 'schema and correction'.[13]

A situation or object, whether represented or *to be* represented, is searched for elements that evoke existing schemas to help make sense of it; the mind fills-in whatever blanks are judged to be relevant for a 'completed' representation, with information provided by whatever schema is employed.[14] Gombrich's application of schema theory to the study of representations helps to demonstrate that the existence, outline and functions of schemas are never more apparent than when

---

[10] F. C. Wallace, *Culture and Personality*, 2nd edn (New York: Random House, 1970), 84–109; see also Neisser, *Cognition and Reality*, 186–8.
[11] E. H. Gombrich, *Art and Illusion: A Study in the Psychology of Pictorial Representation* (Oxford: Phaidon Press, 1959), 24, 55–78.
[12] Popper, *Conjectures and Refutations*, 34.
[13] Gombrich, *Art and Illusion*, 24. To simplify greatly, perhaps the most obvious link between Kant, Neisser, Gombrich, Popper and Peckham can be found in their shared belief that new understanding always proceeds from old understanding: 'tradition and innovation' is a characteristic schema of many of their ideas. As we have suggested in Chapter 1, this is also perhaps a primary element of Romanticism as a discursive concept.
[14] Gombrich, *Art and Illusion*, 63–78.

they are violated. Such violation occurs due to changes in historical context and a conflict between doxa and habitus, when the discontinuous element fails to be absorbed into the schema. These processes can be either conscious or unconscious: 'when we are aware of the process of filling we say we "interpret", where we are not we say "we see"'.[15] We might say that the activation of a schema, representational or otherwise, is a result of a judgement of appropriateness, conscious or unconscious.

Gombrich's linking of schema theory to Popper's philosophy was a fruitful comparison, helping to explain not only the historical development of representational schemas but also schematic cognition more generally in its relation with the critical function of social explanation. We might say that schemas are also similar to theories, inasmuch as they form the *a priori* background knowledge necessary for new epistemological conjectures; they explain something in a satisfactory way while being continually subjected to tests. Popper's comments on the progress of scientific theories can also characterize schemas:

> *Science starts only with problems.* Problems crop up especially when we are disappointed in our expectations, or when our theories involve us in difficulties, in contradictions; and these may arise either within a theory, or between two different theories, or as a result of clash between our theories and our observations. Moreover, it is only through a problem that we become conscious of holding a theory.[16]

There is much in this passage that clarifies the concept of schemas: consciousness of schemas in violation, communication between schemas and their struggle for explanatory supremacy. But Popper is here talking about scientific theories which are characterized by continual and systemic criticism. Non-scientific fields (and even some scientific ones, as Popper often lamented) are often pragmatically content with theories which are merely satisfactory, and even defend such theories against criticism. Representational schemas certainly tend towards this non-scientific type, being merely employed to the extent that they 'make sense' of their explicandum and have a very different criterion for testing and change: clarity, or ease of understanding.

Schemas fill-in blanks in the perception and cognition of a situation or object by extrapolating relevant data from past experiences. In this, they are

---

[15] Gombrich, *Art and Illusion*, 89.
[16] Popper, *Conjectures and Refutations*, 301.

like traditions – pragmatic tools of hermeneutic experience, malleable yet stubborn. Also, like traditions, they can be criticized, defended, adapted and, less commonly, abandoned. Both Gombrich and Popper highlight the fact that their 'truth' is provisional, and any consensus on the truthfulness (rather than the objective truth) of any schema, representation or theory, is dependent on tradition or, more specifically, the constitution of the event of reading – the moment of its entry into discourse – and the power relations which are at play there. In their interpersonal explanatory function, the recognition of 'accurate' elements in a representation (or theory) will depend on the creator, the perceiver and particularly the judge of the perceiver's behaviour, all sharing similar uses for it. As noted in what is perhaps Gombrich's most famous passage:

> To say that a drawing is . . . correct . . . means that those who understand the notation will derive *no false information* from the drawing . . . the correct portrait, like the useful map, is a . . . product on a long road through schema and correction.[17]

But a map is still read and judged to be correct by a perceiver who is trained to make sense of it in certain ways. The claim to truth made by the schema or schematic representation is always illusory in its constructivism, yet often indistinguishable from reality when framed by a corresponding code.

This question of realism introduces another important point that is beyond the purview of cognitive psychology as a scientific discipline. Richard Dyer reminds us that although such constructs of knowledge dependent on tradition are vital to our ordering of the world, they lie at the root of many dangerous ideological mystifications.[18] Schemas define boundaries, maintain norms, guide 'correct' behaviours and impose a sense of Otherness on certain categories.

It is here that we are reminded of the political element of the aesthetic, what Ricœur calls the 'imaginative variations' that the hermeneutic circle carries out upon 'the real', and what Rancière, in turn, calls 'dissensus' or explanatory interventions in 'the distribution of the sensible'.[19] It is important to bear in mind this latent political dimension of the intuitive 'putting together' enacted by schematic cognition. We will return to these ideas, their Romantic aspects and the role of film in the conclusion to this book.

---

[17] Gombrich, *Art and Illusion*, 77–8.
[18] Richard Dyer, 'The Role of Stereotypes', 1979, in *The Matter of Images: Essays on Representation*, 11–18 (London and New York: Routledge, 1993), passim.
[19] Ricœur, 'Phenomenology and Hermeneutics', 34; Rancière, *The Politics of Aesthetics*, 7.

For now, we can summarize the explanatory framework offered by schema theory by stating that schemas, like theories, types and images, are tools which help us make sense of the world. They mould our perceptions of both representations and the world that such representations claim to mimic, dependent upon culturally and historically localized traditions. At the stages of both production and consumption, a representation enters an existing history of schemas; during perception and cognition, the representation is searched for elements that meet expectations constructed from that history, and, if 'releasers' are recognized – elements which trigger the activation of a schema – the representation is sublimated under a category which forces its meaning. Due to a feedback process of violation and correction, schemas which no longer appear to match reality are reshaped to once again become indistinguishable from the 'essence' of their associated concept. The following model of cultural image and schematic types develops from this basis.

Cultural image and schematic types

The model outlined further has been developed in response to a failure to find an existing methodological model of representation based on a combination of schematic cognition and audio-visual explanation. However, this proposed model appears to explain something so fundamental to the way that many representations work, that it may turn out to be a redundant compensation for one that already exists, yet is unknown to the author. Even if the following model is judged to be simply an old idea in new clothes, it still has practical value in approaching the subsequent analysis of filmic representations of Romanticism, exemplified by the figure of Franz Liszt.

Modern historical theorists agree that history is an activity that selects and reshapes surviving documents in order to represent an ultimately unknowable past.[20] In Popperian fashion, such representations are held as the provisional truth while being subjected to tests. Modern historians have also addressed the important role played by cinema in this activity of 'doing history'.[21] Filmic

---

[20] See Hayden White, 'The Burden of History', 1966, in *Tropics of Discourse: Essays in Cultural Criticism*, 27–50 (Baltimore and London: The John Hopkins University Press, 1978), 40–1.

[21] Robert Brent Toplin, 'In Defence of the Filmmakers', in *Lights, Camera, History: Portraying the Past in Film*, ed. Richard Francaviglia and Jerry Rodnitzky, 113–35 (College Station: Texas A&M University Press, 2007), passim.

representations participate in Romantic or Lisztian discourse not by solidifying their image as part of any single cultural type derived from their actual historical situation, but rather by constructing a mobile agent of symbolic relations that change over time, between texts and between the various ways that texts are encountered, understood and talked about. This agent is active both within and between the various 'cultural codes' which regulate the constitution of any particular culture, as theorized within the discipline of cultural studies.[22] An individual awareness of this agent is what is meant by *cultural image*. The cultural image of Liszt, for example, is constructed through cultural activity and participation; it is what enables us to talk about, write about or see a representation of Liszt, and know that they refer to, and tell us something about, the 'same' thing. To have a cultural image of Liszt is to have an awareness of his historical being.

Even if this definition is deemed redundant, it still aids in understanding the related concept of changeable and combinable schematic types; for the cultural image functions in relation to a multitude of such types that it encounters in diverse representations, enacting a continual transformation of these types themselves.

Despite the familiarity of the concept of representational 'types' to Film Studies methodologies – having been previously elaborated by, for example, Richard Dyer[23] – it is perhaps worth addressing this concept in greater theoretical detail. What is meant by *schematic types* are typical and regular formations of connotive meaning, where 'typical' means readily available for partly-structured symbolic signification, and 'regular' means frequently employed and disseminated by cultural products. Schematic types can be judged as typical and regular through the analysis of specific textual representations. This happens as we make judgements about the cultural 'significance' of such representations and the elements they are understood to contain.[24] The interactions between cultural

---

[22] See Stuart Hall, *Representation: Cultural Representations and Signifying Practices* (London: SAGE Publications, 1997), 21–2.

[23] Richard Dyer, *Stars*, 1979 (London: BFI Publishing, 1992), 53–4.

[24] The methodological weaknesses of such models are obvious. First, how can we ascertain the 'significance' of certain textual representations over others? Only by making judgements of appropriateness that have to be defended against tests. Second, if the cultural image is a hypothetical construct, how can speculations as to its processes be verified, and how can its contents be measured? They cannot. Even if, for example, we compile 'facts' by handing out questionnaires to evidence the processes our model attempts to explain, these 'facts' are still subject to the various selection and interpretation biases typically troublesome to scientific method. Yet these objections do not contradict the hypothetical soundness of the model, and, more practically, it has an immediate use value.

image and schematic types are therefore identifiable and observable in specific textual representations, yet remain dependent upon individual competencies and dispositions towards recognition, recall and investment.

As this chapter progresses through the analysis of specific Lisztian schematic types and their employment in film, the applicability of these ideas will become clear. But a number of further theoretical comparisons might initially assist in explaining their proposed characteristics.

First, the cultural image is analogous to F.C. Bartlett's 'central' memory cluster ('Liszt'), which is continually reconstructed according to relationships with overlapping and subordinate schematic 'clusters' (types).[25] A primary object of attention is crossed and re-crossed by secondary 'interests' or biases that both determine and are determined by the 'weighting' of elements perceived from the primary object.[26] Bartlett also clarifies how schematic cognitive processes, or what he calls the 'image-function', can possess an intuitive explanatory character: no system of language 'comes anywhere near matching the delicate distinctions of affective response' generated by schematic cognition, 'consequently, in many instances the images are merely described or named; their significance is left to *tacit understanding*'.[27] This neatly describes the status of the schematic types explored in this chapter – they can be named and described only with the understanding that this does not exhaust them. Bearing in mind the methodology of risky archaeology we introduced in the introduction, we could say that the identification of a schematic type is the identification of what we judge to be an observable and distinct layer of sediment within which an artefact has been discovered – a typical and regular formation of connotive meaning. It stretches far underground, away from the object of analysis, and makes contact with multiple others, many of which – but not all – are buried and unobservable from the perspective of our excavation.

Second, to use terminology associated with Roland Barthes, the cultural image might be described as a polysemous and open-ended chain of signification ('Liszt') that is subject to various processes that attempt to 'fix' its meaning by connoted messages (types). Like Barthes's famous example of connotive meaning, 'Italianicity', the character of a schematic type can be merely vague

---

[25] Bartlett, *Remembering*, 313.
[26] Bartlett, *Remembering*, 217, 221.
[27] Bartlett, *Remembering*, 223.

and suggestive.[28] In a similar way, Neisser noted that schemas are like genotypes in genetics: they enable 'development', or understanding, 'along certain lines, but the precise nature of that development is determined only with an interaction with an environment', or, we might add, in relation to the combined conflict and reciprocity between doxa and habitus.[29] If the terminology of Barthes's *S/Z* (1973) is helpful here, then perhaps we could say that those textual moments when cultural image and schematic type meet are also a kind of *lexia* for a Gnomic/'*cultural code*': a mode of textual reference to the authority of an external body of cultural knowledge.[30]

Third, these concepts may be illuminated by Edward Said's description of the titular concept of *Orientalism* (1978) as 'that created consistency, that regular constellation of ideas as the pre-eminent *thing about* the Orient', or 'Liszt', or whatever other ideas we might wish to understand.[31] This 'thing about' something is built from surface features of diverse and innumerable representations (types), whose correspondence with the truth is partly irrelevant. This reference to Said may also clarify that the cultural image is constructed but not authored – it grows and changes over time as a cultural schema; however, the term cultural *image* is retained to clearly distinguish it from subordinate schematic types.

As mentioned earlier, the criterion of test and alteration for representational schemas may be the principle of clarity, or ease of understanding. The employment of features commonly associated with any particular schematic type can enable audiences to effortlessly engage with a representation and to quickly and unproblematically make sense of it. But schemas have to be 'activated' in order to function; this might be understood as the recognition of 'releasers', those specific elements in representations that determine the activation of an associated schema – what psychologists call a 'weighting' or 'trigger'.[32]

Schemas are also like 'cultural commonplaces', insofar as they encourage audiences to engage with prior experience, and facilitate certain responses without unnecessary reflection on how or why this is encouraged.[33] As Robert

---

[28] Roland Barthes, 'The Rhetoric of the Image', 1964, in *Image-Music-Text*, 32–51 (London: Fontana Press, 1977), 34.
[29] Neisser, *Cognition and Reality*, 56.
[30] Roland Barthes, *S/Z*, 1973 (Oxford: Basil Blackwell Ltd., 1990), 13–20.
[31] Edward W. Said, *Orientalism*, 1978 (London: Penguin Books, 2003), 5, 20–2; italics added.
[32] Bartlett, *Remembering*, 302–3.
[33] The phrase is appropriated from Noël Carroll, who uses it in a different way in 'Film, Rhetoric and Ideology', 1993, in *Theorising the Moving Image*, 275–89 (Cambridge: Cambridge University Press, 1996), passim. Although his phrase is useful in this context, I would suggest that schematic types are far less specific in function than a comparison with Carroll's commonplaces, derived from the Aristotelian enthymeme, would suggest.

Allen and Douglas Gomery noted, biopics similarly present 'attitudes, gestures, sentiments, motivations and appearances' based on 'general notions' about how the represented figures are '"supposed" to act', in addition to how they are supposed to appear as entities.[34] This highlights the schematic role of expectation in filmic representations of historical figures.

Liszt biopics, like other representations, utilize schematic types in this way to fill-in gaps or make sense of their subject. In a generative process operating at levels of both production and consumption, schematic types assist film audiences seeking a grasp of what a given representation might mean. In doing so they contribute to the maintenance or development of Liszt's cultural image, or his historical being.

But at this stage, it is fair to ask: Why, of all subjects, does the analysis of filmic representations of Liszt and his music, specifically, benefit from this model we have outlined? Again, the answer lies in considering his role as a privileged exemplar of the concept of Romanticism itself.

Making sense of Liszt's cultural image with schematic types

Liszt's cultural image can accommodate a great variety of schematic types, including what might be called the artist as magician, warrior, demon, priest, Don Juan or superstar types, and many of these hypothetical constructs have histories far older than Liszt. Yet this diversity explains why Liszt frustrates categorization as a composer, even broadly, since if we pin-down one aspect of his cultural image which seems to demand the restraint of a type, it is often the case that another contradictory aspect soon points in a different direction. Liszt scholars Dana Gooley and Susan Bernstein agreed that when dealing with Liszt 'disconnectedness is inherent in the subject matter'.[35] In his own lifetime, Liszt was associated with representations of saints, magicians, statesmen and classical heroes.[36] It is this element of bricolage or malleability, apart from anything else, which makes Liszt seem comparable to modern stars – the ability to slip between

---

[34] Robert C. Allen and Douglas Gomery, *Film History: Theory and Practice* (New York: McGraw-Hill, 1985), 158.
[35] Gooley, *The Virtuoso Liszt*, 6, 14; Bernstein, *Virtuosity of the Nineteenth Century*, 109.
[36] See Pauline Pocknell, 'Clandestine Portraits: Liszt in the Art of His Age', in *Analecta Lisztiana II: New Light on Liszt and His Music*, ed. Michael Saffle and James Deaville, 123–61 (Stuyvesant: Pendragon Press, 1997), passim.

schematic types dependent on context without appearing half-invested, without apparent contradiction.

This malleability can make Liszt a highly significant subject in reference to such schematic types as representations may be judged to evoke. The utilization of a schematic type in a film is, again, based on a judgement of appropriateness; it must correspond to an expectation – a 'correct' way of doing things. If filmmakers choose to represent Liszt as a diabolic figure it is because it simply makes sense to do so. To repeat Gombrich's useful phrase: the successful schema contributes 'no false information' to the representation, but only so far as the terms 'success' and 'falsity' imply normative explanatory judgements. Part of what makes Liszt interesting in this respect, and perhaps the definitive subject for an examination of the interactions between cultural image and schematic types, is that, thanks to his Romantic disregard for epistemological boundaries, there appears to be so many, often contradictory, 'correct' ways of representing him.

Part of why Liszt's cultural image exists in this state can be understood by considering his specific historical condition as a Romantic virtuoso. During the nineteenth century, the piano became an object invested with not only the technological, industrial and social advancements of the age but also a significant potential for cultural transcendence. Musicological studies by Dana Gooley, Gary Thomas and Richard Leppert have treated the piano as a powerful symbolic object – a location for creating and exploring the fluidity of private/public, male/female, original/reproduction and conservative/progressive binary constructs.[37] The virtuoso performance is an event when ideas about what seems possible are invited to be stretched. By becoming an icon of Romantic virtuosity, Liszt potentially embodies all these possibilities as well, resulting in a multifaceted cultural image with great potential for schematic diversity.

This capacity also extends to Liszt's music, complicating the dominant understanding of musical codes that supposedly establish a set symbolic function in a film soundtrack with a variety of associations, many of which are allied with the cultural types explored in this chapter. The schematic reading of Liszt's music further in the chapter has a certain similarity with 'registers', being (as we noted in Chapter 2) conventional systems of classification 'based

---

[37] Gooley, *The Virtuoso Liszt*, 1; Gary C. Thomas, 'Men at the Keyboard: Liminal Spaces and the Heterotopian Function of Music', in *Beyond the Soundtrack: Representing Music in Cinema*, ed. Daniel Goldmark, Lawrence Kramer and Richard Leppert, 277–91 (Berkeley: University of California Press, 2007), passim; Richard Leppert, *The Sight of Sound: Music, Representation, and the History of the Body* (Berkeley: University of California Press, 1993), 153.

on words, syntax, form and sounds' or 'conventionalized lexical, syntactic and prosodic choices' that are 'commonly shared by a community'.[38] For Michael Long, the study of mixed resisters in cultural products can expose the various functions such registers perform.[39] The use of previously existing music in film can create complex networks of associations between film and quoted source, as the schemas or registers they each evoke become entangled and negotiated. As K.J. Donnelly has noted, film music can act as a kind of 'spiritual' signifier, instructing an audience to respond to the images in reverential or ritualized ways that often go unquestioned.[40] Representations of Liszt and his music, too, often encounter such ritual formations, or intuitive normalized readings. They also tend to function around distinct 'musical moments', or moments when the traditional cinematic hierarchy of vision over sound is rebalanced.

The following list presents a number of schematic types commonly evoked to explain Liszt's cultural image, and the remainder of this chapter will explore each of them in reference to a selection of filmic representations. Needless to say, each theme carries the potential for rich explanatory significance with regard to Romanticism itself:

1. The romantic genius type 1: Cultural transcendence
2. The romantic genius type 2: The mad genius
3. The virtuoso type 1: Performance and vision
4. The virtuoso type 2: Sex and the body
5. The warrior type
6. Diabolic and magical types

The potential and limits of schematic reading

Before we investigate these schematic types in detail, however, and since the current employment of schematic reading may be unfamiliar, it is perhaps necessary to explore the potential and limits of schematic reading with regard to Liszt's music in particular.

The ballet sequence in *Hans Christian Anderson* (1952) neatly illustrates the potential schematic variety of Liszt's music. In this film, extracts from several

---

[38] Long, *Beautiful Monsters*, 5, 12.
[39] Long, *Beautiful Monsters*, 22.
[40] Donnelly, *The Spectre of Sound*, 37.

of Liszt's compositions become ambiguously diegetic motifs accompanying certain images, characters and locations, and they create various moods that capitalize on rich histories of schematic topical associations and registers. The proto-impressionistic 'Au bord d'une source' (1834–55) accentuates, in a vague way, the 'watery' qualities of the water scenes; *Mephisto* Waltz No. 1 (1859–62) accompanies a scene with sea devils, mobilizing schematic associations with demonic types; 'Gnomenreigen' (1862–3) accompanies a mermaid's dance, potentially activating the piece's programmatic association with mythological spirits. The mermaid herself is more overtly associated with an extract from the secondary theme of Liszt's Piano Sonata in B minor (1854), which can be read to function according to the typical gendering of primary and secondary themes in sonata form.

This kind of analysis is fairly simple, yet it neatly illustrates the schematic character and variety of certain kinds of audio-visual associations, connotations, registers and topics apparent in the use of Liszt's music in film, and how they can enable or encourage certain explanatory 'meanings'.

But how complex can such schematic reading become as a method of textual analysis? To explore the potential and limits of schematic reading, two further case studies display a noteworthy opposition. On the one hand, *The Black Cat* (1934), a canonical example of non-diegetic compilation score appropriated from the classical repertoire densely layered with music by Liszt and other Romantic composers; on the other, *Violent Playground* (1958), with a moment of diegetic music during which Liszt intrudes into a British 'social problem' film. Where one film presents a wide-ranging employment of Liszt's work throughout an entire soundtrack, the other presents a brief moment of only a few seconds duration.

The Black Cat stars Boris Karloff and Bela Lugosi as a former war criminal and a man seeking revenge for his wife's death. The soundtrack, arranged by Heinz Roemheld, employs many extracts from the Romantic canon, including works by Tchaikovsky, Schubert, Brahms, Beethoven, Schumann and several by Liszt. Roemheld himself was educated 'under Lisztian disciples', and was involved in compiling music for the Liszt-employing Flash Gordon series.[41] The use of previously existing classical music not only decreased production costs, time and efforts for composition but also provided films with symbolic capital

---

[41] Richard H. Bush, 'The Music of *Flash Gordon* and *Buck Rogers*', in *Film Music 1*, ed. Clifford McCarty, 143–65 (New York: Garland Publishing Inc., 1989), 146.

while ensuring protection from copyright infringement. Although the use of pre-existing music in *The Black Cat* generally conforms to a standard and widely accepted economic and aesthetic practice of mood creation and character motif stabilization, the use of Liszt's music in particular is worth examining for a more complex system of schematic associations that the film may be read to construct.

Before turning to Liszt, the following examples illustrate how the soundtrack of *The Black Cat* employs classical musical extracts for the creation of distinctive audio-visual meanings. The slow movement of Schumann's Piano Quintet (1842) plays when Poelzig (Karloff) leads Werdergast (Lugosi) down a set of spiral stairs to the lower levels of his castle in order to show him the preserved body of Werdergast's wife. The dialogue emphasis on death draws attention to the 'funeral march' register of the music. After Werdegast's attempt to kill Poelzig is interrupted by the appearance of a black cat, the slow movement of Beethoven's Seventh Symphony (1813) appears, next accompanying Poelzig's proposal of a game to settle their vendetta. The narrative themes of fate and death are underlined by the music's stately, sombre, quasi-funereal qualities of rhythm and melody. Bach's Toccata and Fugue in D minor (c1704–50), as performed by Poelzig on the organ, enters, as we will see further, into a long history of cinematic association between organ performance and supernatural villainy.

But most importantly for our purposes, the film presents motivic treatment of themes from Liszt's Piano Sonata in B minor and *Tasso*. The latter is broadly associated with Werdegast, while one of the primary themes in the Sonata in B minor is allocated to Poelzig. Several times, when Poelzig enters a scene, the Sonata announces his appearance in such a way that explicitly links the motif with his character through synchresis (the cognitive bonding provoked by simultaneous sense impression). Both themes appear one after the other in the scene in which both characters meet; first the Sonata theme, when Poelzig enters, and then the *Tasso* extract when Werdegast approaches to face him. This same dynamic of 'call and response' with musical themes appears in other scenes featuring the two leads, although presented with variations in timbre, orchestration and rhythm. When Werdegast discovers the body of his daughter, the *Tasso* theme is distorted to emphasize his emotional distress; this is followed by Poelzig descending the stairs, the Sonata theme accompanying in a similar state of dramatic disarray.

It is during the following climactic fight that the Sonata's later sections are exploited for their 'confrontational' suggestions, and in such a way that suggests

Figure 2 *The Black Cat* (1934)

unusual thematic depth. Throughout the Liszt Sonata, several themes are dramatically counterpointed in a way that is possibly suggestive of a 'battle' between musical 'characters'.[42] In one section (bars 569–81) two principal motifs appear to function against themselves, is as if the themes, ideas or characters they represented had exchanged costumes. By the end of the climactic fight in *The Black Cat*, the tables have turned on the previously threatening Poelzig, and Werdegast, the erstwhile tragic victim, becomes the more villainous presence as he proceeds to skin Poelzig alive. The Sonata 'battle' accompanies on the soundtrack, with the thematic inversion mirroring the dramatic inversion of power between the two characters. Allowing for the fact that these details of Liszt's sonata would almost certainly be known by only a tiny fraction of the film's audience, *The Black Cat* may be employing its soundtrack in a correspondingly inventive way to the Sonata, given the choreography of the fight between Poelzig and Werdegast, and the Lisztian education of the musical arranger. Even if we put aside speculations concerning authorial intention, the film can still be read in this way.

As a horror film, *The Black Cat* employs Romantic music to reconstruct and bolster audio-visual associations between its representational contents and

---

[42] For an overview of the interpretive possibilities presented by Liszt's Sonata in B minor, see Michael Tanner, 'The Power of Performance as an Alternative Analytical Discourse: The Liszt Sonata in B minor', *19th-Century Music* 24, no. 2 (2000): 173–92; and David Brown, 'The B Minor Sonata Revisited: Deciphering Liszt', *The Musical Times* 144 (2003): 6–15.

related schemas. Liszt's music is employed in central roles to explain horror-genre characters played by Lugosi and Karloff, even to the extent of forming the background of their conflict, and, as such, potentially strengthening their schematic ties to the diabolic, magical and warrior types explored further. The cultural image of Liszt, his music and the associated schematic types form a rich symbolic palate from which film such as *The Black Cat* can draw to consolidate audio-visual explanations of textual meaning. This communication also functions both ways by simultaneously affecting Liszt's cultural image. Although we might argue with Susan Bernstein for taking this hypothesis as far as she does, there is certainly some potential behind the view that, in *The Black Cat*:

> as Bela Lugosi's hair becomes wild and dishevelled ... can we be certain that we are not somehow seeing Liszt?[43]

Bernstein's comment neatly demonstrates the loose associative logic of the cultural image concept, and the risky character of archaeological statements made in its name.

Schematic reading is by no means a totalizing explanation of film music's various functions. The textual analysis of such content can be informative, but is, as always, based on, and evaluated by, various judgements of appropriateness which may refute the risks taken to make sense of something. It is also worth demonstrating, therefore, how Liszt's music can appear in a film soundtrack without seeming to justify an employment of schematic reading. This can be achieved by analysing one very brief scene in *Violent Playground*, when Liszt's 'Liebesträume' No. 3 appears to function as an uncomplicated signifier of symbolic capital as class distinction, and nothing more.

Johnny the arsonist, the focal point of the film's exposé/exploitation of juvenile crime, is caught in the act by the police. He makes his getaway through the upper floors of a house. Having momentarily lost his pursuers, Johnny looks around for a way to escape. The location's set design, including a chandelier that appears prominently in the frame, designates this location – the place under attack by Johnny (the embodiment of the social problem presented by the film) – as indistinctly non-working-class. Most other locations in *Violent Playground* establish a lower-class environment of council houses and crowded streets as the primary spaces of Johnny's social type.

---

[43] Bernstein, *Virtuosity of the Nineteenth Century*, 110.

A slow string version of 'Liebesträume' functions as a musical validation of the location's difference. Barely seven notes play before Johnny escapes through a window back onto streets rife with juvenile crime. It is reasonable to assume that the music is diegetic, perhaps coming from some unseen record player or radio; the film has previously used diegetic music prominently to establish locations and their attendant social values during the 'Play Rough' scene. The non-working-class nature of the environment is validated by the symbolic capital attendant of the classical music.

The house Johnny briefly enters is potentially a metaphoric space of class distinction. It may be read as the momentary visuality that Johnny's criminal type attains to the dominant classes, or the momentary, perhaps constant, vulnerability of the dominant classes to harmful intrusion, which, as the film's implied filmmakers (Michael Relph and Basil Dearden) suggest, is the 'social problem' to be highlighted. *Violent Playground* constructs a spatial ecosystem of classes, agents and mobility, and Liszt's music plays a small role in compartmentalizing this world.

Interesting as such musical moments are, the question they raise here is this: Why is Liszt's music used in particular? Recognition is a key element. Only a few notes of 'Liebesträume' are heard; enough certainly to signify 'classical music', but perhaps not enough to signify 'Liszt', except only to those familiar with this particular work. By adopting schematic reading, we may ask whether any other elements of the scene correspond to Lisztian schemas, such as the diabolic, the holy, the genius, and the sexual, as outlined further (with the attendant proviso that such schemas do not exclusively denote Liszt). The result would appear to be that with a hypothetical substitution of music with a similar register by many another composer – Schumann, Chopin or Beethoven, for example – the scene's musical meaning would not substantially change from that identified earlier.

The use of 'Liebesträume' in *Violent Playground* would therefore appear to be an arbitrary choice, perhaps determined by industrial factors, such as the ease of musical licensing for pre-existing music in film soundtracks, combined with the fact that 'Liebesträume' is a canonical piece of 'light' classical music. If this method seems reasonable, then the only schemas the music appears to evoke according to the narrative context are those associated with classical music more generally.

Violent Playground presents a case where deeper schematic reading does not appear to be justified, but it is worth noting that *this judgement is just as risky* as the one made when approaching the analysis of *The Black Cat*. In both cases, we have selected certain textual elements, based upon pragmatic interests for analysis, and filled-in gaps using schematic information to produce interpretations. Yet – and this is the crucial point – one interpretation has given us, as Popper would say, much more 'new and interesting' information than the other. This methodological factor of risky archaeology will remain present throughout the following elucidation of selected schematic types that are often used to explain Liszt's cultural image.

The romantic genius type 1: Cultural transcendence

Liszt is himself . . . a component of the contradictory 'atmosphere of Romanticism' that forever clouds its 'essence' as a concept.

—Susan Bernstein[44]

Foremost among the concepts used to contextualize representations of Liszt, filmic or otherwise, is that of Romanticism itself. As we saw in Chapter 1, Romanticism can be partly characterized by a certain paradoxical attitude towards the concept of genius, one that is usefully brought back into focus by expanding upon Morse Peckham's concept of cultural transcendence. While the Romantic individual transcends the ideologies of their culture by standing apart from society, and adopting and developing oppositional schemas such as 'solitude', 'excess', 'imagination', 'madness' and 'nature', their unique perspective is also expected, through the value ascribed to that oppositional position, to improve culture and society itself. However, because the exact potential for innovation embodied by the Romantic individual is not valued *a priori* as either 'good' or 'bad', 'genius' or 'madness', their cultural function often becomes that of testing the boundaries of cultural acceptability. The Romantic type is expected to 'go too far' – to expose the arbitrary lines of distinction drawn by cultures, alter them for better or for worse, and perhaps, by failing, becoming a martyr for ideals whose subsequent value is negotiated by various representational means, thereby reinforcing the dominant ideological constructs against which they had fought.

When we examine various filmic representations of Liszt and his music, we can see how cultural products can work-through this problematic by way of a variety

---

[44] Bernstein, *Virtuosity of the Nineteenth Century*, 130.

Figure 3 *Lola Montès* (1955)

of schematic audio-visual explanations. Liszt's cultural image often functions in accordance with this Romantic programme of cultural transcendence, inviting the contemplation and valuation of alternative ways of living. Arguably, Liszt's brief appearance in *Lola Montès* (1955), travelling through Europe in a luxurious carriage during an affair with the famous dancer, exemplifies his literal detachment from social fixings, both habitational and moral.

A self-proclaimed humanist with a belief in equality and a tendency to romanticize the working classes, Liszt was instrumental in breaking down the social barriers that existed between musicians and aristocrats, and between the artistic forms favoured by the cultural elite and popular audiences respectively. The virtuoso must become, in Liszt's words, 'no longer just a nobleman's favourite ... [but] the people's chosen one, the nation's artist'.[45] Films such as *A Song to Remember* (1945) and *Song Without End* (1960) present their piano virtuoso protagonists inverting the power balances between traditional power structures and social groups, between the artist, their aristocratic benefactor and a romanticized representation of the lower socioeconomic classes. Respect for music – that most valued and ineffable of Romantic arts – provides the means for social elevation, even above tsars and kings. These scenes will be addressed in more detail in the next chapter.

In certain cultural representations, the tension inherent in the paradox of the Romantic genius type creates a sense of thematic significance around a kind of subjective spiritual pain. An affective expression of that ideological tension, this pain then must become reconciled, accepted, and even desired by the Romantic individual as a signifier of their fidelity to the programme of cultural

---

[45] Liszt, *An Artist's Journey*, 155.

transcendence. This, in other words, names another of the most notable Lisztian Romantic tropes: that of suffering, or martyrdom for artistic ideals.

As Franco Moretti explained, it was during the late eighteenth century that the concept of a negative personal experience acquired an 'additional' or progressive quality in Western cultural products.[46] The trial is no longer an obstacle to be overcome, but, rather, a valuable opportunity for subjective development – something which must be assimilated without losing an awareness of its Otherness. The concept of progressive suffering resulting from a divided self, which took a central role in the development of Romantic schemas, was derived from religious myths and the influence of German Pietism. One common cause of Romantic suffering is the abstract ideal (what Frank Kermode called the 'Image')[47] that was known by, but always eluded, the artist. The joy and suffering that this ideal affords them guarantees their distinction as artists. But, in broader terms, the suffering genius type is a location for the intersection of pain and spiritual development as a criterion of creativity itself. Struggling with his status as an artist, Liszt once wrote, with quintessential Romantic rhetoric:

> Two opposing forces are fighting within me: one thrusts me ... up to the heavens; the other pulls me down towards ... regions of calm, of death, of nothingness ....
> I stay nailed to my chair, equally miserable in my strength and my weakness.[48]

To mythologize pain, or to turn pain into a kind of pleasure, cuts to the heart of Romantic liminality and its malleable explanatory potential. The trope of the suffering musician collapses the boundaries between physical and mental, bodily and spiritual modes of cultural expression; and the resultant representations of suffering can suggest of a kind of 'energy' channelled in various ways, perhaps towards an exterior social ideal, and casting a shadow of elusive meaning and mythic value over the various social and political concepts which might also be evoked alongside it – what we have previously called explanans. For example, *Song Without End* presents Liszt as divided and suffering when he states: 'I am part gypsy, part priest ... at war with myself.' Once evoked, this divided-suffering energy is then able to validate and mythologize Liszt's quest for a more authentic means of musical expression, although the more threatening aspects

---

[46] Franco Moretti, *The Way of the World: The Bildungsroman in European Culture* (London and New York: Verso, 1987), 46–8.
[47] Kermode notes that this image is commonly embodied in the idea of the female body and the tree as emblems of the importance of irrationality and organic growth to Romantic art; Frank Kermode, *Romantic Image*, 1957 (London and New York: Routledge, 2002), 1–14, 53.
[48] Cited in Walker, *Franz Liszt: The Virtuoso Years*, 269.

of this drive for cultural transcendence are negotiated by the film's own audio-visual explanation of those elements.

The ability of the Romantic hero to transcend suffering can have a cathartic effect on the consumers of their story; their martyrdom negotiates the attendant valuations that accompany their uniqueness within a fictional social context. Again, in Chapters 4 and 5, we will explore this process in greater depth by seeing how individual biopics of Liszt can negotiate the meaning and values of the Romantic genius in different ways.

The romantic genius type 2: The mad genius

As suggested earlier, if the Romantic genius strives to find self-worth outside of established social systems, then this radical symbolic potential must be continually reconciled to varying ideological contexts. Consequently, the genius type is often reconfigured in cultural representations through the development of various relationships with mediating cultural types that can defuse its more radical symbolic potential. Rephrasing this in the more specific theoretical terms already introduced, we can seek to expose the erased explanans of audio-visual explanations – those ancillary judgements, values and schemas it is apparently necessary to take for granted in order to render an explanation intelligible and relevant to a given situation.

One of the most effective means of rendering the genius figure ideologically 'safe' in this way is by developing a schematic association with madness. Romantic composers are commonly associated with madness due to cultural connotations of sensitivity, emotion, fantasy and excess. Perhaps the two most obvious examples of this association are Schumann and Wolf, who both lived in asylums in later life; but the temperamental and egoistic cultural images of Beethoven and Wagner may also encourage certain associations with madness. Liszt, too, can potentially be conceptualized through schemas of the 'mad genius' type, which is frequently employed in films to reduce the distances between the artist, their work and the film audiences who may have difficulty negotiating their attendant symbolic capital.

Albert Boime suggested that the persistence of 'the mad genius' type in Hollywood films may function to negotiate audience fears of creativity.[49] 'Fear of creativity' could perhaps be expanded here in a broader sense to suggest the positivist or Platonic fear of change, in opposition to the Romantic philosophical viewpoint which underlies German Idealism, schema theory and philosophical hermeneutics (in addition to Critical Theory and Popper's critical rationalism) – one which hypothesizes the mediated, historical and criticizable nature of perceived reality. The practice of 'explaining away' Romantic creativity via the employment of negatively valued explanans, such as madness, therefore, is a common technique in filmic representations.

By having the conducting Schumann collapse on the podium during the climactic concert in *Song of Love* (1947), for example, the film is potentially rendering the music 'palatable' to audiences who, due to variations in personal disposition, may not relate to its status as a musical 'masterwork'. By collapsing on stage in the throes of artistic commitment, Schumann is represented as a victim of his own musical genius and, therefore, inherent 'weakness', according to the explanans mobilized in this context. Although the Romantic creativity evidenced in Schumann's music contains a latent radical potential, it is possibly rendered ideologically harmless by being audio-visually explained as the very product of 'genius' itself – a production of one whose world view and potentials for action are radically different from members of society as a whole, no matter how much audiences might sympathize with his character and the values they embody in the narrative more broadly.

Obviously, there is no shortage of films in which Romantic music is linked with madness. Another illustrative example of the association can be found in an early scene in *Gaslight* (1940), when the central couple, Bella and Paul, attend a piano recital. The music being performed is Liszt's 'Sonetto 123 del Petrarca' (1838–42), and the theme is afterwards woven into Richard Addinsell's orchestral score, typically accompanying moments which are suggestive that Bella is grappling with a fear of losing her mind. In one notable instance, Bella runs down the hall stairs to the front door of her home in order to greet who she believes to be her cousin – a possible saviour from the sinister oppression of her husband Paul. Liszt's theme is repeated on the soundtrack quickly in rising tones, suggestive of the passionate, 'romantic' and suspenseful musical

---

[49] Albert Boime, 'An Interview with John C. Tibbetts', in *Liszt: A Chorus of Voices*, ed. Michael Saffle, John C. Tibbetts and Claire McKinney, 31-7 (Stuyvesant: Pendragon Press, 2012), 35.

registers of Wagner's 'Liebestod' from *Tristan und Isolde* (1865) – an opera saturated with notions of irrationality, emotion and madness both in content and reception contexts. That Liszt's music is seen fit to be treated in this way is suggestive of a certain confluence of musical iconography between Liszt's 'emotional', and therefore 'irrational', style and broader notions of the mad genius type.

Returning briefly to the concerns of the previous chapter, another more specific element of madness schemas can help us clarify why Liszt lacks a more solid foundation for his status as a canonical Romantic composer, explaining, in the process, why his potential to be situated as a progenitor of cinema was undeveloped in film and film music discourse.

Alan Davison investigated Liszt's relationship with phrenology, a pseudo-science which was popular in the 1890s.[50] He concluded that by living in a certain historical period and by displaying certain kinds of facial features, Liszt fell victim to another kind of critical oversight. In the years between c1890 and c1935, the dominant categories of bodily and facial characteristics associated with the Western male genius – including madness, physical impairment, constitutional weakness and slight stature, a selection of categories Davison calls 'degenerate' – applied to many canonical composers including Chopin, Beethoven, Schumann and Mozart, but not to Liszt. As Davison summarizes:

> artistic genius . . . changed dramatically in the second half of the nineteenth-century . . . [from the divided soul type to the degenerate type] some musicians came out well – in the sense of being sick enough. Others did not.[51]

In other words, by the first decades of the twentieth century, Liszt's cultural image was 'too handsome', or 'too healthy', to be that of a genius when judged by the standards of the time. But, as Davison suggests, things changed again around 1934, with the publication of Ernest Newman's famous Liszt biography.[52] The composer was now situated back within a cultural template of the genius which was dominant in the early nineteenth century: the divided soul type.

---

[50] Alan Davison, 'Liszt among the Degenerates: On the Vagaries of being a Musical Genius, c. 1890-c. 1935', in *Liszt's Legacies*, ed. Michael Saffle and James Deaville, 236–58 (Stuyvesant: Pendragon Press, 2014), passim.
[51] Davison, 'Liszt among the Degenerates', 237.
[52] Davison, 'Liszt among the Degenerates', 254–5.

Newman's emphasis on Liszt's 'dual nature' fitted emerging and increasingly dominant ideas about genius, and also had the advantage of accounting for Liszt's uneven output and challenging works. . . . Newman's biography marked . . . a turning point in the Liszt reception, for it reattached Liszt to a Romantic trope current in his own lifetime.[53]

The period between c1890 and c1935 was, in a sense, time lost for the cultural solidification of Liszt as a musical genius. As we have seen in Chapter 2, this was also the decisive time for the appropriation of Wagnerian aesthetics within film and film music discourses. During this crucial posthumous period for canonization following Liszt's death in 1886, he simply did not 'look' like a genius when judged by the cultural schemas of the time. Consequently, his artistic persona remained without a fixed status as an artistic genius type, resulting in the uniquely fluid and inconsistent canonical position he occupies in the history of Western music to this day.

Despite this complicated history, there survive certain iconographic elements to Liszt's cultural image that are commonly associated with more modern Western schemas of the musical genius: long white flowing hair, the black cassock and gestural performance styles. However, these elements also overlap with other schematic types which pull their meaning in different directions, including, as we will see further, the magical and the diabolic.

Liszt's cultural image lies in this fertile space of liminality between the solidified genius status of the great and tortured Beethoven, Wagner, Schumann and others, and the vacuous yet glamourous virtuoso. This condition also introduces another essential element, not only for Liszt's particular relationship with the Western genius myth but also one that is at the heart of Romantic virtuosity itself: that of being 'in the middle' – a mediator.

The virtuoso type 1: Performance and vision

The virtuoso . . . becomes the very site through which tradition, like the musical composition, passes.

—Susan Bernstein[54]

---

[53] Davison, 'Liszt among the Degenerates', 255.
[54] Bernstein, *Virtuosity of the Nineteenth Century*, 86.

At the heart of Liszt's cultural image lies the virtuoso performance, an event with the symbolic potential to collapse a host of binary distinctions between private and public, original and reproduction, freedom and control, and authenticity and artificiality. This potential to problematize such kinds of social ordering is rooted in the essential function of the virtuoso as both a cultural and an economic agent: they must embody a potential to exceed expectations.

But the concept of virtuosity is more complex than this. It also has a distinct historical character, emerging as a significant cultural and economic phenomenon during the early nineteenth century due to the development of social and economic trends, as well as technical innovations in instrument design. In addition, the audio-visual and ritualistic character of virtuosity means that it is not something possessed by certain individuals, but is rather something constituted by a complex of relations between perception, expectation and judgements of personal and procedural appropriateness. Virtuosity might be dependent upon a perceived imbalance between the visual 'proof' of the human source of sound production ('only human') and the character of the sounds heard ('more than human'), in a play of what is shown and not shown. This occurs alongside several further judgements of appropriateness: (1) that these combined audio-visual impressions are 'musical' and (2) that the right person is making them in the right way and in the right place. Accordingly, virtuosity appears to be perceived, recognized and organized in the judgement of others, activating secondary schematic expectations and associations.

Along with figures such as Paganini and Jimmy Hendrix, Liszt remains today an archetypal virtuoso. Historical discourse has raised his playing to mythic status. Among a new generation of pianist-composers to emerge in early nineteenth-century Europe, Liszt sought to exceed what was thought possible in terms of physical technique and sonic effect. As Johnathan Dunsby asserts, the piano music of the nineteenth century was 'in its purely physical demands ... more or less at the limits of possible human achievements'.[55] Liszt's supposed uniqueness developed in accordance with a powerful mythologizing discourse. His fellow composers, the public, the critics, and even some who had never heard him play, proclaimed that his pianism was unprecedented, 'absolutely overwhelming' and 'almost terrifying in its intensity'.[56] Some contemporaries

---

[55] Johnathan Dunsby, 'Chamber Music and Piano', in *The Cambridge History of Nineteenth Century Music*, ed. Jim Samson, 500–19 (Cambridge: Cambridge University Press, 2001), 511.
[56] Vladimir Stasov, 'Liszt, Schumann and Berlioz in Russia', 1889, in *Selected Essays on Music*, 117–94 (New York: Da Capo Press, 1980), 121; Arthur Loesser, *Men, Women and Pianos: A Social History* (New York: Simon and Schuster, 1954), 367.

recognized that these remarkable effects were due to the extraordinary visual and theatrical characteristics of his performances, which were often rooted in easily exploited Romantic tropes such as madness, religious ecstasy, freedom and nature; 'Storms', Liszt once said, 'are my *forte*'.[57]

Dana Gooley has summarized the curious self-fulfilling prophesy which sustains Liszt's mythic status in historical discourse:

> On the one hand, Liszt's audiences applaud enthusiastically because he is a great artist; on the other, Liszt is a great artist because his audiences applaud enthusiastically.[58]

The historical absence of audio recordings means that word-of-mouth and written documents bear the burden of sustaining Liszt's transcendental virtuosity. Biographies have continued to mythologize Liszt by idealizing the absence of his actual musical ability from modern sense perception. Films, as we will see further, also participate problematically in this discourse.

Recent studies have also exposed the myth that virtuosos were unmotivated by profit, and that the supposedly sacred priority of music came before any economic imperatives.[59] The fallacy that composers were singly focused on producing 'art' rather than 'products' – that is, objects and services constructed for exchange and profit, demanding the maintenance of a relationship with a market – is the result of selective critical history.

Throughout Liszt's life, the press, social events, biography and word-of-mouth fostered a desirable image of him as a redoubtable pianist, and a progressive and altruistic upholder of post-Beethoven Romantic artistic ideals.[60] One key instance is the *Weihekuss*, Liszt's legendary encounter with Beethoven in 1823. A conscious authoring of this event has long blurred the line between fact and fiction, to the benefit of Liszt's cultural cache.[61]

All this highlights the fact that Romantic virtuosity is intimately associated with the concept of modern fame or celebrity in both its economic and its performative aspects. It seems reasonable to accept that Liszt was a key prototype

---

[57] Cited in Kenneth Hamilton, *After the Golden Age: Romantic Pianism and Modern Performance* (Oxford: Oxford University Press, 2008), 8, 44.
[58] Gooley, *The Virtuoso Liszt*, 4.
[59] See Dana Gooley, 'Franz Liszt: The Virtuoso as Strategist', in *The Musician as Entrepreneur, 1700–1914: Managers, Charlatans and Idealists*, ed. William Weber, 145–61 (Bloomington and Indianapolis: Indiana University Press, 2004), passim.
[60] Lawrence Kramer, *Musical Meaning: Toward a Critical History* (Berkeley: University of California Press, 2002), 33.
[61] See Alan Walker, *Reflections on Liszt* (Ithaca and London: Cornell University Press, 2005), 1–10; Gooley, 'Franz Liszt: The Virtuoso as Strategist', 155.

of the star figure. As Joshua Gamson notes, celebrity image-management was 'relatively unsystematic until the growth of professional public relations and film technology';[62] by being conscious of their own image and its relation to market forces, celebrity virtuosos such as Liszt, Paganini and Jenny Lind set a historical precedent for later developments within and around the film industry. This trend eventually led to the institutionalization of celebrity-audience relations and to the development of the star system and its associated social functions. In his lifetime, Liszt's likeness even appeared on a wide variety of merchandise.[63]

Like the Hollywood film star, Liszt's appearance before an audience sometimes created the profound emotional identifying effect that 'they [the audience] were seeing a dear, beloved friend', more accessible than a great military leader or king.[64] Lawrence Kramer has explored Liszt's cathartic effect on audiences who, by being 'sutured' by the music into identifying with the body of the performer, could share his 'impulsive' freedom and power while maintaining a certain distance by the displacement of that pleasure into the process of looking.[65] This process is, in some respects, reminiscent of modern expectations of twentieth-century stardom, facilitated by modern image reproduction and broadcasting technologies. Although there can be no formally established cause-and-effect connection between these two developments, one does provide historical precedent for the other. As we will see in Chapter 5, this connection is explicitly evoked in Ken Russell's *Lisztomania* (1975), where 1830s virtuoso hysteria is riotously compared to twentieth-century rock stardom.

The importance of visual bodily impression in Lisztian discourse is partly a result of historical limitations on recording technology. As mentioned previously, there exist no known audio recordings of Liszt playing the piano. Written accounts, caricatures and the musical scores themselves remain the only 'proofs' of his ability. But the genius myth is here sustained as much by a visual absence as by an auditory one. As one contemporary critic wrote: 'you have to see Liszt's face, Liszt's eyes when he plays'; Schumann concurred: 'I wish I could capture in words a picture of this extraordinary man. . . . It is not easy!'[66] As

---

[62] Joshua Gamson, 'The Assembly Line of Greatness: Celebrity in Twentieth-Century America', in *Stardom and Celebrity: A Reader*, ed. Sean Redmond and Su Holmes, 141–55 (Los Angeles: Sage, 2007), 144.
[63] Pocknell, 'Clandestine Portraits', 123; Kramer, *Musical Meaning*, 91.
[64] Hans Christian Andersen cited in Kramer, *Musical Meaning*, 87.
[65] Kramer, *Musical Meaning*, 85.
[66] Cited in Stasov, 'Liszt, Schumann and Berlioz in Russia', 123; Robert Schumann, 'Franz Liszt: Concerts in Dresden and Leipzig', 1840, in *Schumann on Music: A Selection from the Writings*, ed. Henry Pleasants, 157–61 (Mineola: Dover Publications, 1965), 158.

Susan Bernstein noted, such accounts describe reactions rather than the playing itself.[67] Liszt's appearance was also compared to a 'glorious, powerful eagle', 'thunder' and 'lightning', a 'bird-of-prey' and a 'lion', and even when descriptions of Liszt are less than complimentary, they are often striking in their visual suggestions: 'a freak', 'a scarecrow' or 'a mummy'.[68] It was left to caricatures, such as those by János Jankó, to utilize these 'freakish' elements in communicating the more expressive 'filmic' visual impressions of the way pianists, or any public figures, moved.[69] These were the elements that were expunged by single paintings and photographs. Due to its perceptual absence from contemporary subjective experience, Liszt's pianistic ability remains so entrenched in myth and sublimity that filmic representations of his playing are unfailingly liable to court judgements of insufficiency.

Figure 4 *A Song to Remember* (1945)

[67] Bernstein, *Virtuosity of the Nineteenth Century*, 120.
[68] Vladimir Stasov, 'Letters from Abroad', 1869, in *Selected Essays on Music*, 38–51 (New York: Da Capo Press, 1980), 48; Wilhelm von Lenz, *The Great Piano Virtuosos of Our Time: A Classic Account of Studies with Liszt, Chopin, Tausig and Henselt*, 1872 (London: Kahn and Averill, 1995), 17; Gooley, *The Virtuoso Liszt*, 107; Stasov, 'Liszt, Schumann and Berlioz in Russia', 125.
[69] Alan Davison, 'Liszt and Caricatures: The Clarity of Distortion', in *Liszt: A Chorus of Voices*, ed. Michael Saffle, John C. Tibbetts and Claire McKinney, 68–75 (Stuyvesant: Pendragon Press, 2012), 73–4.

In accordance with the Romantic imperative of audio-visual explanation, visual stimulus remains fundamental to various attempts to give represented musical performances, filmic or otherwise, a kind of meaningful significance. Dana Gooley has suggested that Liszt's audio-visual performance articulation was determined by a combination of textual features and theatrical behaviours. When playing his own edition of Weber's *Konzertstück* (1821), for example:

> Liszt's chromatic octave surge expanded the sonic and visual dramatic amplitude of the gesture that marks the appearance of the hero. The listener could no longer see *through* Liszt to the narrative, for he had *become* the hero who appears over the horizon.[70]

As we have seen, this boundary-breaking visual dimension lies at the heart of Liszt's whole aesthetic philosophy.

To defend Gooley's hypothesis, Rolf Inge Godøy has demonstrated that, according to the motor theory of perception, any conception of meaning in musical performance is intrinsically related to 'sound-motion objects', or the simultaneousness of sonic event and visual cues provided by the gestures of the performer.[71] The musical event is given 'sense', in part, by the visual characteristics of the performance. As suggested earlier, an imbalance between sound and vision, combined with certain judgements, may establish a musical performance as one of virtuosity and its performing individual as a virtuoso. In *The Sight of Sound* (1993) Richard Leppert similarly suggested that public musical performances more generally, live or represented, present a psychological imbalance between the visually observable physical activity of the music-making process and the resulting music as a non-visually observable counterpart.[72] Sight, and particularly sight of the body, becomes a key element in mediating this slippage. Film presents instructive instances of this process in various contexts, as the meaningful effect of the represented music is explained through various visual processes.

To give one example, Lawrence Kramer has suggested that one of cinema's common methods for representing diegetic pianistic performance – the pianist's bodily fragmentation into alternating shots of their face and hands (often a production necessity allowing the insertion of shots of a professional

---

[70] Gooley, *The Virtuoso Liszt*, 104.
[71] Rolf Inge Godøy, 'Postures and Motion Shaping Musical Experience', in *The Routledge Companion to Embodied Music Interaction*, ed. Micheline Lesaffre, Pieter-Jan Maes and Marc Leman, 113–20 (London and New York: Routledge, 2017), 115–18.
[72] Leppert, *The Sight of Sound*, xxi.

pianists' hands) – continues the reliquary fragmentation of the pianist's body for audience pleasure. The isolated, 'impossible', hands fill the screen, becoming 'the cinematic equivalent of the souvenir'.[73] A part of the cinematic pleasure occasioned by a montage sequence comprising of close-up shots of a virtuoso's performing hands lies in the privileged perspective of such images as sights otherwise impossible to see. Kramer's argument finds precedent among the oldest theories of film, including Béla Balász's concept of microphysiognomy – the ability of the close-up shot to reveal the phenomenal world from otherwise unavailable perspectives.[74] As well as providing pleasure in this way, the fragmentation inherent in such representational techniques has the potential to blur the boundaries between the piano and the identity of the pianist. Cinematic conventions such as these continue and enrich debates that first circulated in musical culture during Liszt's own lifetime. Liszt himself expressed the common theme that a pianist can figuratively merge with their instrument: 'My piano is to me what a ship is to the sailor, what a steed is to the Arab . . . my piano is myself, my speech, my life'.[75]

In addition to privileged perspectives, cinematic musical moments also commonly rely on representations of character reactions to confirm the authority of the musical performance being shown. *Song of Love* presents an interesting variation of this technique, while also subverting the cinematic fragmentation of the performance event into privileged shots. In one scene the young Brahms plays the piano while Clara and Robert Schumann stand over the instrument, enraptured by his playing. We are shown no shots of Brahms's hands touching the keys, only his placid expression. The authority of the performance comes from the explanatory facial and bodily reactions of the two listeners. The film's 'refusal' to show the performing hands might seem to decry (from the conservative side the War of the Romantics) the fetishized display of performance through the fragmented montage technique which has, at this point in the film, been associated with Liszt. Yet the camera's refusal to confirm the sound-motion object – refusal to show the pianists' hands – fetishizes Brahms's performance in a different way. Through fragmented absence, instead of fragmented presence, voyeurism is replaced by taboo.

---

[73] Kramer, *Musial Meaning*, 92.
[74] Béla Balász, '[from] *Theory of the Film*', 1945, in *Film Theory and Criticism: Introductory Readings*, ed. Leo Braudy and Marshall Cohen, 5th edn, 304–11 (Oxford: Oxford University Press, 1999), 309.
[75] Liszt, *An Artist's Journey*, 45.

This varied emphasis on vision in musical performance was also a significant element in the changing values of Romantic virtuosity itself. The instrumental virtuoso was now, by being situated in a market position where they are expected to display their skills visually as well as audibly, vulnerable to accusations that the value of the visual display superseded the value of the music itself. As the Brahms example from *Song of Love* demonstrates, a certain kind of conservative formalism prejudices music to the extent that it accentuates the visual impression of its method of production.

Arthur Loesser describes the changes in European musical culture during Liszt's retirement c1850 that clarify this alteration in the hierarchy of sensory elements.[76] A growing musical press evidenced the rise of a musically educated post-revolutionary bourgeoisie, and a gradual transformation of the virtuoso concert ensued. The informal performance styles of Liszt and Sigismund Thalberg gave way to the more solemn recitals of Anton Rubinstein and Hans von Bülow. Visual performance effects – such as Liszt theatrically brushing-back his hair[77] – were considered sites of visual excess, problematizing the reception of the music as 'good' music, despite negatively reinforcing the importance of vision and individuality as being essential to the concept of virtuosity itself. Performances with a self-consciously visual dimension were seen to 'submerge the music in the spectacle of the musician' – an effect to which many critics objected.[78]

For Bartók, what 'repels' about Liszt's cultural image is his 'many-sidedness, his eclecticism and his over-susceptibility to all musical sensations, from the most commonplace to the most rare'.[79] Such value judgements privilege the purity of exclusive categorizations while devaluating audiences who are judged to be easily impressionable. Bernstein continued this point by stating that, for Liszt, 'stealing, the theft that devalues the origin and the original, is permitted'[80] – a privilege which furthers the potential of Liszt's cultural image to destabilize cultural values.

Despite such criticisms, many historical accounts also validate Liszt's capacity for genuine musical 'greatness'. What is potentially disturbing is that greatness and artificiality both appear to be within Liszt's grasp, both appearing

---

[76] Loesser, *Men, Women and Pianos*, 422–32.
[77] Kramer, *Musical Meaning*, 73; Samson, *Virtuosity and the Musical Work*, 77.
[78] Kramer, *Musical Meaning*, 87.
[79] Cited in Bernstein, *Virtuosity of the Nineteenth Century*, 93.
[80] Bernstein, *Virtuosity of the Nineteenth Century*, 106.

fundamental to Liszt's artistic makeup, interchangeable or equal. He achieved something which was problematic for cultural hierarchies: he could 'imitate the inimitable', undermining the structuring distinctions between high and low, genius and vessel, and original and reproduction. As Wagner put it, it was often unimportant what music Liszt played at all.[81] It is this capacity to encompass and compress extremes of value that makes Liszt such a potent agent of cultural liminality, and also seem particularly modern. Mendelssohn, too, famously stated: 'Liszt's way in everything . . . is a perpetual fluctuation between scandal and apotheosis'.[82] Contemporary critics often stressed the shocking effect made by a virtuoso who, for example, sometimes instead of 'using the steps . . . leaped onto the platform'.[83] His scandalous behaviour and private life was matched by an equally outrageous musical output (see Chapter 2). As we will see in Chapter 5, it is this element of obscenity – the potential to transgress the decent – which informs Ken Russell's approach in the self-consciously scandalous *Lisztomania*.

The virtuoso type 2: Sex and the body

So the body of the performer and the process of looking often play central roles in musical meaning. In film too, diegetic musical performances often appear to encourage embodied musical cognition, where the display of the performing musician mediates the slippage identified by Leppert earlier. The result is often a combined horizontal and vertical montage of sound-motion objects, and diegetic responses to such objects, which combine to enforce their meaning by audio-visual explanation.

This is often centrally accomplished by the represented performing musician being watched by other diegetic characters. Such musical spectacles are sometimes sexualized through the evocation of a voyeuristic register. Performance activity itself can be sexualized through the combination of heightened emotion and the physical prowess required for virtuosity. Lawrence Kramer has explored how recitals can be read as moments of sexual connection, as a sonic 'envelope' forms between performer and listener, functioning as 'an

---

[81] Bernstein, *Virtuosity of the Nineteenth Century*, 13; cited in Samson, *Virtuosity and the Musical Work*, 102.
[82] Cited in Kramer, *Musical Meaning*, 69.
[83] Stasov, 'Liszt, Schumann and Berlioz in Russia', 120–1.

extension of touch'.[84] A diegetic relationship between performer and on-screen listener is often potentially sexual, particularly when the performer's body itself becomes the focus of the gaze. Desire for the music is recontextualized through the voyeuristic process as a desire displaced onto the image of the performer's body. This device turns the performance into one centrally determined by its visual element, functioning to compensate for the absence or slippage inherent to dominant cultural formations of classical music in general. The culturally determined 'greatness' of classical music, and the potential absence of this recognition from the perspective of the audience, is overcome by a visual bridge. Sex, like the madness schemas explored in a previous section, provides such a bridge from the emotional absence demanded by 'high' cultural values to an intuitive emotional understanding of value. In other words, films can employ a voyeuristic structure to help audiences engage with music that may otherwise alienate them. In the process of explaining 'difficult' classical music to audiences, films displace it by a supposedly more 'universal' sexual register.

In a more specific and formal sense, the erotic potentiality of Romantic pianism is typically displayed through an equation between digital activity and sexual touching – an effect sometimes created through montage. In *Letter from an Unknown Woman* (1948), for example, the teenage Lisa listens in a reverie while the object of her unrequited affection, Stefan, practices Liszt's 'Un sospiro' in an upstairs room. Lisa's friend gossips about a boy, mentioning his wandering hands; the moment is interrupted with a close-up shot of Stefan's hands playing a crescendo on the high notes. This edit links virtuosic pianism with a desirous and somewhat illicit sexuality – illicit due to the element of auditory voyeurism introduced by Lisa's secret listening to Stefan's private practice. Similarly, during *Lisztomania*'s Chaplin sequence, a descending chromatic run of notes accompanies a shot of Liszt's kisses running up Marie's arm. In such scenes the virtuosity, passion, sensitivity and prowess of pianistic performance become implied elements of sexual performance as well.

At its most extreme, this tendency associates the piano with the female body itself, strengthening the ideologically problematic schematizing of male control and female Otherness. Both Gooley and Kramer have suggested that the common virtuoso motif of 'blood on the keys' can suggest rape or loss of virginity on the part of a feminized piano.[85] Liszt's own performances were occasionally

---

[84] Kramer, *Musical Meaning*, 34; Kramer, 'Classical Music – Virtual Bodies – Narrative Film', 358.
[85] Kramer, *Musical Meaning*, 84, Gooley, *The Virtuoso Liszt*, 108.

described in terms of a romantic embrace, with the performer dominating a submissive female piano.[86] This was validated by sexualized discourses surrounding Liszt himself as a womanizer. Some commentators went so far as to brand Liszt an 'erotomaniac'.[87] (This term expresses an extremeness given full reign in *Lisztomania*.) In the next chapter, we will see how representations of pianism can explore the boundary between public and private expressions of sexual desire.

On a related note, the potentially transgressive nature of this sexual dimension is also sometimes tempered by the piano's partly domestic functionality.[88] Cinematic representations of Lisztian pianism often encounter this conflict between artistic passion and sheltered homelife. Liszt's first scene in *Impromptu* (1991), for example, alternates between a dramatic piano improvisation and its effect of disturbing a baby in the next room. Interestingly, both conflicting 'worlds' are disturbing *and* disturbed, communicating values between them with equal suggestiveness; comically deflating the seriousness of the music, and bringing a quality of sexualized passion into the domestic environment. In the clarity and potency of its symbolic content regarding relationships, art, society, sex and violence, the image of a pianist disturbing a crying baby and a crying baby disturbing a pianist could function as an exemplary cliché of the composer biopic.

The warrior type

Extending this ideologically charged tension between passion and domesticity – public and private – represented Romantic composers are often situated between introverted artistic isolationism and extroverted social duties and conflict.

Romantic artists were sometimes defined by their 'womanish' isolation in a 'padded' world.[89] Romantic composers are also feminized in a variety of ways that contrast them with conventions of masculinity. This is demonstrated in *Impromptu* when Liszt and Chopin are described as 'perfumed prancers'

---

[86] Gooley, *The Virtuoso Liszt*, 108.
[87] Max Nordau cited in Davison, 'Liszt among the Degenerates', 247.
[88] Kramer, *Musical Meaning*, 42.
[89] Lenz, *The Great Piano Virtuosos*, 46; cited in Asa Briggs, 'Manners Morals and Tastes: Changing Values in Art and Society', in *The Nineteenth Century: The Contradictions of Progress*, ed. Asa Briggs, 291–326 (London: Thames and Hudson, 1970), 321.

while playing a duet. Framed in long shot, sitting close together, their bonding is ironically presented as a kind of homosexual encounter. At the same time, Romantic qualities of dynamism and vitality contradict this 'padded' and feminized stereotype, sometimes evoking various contemporary social and political realities in cultural representations. In typically contradictory fashion, Liszt can be read as the quintessential 'padded', 'long-haired' recluse and the quintessential proactive, socially-minded warrior.

Once again, contemporary historical context illustrates the development of this Romantic tension. The fusion of European art and politics during the early nineteenth century mingled with the rising importance of the press who reported the activities of famous personalities. Romantics like Lord Byron, who took part in the Greek War of Independence, and Wagner, who was forced to flee Germany following the Dresden May Uprising of 1849, were politically active individuals, closing a perceived gap between artistic ideals and public action. This sometimes results in a tension between art and revolution in classical music biopics, often seemingly exploring that image provided by Theophile Gautier: '[Art] is only aware of revolutions when the bullets break the windows'.[90] This metaphor was employed, sometimes literally, in *Lisztomania*, *Wagner* (1983) and *The Pianist* (2002) to symbolize the divide between insulated high culture and the violation of its spaces by the demands of history and the wider public domain. Composer biopics often situate their protagonists alongside political or military conflicts in opposition to the domestic confinement which provides its counterpart.

Figure 5 *Lisztomania* (1975)

[90] Cited in Tim Blanning, *The Romantic Revolution* (London: Phoenix, 2010), 54.

This vague and suggestive warrior type is also often located, once again, in the dynamism and potential subversion of Romantic pianism itself. Liszt's critics, positive or negative, often circulated descriptions in which the virtuoso defeated his audience in strikingly visual metaphors of Napoleonic combat: 'All he had to do was hurl one colossal bomb – the *William Tell* overture – and Odessa was taken by storm', as one critic wrote, also comparing Liszt with Alexander the Great.[91] Biographer Alan Walker similarly writes of Liszt possessing a 'warrior spirit', and of his becoming a 'crusader' during the Weimar years.[92] The military topics of pieces such as *Grand Galop Chromatique* (1838) inspired descriptions and drawings of Liszt as a solider riding his piano into battle.[93] Further metaphors of enslavement, domination and destruction are common among contemporary descriptions; as Kramer notes, 'the Napoleon of the piano' was one of the most common metaphors used to draw Liszt into an 'orbit' of military-themed representations.[94] The biopic that perhaps most notably engages with the warrior type is, again, *Lisztomania*, in which Liszt (as we will see in Chapter 5) engages in a swordfight, marches across a stage wearing Hungarian military uniform and slays Richard Wagner with a flame-throwing piano.

Diabolic and magical types

During one scene in the horror film *White Zombie* (1932), Liszt's 'Liebesträume' No. 3 is played by Madeleine, who sits at a piano in a high-ceilinged castle chamber. Her sole spectator Charles sits listening. Charles has conspired with Murder Legendre (Bela Lugosi) to enslave Madeleine with voodoo powers, and this scene presents the central narrative reveal of the consequences of Charles's actions, accentuated by atypical camera movements. This is the moment when he realizes the dissatisfaction, and eventually the horror, of his situation. One camera movement, accompanied by a momentary musical crescendo, tracks-in on Madeleine's face to emphasize a remarkable disparity. She sits perfectly still with expressionless eyes staring forward unblinkingly, not reacting when Charles places jewellery around her neck. The unsettling quality of this uncanny

---

[91] Cited in Stasov, 'Liszt, Schumann and Berlioz in Russia', 142.
[92] Walker, *Franz Liszt: The Weimar Years*, 339.
[93] Bernstein, *Virtuosity of the Nineteenth Century*, 115.
[94] See for example, Kramer, *Musial Meaning*, 68–71, 87; Gooley, *The Virtuoso Liszt*, 78–116.

domestic scene is accentuated by the discontinuity between Madeleine's vacant expression and the expressive music she plays.

Again, the key questions are: What difference does the selection of Liszt's music make? What secondary associations might it evoke that Chopin's or Schumann's music might not? This example highlights the way a cultural image of a composer and his music can contribute to a broader array of schemas without being required to communicate with them in any *specific* sense – knowledge of the name of the work or the composer is not necessary for an awareness of the associative potential of the music. This example also neatly encapsulates two further Lisztian schematic types: the diabolic and the magical.

The association between Liszt's cultural image and Mephistophelian or diabolic imagery was variously constructed by Liszt's physical appearance, performance practices and musical compositions, and according to Dana Gooley, 'to this day it remains the favourite metaphorical analogy' used to characterize Liszt.[95] The virtuoso Liszt had inherited some of the sinister and cadaverous aspects of Paganini's earlier celebrity image. Some of Liszt's audiences saw him as 'a demon, venting his rage upon the piano and destroying it in the process . . . it became commonplace to see something demonic in Liszt's playing', but simultaneously something of the miraculous as well.[96] Liszt's diabolism, beyond an image inheritance from Paganini, was also intimately determined by cultural formations of the musical creative process. According to Gooley, Liszt presented audiences with a 'discourse of demonic possession and exorcism, and culminating in a glow of goodness'.[97] This 'exorcism' is supposedly located in the audio-visual performative mode itself, independent of the topical or programmatic content of the work being played.

This point is highly suggestive, for the mythic production of the virtuoso mode itself contains an implicit conflict between the paradigmatic extremes of cultural value – 'good' and 'evil' – free creativity, against its negation in mere reproduction. Art, of course, by its philosophical valuation under Romanticism, triumphs in the name of good – Liszt's ability to 'play' with diabolic ideas has already inscribed the positive power of art to usurp and ascribe to them a similar positive value; but the inherent drama the virtuoso (and perhaps all art) presents between original and reproduction, seen and unseen, light and darkness, clarity

---

[95] Gooley, *The Virtuoso Liszt*, 239.
[96] Cited in Stasov, 'Liszt, Schumann and Berlioz in Russia', 128.
[97] Gooley, *The Virtuoso Liszt*, 239.

and obscurity, determinacy and indeterminacy, is, as we know, vital to the conceptualization of Romanticism itself.

Despite this, Liszt's association with diabolism has survived largely independently of claims to the social position of the Romantic genius figure, and their negotiation and delineation of values in the work of art. His diabolism also makes more direct contact with schemas of satanic magic; an effect augmented by the intertextual reception of Liszt's use of chords and melodies topically associated with 'evil'. Liszt produced a variety of pieces that specifically express diabolic ideas and associations; the most commonly cited of these include the *Dante* Sonata (1849), *Mephisto* Waltz No. 1 and the *Faust* (1854; 1857) and *Dante* Symphonies, with their dramatic, playful and ironic evocations of Mephistopheles and hell. CD artwork selections often accentuate the demonic schematization of these works by employing artwork by Goya, or pictures of gargoyles.[98] Persistent readings in these terms lead to certain interpretive traditions. As one commentator states: 'the devil lurks everywhere' in Liszt's music and cultural image.[99]

Lisztian diabolic tropes find significant expression in film, where perhaps the most notable example remains the 1943 version of *The Phantom of the Opera*. This famous horror film implies a certain comparison between Claudin the Phantom (Claude Rains) and Franz Liszt, a fictional embodiment of whom is recruited to aid in the villain's capture. It is a comparison which may suggest similarity as much as difference, with Liszt's associations with isolated genius and madness either heightened or disarmed by the proximity of the exaggerated case of Claudin – the diabolic composer-type rendered monstrous. The behavioural and visual eccentricities of Claudin may frame Liszt's similar eccentricities as socially acceptable, even valuable, by comparison; their dangerous excesses are purged by being displaced into Claudin.

The black cassock, long white hair and religious piousness which formed a central part of Liszt's later-life image do not invalidate the activation of demonic schemas (recall Gombrich's phrase: 'no false information'). But with the addition of one significant element – that of unique 'knowledge' or the 'ability' associated with virtuosity – this accumulation of iconographies can also lead to schemas of the magician.

---

[98] See for example, Hyperion, Leslie Howard, *The Complete Liszt Piano Music*, CD 20, *Liszt Waltzes*; EMI Classics, 2005, Sir Thomas Beecham, et al., *Liszt - Faust Symphony, Tone Poems, Pslam XIII*.

[99] Ophra Yerushalmi, 'Benediction to Liszt in His Solitude', in *Liszt: A Chorus of Voices*, ed. Michael Saffle, John C. Tibbetts and Claire McKinney, 370–5 (Stuyvesant: Pendragon Press, 2012), 372.

The widespread cultural tendency to associate both Liszt and his music with magic developed through a combination of specific visual iconographies, music and performance tropes and, as Kenneth Hamilton notes, a vague 'quasi-mystical' aura around Liszt's personality and cultural image.[100] The magical element in his physical appearance developed in the 1840s, mostly as a consequence of post-Paganini virtuoso reception, complemented by Liszt's demeanour, long hair and black clothes. For pianist Amy Fay: 'He made me think of an old time magician. . . . I felt that with a touch of his wand he could transform us all', and, for Wagner, Liszt was able to conjure 'magic without parallel'.[101] The 'magic' that Liszt conjured was, of course, his mythologized pianism; an unprecedented power to summon his listeners' emotions combined with seemingly 'impossible' keyboard acrobatics. Liszt's perceived affinity with the piano sometimes provoked metaphors in which the piano 'disappeared' under Liszt's touch.[102] As well as entrancing his audiences, Liszt would conduct without a baton and wearing a long black frock coat, providing a precedent for the equation of musicianship with magic later popularized by *Fantasia* (1940).[103] Liszt's cultural image appears to accommodate, easier than most composers, associations with the extra-human.

What is perceived as 'magic' transgresses the culturally and historically determined boundaries of the natural and the holy, and, as such, the schematic cultural legacies of Liszt's musical magic are often articulated as something dangerous or uncanny, as *The Mephisto Waltz* (1971) illustrates. This horror drama takes its name, and part of its soundtrack, from Liszt's *Mephisto* Waltz No. 1. The music accompanies the introduction of the antagonist, pianist Duncan Ely, first seen playing the difficult piece when Myles Clarkson, his future victim of body-swapping, arrives for an interview.

A commonly understood cinematic convention stipulates that any character appreciative of, or associated with, classical music is potentially villainous. The keyboard, in particular, has a long history in horror film iconography. From *The Phantom of the Opera* to *20,000 Leagues Under the Sea* (1954), an organ-playing villain can suggest isolation and a certain inhuman quality. Even before Ely has put his diabolic plan into action – to steal Myles's body so he can seduce his own daughter – Liszt's music has potentially told all we need to know about his narrative role. An element of perversity, something dangerous and beyond-the-

---

[100] Hamilton, *After the Golden Age*, 226.
[101] Cited in Walker, *Franz Liszt: The Final Years*, 235, 280, 380.
[102] Cited in Kramer, *Musical Meaning*, 73, 298.
[103] See Walker, *Franz Liszt: The Final Years*, 240–1.

pale, is also introduced through Ely's statement that 'blood on the keys' is the desired result of artistic commitment, expressing an element of bodily sacrifice intimately connected with both the film's satanic themes and, as Theodor Adorno suggests, the certain ritualistic and sacrificial character of Romantic pianism itself.[104]

Throughout *The Mephisto Waltz*, the titular music recurs dietetically and non-dietetically, notably during illicit amorous embraces to reinforce an association between pianism and sex. When Myles's usurped body awakes containing the soul of Ely, the waltz is recognizable on the soundtrack through distorted electronic sounds, muted, distant and heavily reverberated, accentuating the scene's dreamlike confusion and otherworldliness. Since the film does not obviously imply that the body-swap has occurred (it remains ambiguous, although strongly implied), and since the waltz has been previously associated with Ely, the music functions as a character motif, suggesting the presence of Ely's soul in Myles's body. The music reaches a crescendo, and Myles/Ely raises his pianist's hands towards the camera until they nearly fill the screen – an image potentially expressive of self-awareness, self-discovery and dominating control. The virtuoso's 'ability', located in his hands, is here associated not only with magic and the supernatural but also with a sense of transcendent sublimity – that vacuum in which other concepts can flourish without impinging on each other's sense of authority.

Figure 6 *The Mephisto Waltz* (1971)

---

[104] Theodor Adorno, 'The Natural History of the Theatre', 1931–33, in *Quasi Una Fantasia: Essays on Modern Music*, 65–78 (London and New York: Verso, 2011), 66.

Again, the question 'Why Liszt's music?' can be answered by recognizing the schemas at work in the film, and identifying those which correspond to Liszt's cultural image while not necessarily overlapping with those of other composers. Diabolism and magic are, therefore, the key representational schemas employed by the inclusion of Liszt's music in *The Mephisto Waltz*; so much so that the relationship between them would appear to be fundamental to the construction of the film, down to the title itself.

Conclusion

The critical dialogue between intuitive understanding and social explanation restages the typical Romantic conflict between tradition and innovation, fore-structures and violence, and society and genius which is so well embodied by the image of the virtuoso. By itself, this realization merely Romanticizes all cyclical schematic cognition, as well as philosophical hermeneutics, more generally, in distinctly problematic fashion. But if we combine it with the complementary hypothesis that *audio-visual* explanation, specifically, is a quintessentially Romantic phenomenon, then we can re-state, and perhaps intuit an answer to, that question posed by Jacques Rancière: In what sense can film – that technological epitome of modernism – be considered a Romantic medium?

In this chapter, we have advanced from this recognition to develop and test a methodological model of cultural representation, suggesting that a cultural image can be constructed and developed through the employment of schematic types. This has enabled a continuation of our examination of that Romantic idea of audio-visual explanation in reference to an array of filmic representations of typical Romantic concepts. Once again, the figure of Franz Liszt provided a leitmotif to guide us through a selection of representations while enabling a wider reference to the interplay between audio and vision in both film and Romantic aesthetics. Schemas associated with notions of genius, virtuosity and demonic magic are among those most pertinent for an understanding of how the Romantic composer and virtuoso Franz Liszt has been portrayed in films, and how his music and image has often been used to create meaning. This has also demonstrated how a generalized cultural image of, in this case, a pianist and composer, can be contextualized in filmic representations through contact with such secondary schematic types to meet a variety of institutional, narrative comprehension– aiding and explanatory needs.

The schematic types explored earlier in reference to filmic representations of Liszt and his music offer only a selection of typical and regular tendencies for connotive meaning formation rather than a complete taxonomy. Any catalogue claiming to be complete would be unreliable. These schematic types have also been placed within contextual histories to illustrate how they can be read to perform certain explanatory functions, often relating to wider aspects of Liszt reception, biography and various wide-ranging debates in nineteenth-century European culture. Having established these important recurring themes, the following chapters present case studies of films which, due to their differing national, historical and industrial contexts, take very different approaches to the representational issues identified above.

4

'Nothing untrue, simply convenient'

Song Without End (1960) and the Hollywood composer biopic

Don't entangle yourself in too many details. My biography is far more to be imagined than taken down in dictation.

—Franz Liszt[1]

She did much worse than insult me, my dear. She described me!

—Franz Liszt (Henry Daniell) in *Song of Love* (1947)

Introduction

Song Without End (1960) was the last in a series of Hollywood biopics based upon the lives of canonical European Romantic composers. Columbia gave Chopin's life the Hollywood treatment in 1945 with *A Song to Remember*, MGM chose Schumann for 1947's *Song of Love* and Republic was a step behind with Wagner and *Magic Fire* in 1955; by comparison, Columbia's *Song Without End* is often considered to be an anachronistic holdover. By 1960, post-Paramount decree films had long been breaking boundaries in stylistic approaches, technical methods and the inclusion of sexual and violent content. As John C. Tibbetts, author of *Composers in the Movies* (2005), stated: '*Song Without End*, in style and substance, was already a museum piece by the time it reached the theatre', and was the 'last gasp' of the classical Hollywood composer biopic tradition.[2]

---

[1] Addressed to Liszt's biographer Lina Ramann, cited in Rena Charnin Mueller, 'From the Biographer's Workshop: Lina Ramann's Questionnaires to Liszt', in *Franz Liszt and his World*, ed. Christopher H. Gibbs and Dana Gooley, 361–424 (Princeton: Princeton University Press, 2006), 366.
[2] John C. Tibbetts, *Composers in the Movies* (New Haven: Yale University Press), 72.

The film's 'lateness' was partly due to a faltering production history, dating back to at least 1953, when Columbia's Liszt biopic project was entitled *Dream of Love*; in 1954, it became *The Franz Liszt Story*, then *Crescendo* and remained *The Magic Flame* until as late as 1959.[3] This chapter will address *Song Without End* as a part of this Hollywood composer biopic tradition, presenting an overview of production and reception contexts and a textual analysis. The schemas explored in Chapter 3 will re-merge in relevant sections to contribute to a similarly multifaceted analysis of the representational trends associated with Liszt and Romanticism displayed by a film from a transitional period for Hollywood cinema.

With Dirk Bogarde in the starring role, *Song Without End* represents the life of Franz Liszt from his pianistic 'duel' with Sigismund Thalberg in 1837 to his separation from Princess Carolyne zu Sayn-Wittgenstein in the early 1860s. The narrative presents the working-out of two diegetic conflicts: (1) the one between Liszt's popularity as a virtuoso and a desire to fulfil his feeling of duty towards art by writing 'serious' compositions, and (2) the love triangle between Liszt, Carolyne and his first wife Marie d'Agoult.

The film offers its audiences pleasure on a number of levels, relating not only to narrative and characters but also to music, casting, locations and production design. An initial look at the trailer illuminates the elements of the film which were considered desirable for audiences during its marketing.

The prestige element is accentuated by text announcements: 'Crashing to HEIGHTS the Motion Picture Screen Has Never Before Achieved!' Extracted shots show cheering crowds and Liszt playing fast and loud music on a piano, interspersed with: 'HEIGHTS of MUSIC!' 'HEIGHTS of MEMORABLE PERFORMANCES!' and 'HEIGHTS of SPLENDOR!' A scrolling list of the composers whose music features in the film further advertises the film's high-cultural credentials. Publicity accentuated the film's legitimate musical qualifications, including the Cuban-American pianist Jorge Bolet and the Los Angeles Philharmonic Orchestra playing arrangements by Morris Stoloff and Harry Sukman. The male American narrating voice proclaims Liszt 'arrogant' and 'a triumphant hero, with the courage to defy emperors!', highlighting Liszt's rebellious uniqueness and, therefore, suitability as a biopic subject. Dialogue extracts serve as sound bites accentuating a theme of internal struggle: 'I'm part

---

[3] Tibbetts, *Composers in the Movies*, 75; Carlos Clarens, *Cukor* (London: Martin Secker & Warburg Ltd, 1976), 178–9; John Coldstream, *Dirk Bogarde: The Authorised Biography* (London: Weidenfeld and Nicholson, 2004), 259.

Figure 7 *Song Without End* (1960)

gypsy, part priest . . . at war with myself'. The words 'libertine' and 'scandal' here function as enticements to the prospective audience member. A key selling-point is visual spectacle – the opportunity to see 'the world's great capital cities', their cathedrals, opera houses and theatres, and the 'priceless jewels and gowns that make their women the most alluring of all time'. Heavy emphasis is also given to the pleasure of seeing the lead actress Capucine, 'one of France's great beauties', in addition to the handsome former matinée-idol Dirk Bogarde himself. In this way, *Song Without End* was sold by appealing to visual spectacle, high culture, exoticism, nostalgia and difference.

These advertised pleasures correspond to a number of cultural, legal and financial conditions which effected Hollywood studio production prior to 1960. The dissolution of the studio system, the rise of television and the blockbuster model, the increasing interest in niche audiences and the increased influence of international productions, personnel and markets had all altered Hollywood practices and products.[4] The composer biopic belongs to a certain kind of residual prestige picture trend; *Song Without End* attempts to provide 'the past' and 'high culture' as pleasures still within the gift of Hollywood. The past is generally expensive to film, and the capital that Hollywood studios could afford to invest in their productions meant that the historical biopic presented audiences with something that was largely beyond the means of television or smaller studios: large, historically informed stories, told with lavish sets, costumes and props. By choosing historical subjects drawn from the cultural canon, a Hollywood

---

[4] See John Izod, *Hollywood and the Box Office 1895–1986* (London: The MacMillan Press, Ltd.,1988), 151–70; and Peter Lev, *History of the American Cinema*, 9 vols. (New York: Charles Scribner's Sons, 2003), 7: *The Fifties – Transforming the Screen: 1950–1959*, passim.

studio announced its 'higher' and more prestigious filmmaking concerns. A film such as *Song Without End* provided a studio with opportunities to film at visually attractive non-American locations, such as Vienna's Schönbrunn Palace, presenting a series of impressive European palaces and theatres that American, and many international, audiences may not have seen before. Such locations were also populated with background casts adorned with colourful and expensive-looking costumes.

Audiences might assume that in paying to see a prestige biopic of a classical composer, they could enjoy a visual feast – Hollywood would mobilize all its resources to make a past era come alive on screen. The individual results of this marketing strategy varied, and it might be expected that audiences would have been less impressed by the visual spectacle of *Song Without End* than if it had been made in the heyday of its genre, fifteen years before. In the meantime, Hollywood had pursued bigger and more impressive spectacles.

Composer biopics

The biopic is broadly characterized by generic hybridity and a conscious mediation of history, its images and meanings. Robert Rosenstone suggested that the dominant generic form, with its telescoped timeframe, exaggerated characterization and simplified historical events, typically presents 'a slice of intensified history'.[5] This 'slice' is constructed within a variety of production contexts, meeting numerous demands and with the ultimate aim of appealing to specific audiences. In biopics, authorized written history is subjected to various industrial and cultural needs and influences, becoming the raw material for Hollywood's own historical discourse. Interestingly, this conflict is announced dietetically within *Song Without End* itself when Marie accuses Liszt of self-authoring his cultural image; Liszt's account of himself is carefully constructed – 'Nothing untrue, simply convenient'.

The biopic typically presents audiences with *a* story, pertaining to be *the* story, of a historical individual, constituting a part of their cultural image. As an audio-visual explanation, a biopic makes a 'claim to truth' despite a complex relationship with notions of historical accuracy determined by subject, period,

---

[5] Robert Rosenstone, 'In Praise of the Biopic', in *Lights, Camera, History: Portraying the Past in Film*, ed. Richard Francaviglia and Jerry Rodnitzky, 11–29 (College Station: Texas A&M University Press, 2007), 26–7.

censorship and studio- or production-specific industrial and marketing factors.[6] In his book *Bio/Pics* (1992) George Custen suggests that what makes a biopic's presentation of history financially 'tenable is the extent to which a particular bricolage of known facts contains either a new slant . . . or else "classically" organizes what is already known' according to institutionalized, often studio-specific representational and formal paradigms'.[7] As historical discourse, biopics are limited by space, resources and time, and they must depict specific events over broad analysis and select some events over others. These processes expose the selective inclusion of historical facts and the addition of fictional elements in biopics, altering the subject's narrative to meet multiple, often indefinitely determined, functions. Despite these conditions, biopics, as audio-visual explanations, often reach a larger audience than written histories, and their contributions to popular historical discourse can be considerable.

The sense of authenticity essential to marketing biopics is achieved by the construction of a malleable discourse of realism. Details of costume, setting, location and props typically provide a vague feeling of historical realism, although often at the expense of an 'authentic' presentation of historical events and characterization. Most biopics are obliged to render their subject as entertaining as possible to meet financial imperatives, representing their subject as more 'relatable', 'more human' and less distanced from audiences by their perceived genius and historical displacement, following the logic, as Leo Braudy noted, that in Western discourse 'a famous person has to be a socially acceptable individualist, different enough to be interesting, yet similar enough not to be threatening'.[8] A biopic must maintain a balance between mythologizing its subject – making them seem 'special' or 'unique' enough for it to be worth telling their story – and demythologizing them; making them seem 'human' or

---

[6] George F. Custen, *Bio/Pics: How Hollywood Constructed Public History* (New Brunswick: Rutgers University Press, 1992), 51. Custen presents a Marxist formulation of formal frameworks and representational patterns that mediate the genius myth according to hegemonic discourse, reassuring audiences that 'all ills can be cured' by privileged yet suffering outsiders; Custen, *Bio/Pics*, 32–3, 189–90.

[7] Custen, *Bio/Pics*, 180. Custen also suggests a three-stage model of biopics, including (1) the Big Break idea, (2) peer resistance and support, and (3) conflict between innovation and tradition; Custen, *Bio/Pics*, 70–7, 206–11. Interestingly, Custen's model is upheld by *A Song to Remember* and *Song of Love*, but not *Song Without End*. Since the film begins at the height of Liszt's fame, he experiences no Big Break in the first act. The resistance against his music is not defended by a peer, whose role is amalgamated into that of Carolyne as love interest; and thirdly, there is no presented 'tradition' to contrast against him. The entire progressiveness of Liszt's musical output is subsumed under the romantic narrative, as we will see, presented as transgressive in its conflict with an ethical tradition embodied by the church.

[8] Leo Braudy, *The Frenzy of Renown: Fame and Its History*, 1986 (New York: Vintage, 1997), 8.

'relatable' and not estranged by any supposed audience anxieties over the notion of genius as Other. This conflict can present particularly significant material regarding the interpretation of what a subject's cultural image means. The historical subject is a location for exposing and working through issues between past and present, and, in this sense, the biopic is analogous to the virtuoso performance, in which, as we saw in the previous chapter, music of the past (the composer's 'voice') sounds through a modern performative body expressive of present cultural relations. In similar fashion, the historical figure from the past sounds through the conditions of the biopic; the structure, and what we might call 'attitude', of such a representation is also expressive of present cultural relations. Where Liszt is concerned, these issues often include the selection of schematic types outlined in chapter three: Romantic genius, virtuosity, sex and the body, warrior, diabolic and magical types.

Like other types of film, biopics utilize complex representational structures that seek to explain their contents, or guide an audience's attitudinal response to different characters, situations and events. There will often be moments when a film's rhetorical 'attitude' becomes clear, or when those various things a film appears to value, which are not necessarily what the filmmakers value, become 'mythologized' in Roland Barthes' sense of the term. By appealing to a 'reserve of history ... a tamed richness' of what is already understood, something that is mythologized 'transforms history into nature' and robs language of its polysemy.[9] Put in different terms, myth is a kind of intuitive explanation. Certain elements in films can be read as mythologized in this way – made to seem natural, authoritative or 'good' – and a recognition of these elements can be said to imply a film's attitude or metalanguage.[10]

These attitudinal or explanatory processes (always dependent upon personal interpretive disposition) are also partly constituted by culturally and historically specific filmmaking concerns. As Robert Rosenstone notes, the biopic attempts to make a historically significant person 'meaningful to a new audience' and their sociopolitical contexts.[11] In other words, history is reconstructed to correspond to new prevailing 'attitudes'.

---

[9] Roland Barthes, *Mythologies*, 1957 (London: Vintage, 2009), 138–70.
[10] Despite the criticism Bordwell levelled against Colin McCabe's famous use of 'metalanguage' (Bordwell, *Narration in the Fiction Film*, 18–20), its employment here has perhaps a greater similarity to Ian Jarvie's use of the term 'attitude', as the second of his four layers of film's philosophical address; Ian Jarvie, *Philosophy of the Film: Epistemology, Ontology, Aesthetics* (New York and London: Routledge and Kegan Paul Inc., 1987), 6.
[11] Rosenstone, 'In Praise of the Biopic', 27.

Guido Heldt has provided examples of this process shaping representations of Liszt in several German films made during the Third Reich, including *Abschiedwaltzer* (1934) and *Traumerei* (1944). In these films, Liszt is 'relaxed, noble and self-assured', without a mythologized sense of greatness achieved by struggle; the Hungarian composer is 'Germanised', presented as a 'paternal mentor' to composers such as Schumann.[12] In similar ways, contemporary social and political issues also affect the representation of composers in Hollywood biopics. Perhaps the most notable example is Chopin's accentuated patriotism in *A Song to Remember*, which appears to invite a direct comparison between the composer's self-sacrificing nationalism and the contemporary wartime events in Europe. At the same time, as John C. Tibbetts has noted, Hollywood biopics are subjected to institutional imperatives concerning ideological conditioning and censorship; production executives occasionally intervene to curb what might be seen as immoral or politically problematic elements in the screenplays of the 'Song' films, impacting on their representations of Romantic composers.[13]

In addition, representations are also affected by the industrial necessities of the star system. Star casting often encounters complex histories of associations among individual stars, provoking significant remoulding of a historical figure's cultural image. As Richard Dyer and John Ellis note, a viewing audience, aware of the broader contexts of star image and career progression that a performance enters, negotiate that performance in relation to implied, negated and augmented associations.[14] As we will see, the casting of Dirk Bogarde (and, in Chapter 5, Roger Daltrey) as Liszt opens various possible tributaries of meaning formation dependent on intertextual knowledge and recognition.

It is easy to understand why Romantic composers, specifically, provided attractive subjects for Hollywood biopics. Not only did they provide studio productions with symbolic capital but their life stories were also often exciting enough to sustain biopic treatment. Biopics are typically concerned with historical figures whose cultural image includes adventure, gossip, tragedy and interpersonal unrest. As far as classical music is concerned, therefore, Romanticism takes centre stage – in Aaron Copland's words: 'the nineteenth-century, especially the Lisztian

---

[12] Guido Heldt, 'Hardly Heroes: Composers as a Subject in National Socialist Cinema', in *Music and Nazism: Art Under Tyranny, 1933–1945*, ed. Michael H. Kater and Albrecht Riethmuller, 114–35 (Laaber: Laaber Verlag, 2003), 120.
[13] Tibbetts, *Composers in the Movies*, 76.
[14] Dyer, *Stars*, 146–9; John Ellis, 'Stars as a Cinematic Phenomenon', in *Stardom and Celebrity: A Reader*, ed. Sean Redmond and Su Holmes, 90–7 (Los Angeles: Sage, 2007), 94.

part of it, was the "juiciest" period in music'.[15] In retrospective discourse, Liszt was often considered to be as fascinating as a film star; the apocryphal episodes with Beethoven, Lola Montez and Olga Janina are only the most well-known adventures in his colourful life. Liszt lived with Carolyne in Weimar at a time when adultery was punishable by imprisonment, and he was even suspected of being a spy.[16] Such exciting composers were more attractive subjects for Hollywood biopics than those with less-eventful lives, such as, for example, Bruckner or Ravel. In this sense, Liszt was their antithesis – the inheritor of more Hollywood-malleable Romantic iconographies and schematic types.

In order to clarify the causes and effects of these various contextual issues, and what they often bring to bear on the Hollywood Romantic composer biopic, we can briefly address key Liszt-related issues in *A Song to Remember* and *Song of Love*. This will provide the historical and generic context of the classical Hollywood 'Song' films tradition, which the anachronistic *Song Without End* entered late in 1960.

A Song to Remember

In the opening scene of *A Song to Remember*, the young Chopin interrupts his piano practice with loud, discordant thumps on the keyboard. He has noticed Russian soldiers escorting Polish prisoners past the window. Chopin's nationalist passions are expressed throughout the film by such musical moments which stress the interdependence of musical genius and political duty.

Later in the film, Chopin's musical reputation is secured by 'Liszt *ex machina*'.[17] The Hungarian's rendition of Chopin's Polonaise in A-flat, Op. 53 (1842) at Pleyel's salon secures its composer's social endorsement while establishing Liszt's own authoritative uniqueness. We first hear Liszt's playing from another room, attracting the attention of the other characters who rush to see him. The camera shows their astonished response for several seconds before presenting Liszt at the piano. The difficult music appears to not tax Liszt's ability – he sight-reads perfectly. When Chopin joins in, playing another piano positioned behind the

---

[15] Aaron Copland, *Copland on Music*, 1960 (New York: Da Capo Press, 1976), 118.
[16] Walker, *Franz Liszt: The Final Years*, 4–5, 215, 224, 377; Walker, *Franz Liszt: The Weimar Years*, 5, 11.
[17] 'Liszt *ex machina*' was a function identified by Luigi Verdi in his catalogue of Liszt film types. Although the phrase is useful, Verdi's taxonomy itself of questionable value due to overlapping categories; Luigi Verdi, *Franz Liszt e la sua musica nel cinema* (Lucca: Libreria Musicale Italiana, 2015), 497.

virtuoso, Liszt is able to quickly identify him as the composer without turning around. Liszt's musical authority is therefore secured by elements of dialogue, camera direction and narrative function – a valuation that will soon place him within a sympathetic community of eccentric 'genius' outsiders, including Professor Elsner and novelist George Sand, who will rally to Chopin's aid against an antagonistic community of critics.

At a reception organized by Sand, the social elite are invited to a concert given by the adored Liszt at a time when Chopin is generally disparaged. The room is darkened, to supposedly improve the effect of the music, and the crowd listens respectfully to the now-invisible Liszt's playing. Even the revelation that the music is actually a composition by Chopin cannot shake the prejudiced attitude held by the critic Kalkbrenner, who states: 'anything would sound good played by Liszt'. The dramatic climax comes as Sand enters the darkened room carrying a candelabra, revealing that the invisible pianist they have all been praising is actually the socially derided Chopin. The performers had used the darkness to swap places. The crowd is astonished, Kalkbrenner is deflated and Sand joins the real Liszt, who stands-by while Chopin concludes the performance. As well as representing visuality as a key element contributing to musical meaning and its significance to nineteenth-century culture, this scene also evokes the socially transgressive potential of Romantic virtuoso experience, or its potential for cultural transcendence – exposing and criticizing the dominant social standards prevailing at a given time and place, and the explanatory valuations they implicitly uphold.

Later in the film, this outsider group is fragmented; Liszt becomes relegated in favour of a contrast between Elsner and Sand. From his musical opinions to his rustic gait, Elsner remains an outsider, while Chopin earns acceptability among the social elite. With Sand acting as the voice for Chopin's personal success, Elsner eventually turns Chopin towards nationalistic self-sacrifice. During his intervention, Elsner calls Chopin a 'fop' and Sand a 'debased . . .': the sentence is interrupted, yet the implication may be directed against Sand's transvestism or controlling 'masculine' personality. The film's attitude would appear, given the self-sacrificing wartime nationalism that it endorses, to prioritize Elsner's perspective; the mentor's moral outrage is also the outrage of the film's metalanguage, directed (explicitly) against the 'foppish', 'padded' element of Chopin's cultural image, moulded by the intervention of an authoritative male superior to the 'right' course of masculine self-sacrificing action and directed (implicitly) against the sexual transgression embodied by Sand. It would have been different, for example, if the narrative functions of Sand and Elsner were reversed. Their attendant schemas would have exchanged values to prioritize the authority of the otherwise devalued and dangerous 'outsider-transgressive' female over the 'outsider-genius' male. This illustrates how explanatory filmic representations of Romantic cultural transcendence can distinguish between 'good' and 'bad' kinds of embodied individual values.

Sand tells Chopin that, considering his deteriorating health, a prospective tour to raise money for the oppressed Polish people is 'literally and actually suicide'. This scene – presenting both Sand's tirade against Chopin's fateful decision, and Chopin sitting unspeaking at the piano, playing fragments from the Polonaise – evokes compelling musical symbolism. Sand's belief that the Polish struggle is none of their business, and that to aid them would be an act of weakness, is unanswerably contested by the 'argument' of the music, Chopin's only response, which, like the ineffable 'language' that Romantic music was supposed to be, cuts past all 'reasoned' objections to an intuitive explanation of the film's attitude. Sand ultimately storms out, unable to effectually respond to the Polonaise, which is speaking with unanswerable power on behalf of its countrymen, Elsner and the film's metalanguage.

The film's climactic montage sequence presents Chopin's tour of Europe, during which twin narrative threads are united and resolved: (1) Chopin winning social recognition for his music, and (2) Chopin honouring his artistic/political duties. Momentary flashbacks place this struggle into a summary context: this is the artist's 'suicidal fight' for his homeland. The music's continual physical demands have taken their toll on Chopin's heath; as the sweat on his face increases, the evocation of the warrior type is strengthened when a splash of blood lands on the keys – this tour is Chopin's 'battle'. Shots of thunder and lightning unite the authority of the music's Romantic 'storms' with mythologizing natural symbolism. This sequence culminates with the Polonaise – a piece that is situated as Chopin's 'masterpiece', contrasted, as it has been throughout the film, with 'lesser' Waltzes, Impromptus and Nocturnes. The famous thundering octave passages recall the young Chopin slamming his hands on the keys when angered by the sight of Russian soldiers. This connection establishes the sound-motion object of fortissimo chord/octave repetitions as expressive of social/political energy; this is in addition to the visual correlative of the performer looking beyond the instrument to the non-musical realm of ideals. This Polonaise also displays similarities with Liszt's 'Funérailles' (1849) – a piece which is put to similar use, as we will see in Chapter 5, symbolizing nationalistic revolutionary energy in *Lisztomania*.

1945's *A Song to Remember* displays several conventions that will inform *Song Without End* fifteen years later. Both resolve twin narrative threads, musical and romantic, by playing them against each other. Both fill-in gaps in the one by appealing to mythologized explanations provided by the other. Each film features a final public concert which functions as the narrative climax, providing conformational 'proof' of the composer's greatness being recognized by their public. The status of *A Song to Remember* as wartime propaganda accentuates represented elements of nationalism, masculinity, individuality, duty and self-sacrifice which find different expression in *Song Without End*.

Song of Love

In contrast to the political struggle faced by the Romantic virtuoso over an engagement with the wider public domain, *Song of Love*, a 1947 biopic of Schumann, explicitly links mid-century conservative musical traditions with the pleasures and restrictions of domesticity. The sound of Schumann composing at the piano forms a diegetic soundtrack permeating many scenes of domestic life with his wife and fellow composer Clara, their children, their servants and their friend Brahms. Liszt provides a contrast to this domesticity, becoming a represented element that Schumann's music, as well as the ideals of Clara and Brahms, can define themselves against.

The first diegetic music in the film is the opening bars of Liszt's Piano Concerto No. 1, played by Clara on stage. Her domineering father sits behind her, providing corrections and ill-tempered encouragement. This loud and taxing piece is then contrasted with a performance of 'Träumerei' (1838) by Schumann, which is selected by Clara in defiance of her father's wishes. In this way, the Liszt piece is associated with the restrictive and demanding father, while the Schumann piece is associated with the independence and artistic idealism of Clara. The royal family of Dresden, for whom Clara is performing, are shown to prefer the Schumann piece to the Liszt Concerto, and the whole scene is weighted to accumulate audience sympathies for the film's central romantic couple: Clara and Robert Schumann. Liszt's music functions as a symbol of 'lesser' worth, something to be overcome or 'done away with' in pursuit of the 'authentic' ideal that is embodied, for classical Hollywood, in the monogamous heterosexual couple.

However, the character Liszt soon appears to complicate this simple dichotomy of 'good' and 'bad' music. During a court scene in which Clara and

Schumann appeal for their right to marry against her father's wishes, 'Liszt *ex machina*' returns as a kind of musical character-witness. Liszt's great attribute here is the ability to command his audience – they know him by sight, murmur with anticipation as he approaches the front of the court, announce his name *en mass* and laugh at his jokes. When Liszt finishes his speech praising Schumann's music, he takes his hat and gloves and receives applause from the audience. Liszt is shown to not even need a piano to win over an audience. In this way, Liszt's cultural image serves two masters in *Song of Love*: his music is used to delineate an opposition between 'good' and 'bad' music that establishes the value of the central romantic couple, while the mythology of his personal presence and charisma, an ability to command his public – extending his virtuosity (the potential to exceed) beyond the confines of musical performance – is used to progress the narrative.

When Schumann's opera is rejected at a critical moment for his mental wellbeing, their friend Brahms turns to Liszt for help. The following concert scene is implied to have been arranged by Liszt for the purpose of seducing the influential conductor Reinecke, who sits next to one of Liszt's female 'associates'. She is tasked to win Reinecke's favour on Schumann's behalf. While on stage Liszt plays his difficult *Mephisto* Waltz No. 1, whose diabolic or magical schematic associations highlight the 'puppet master' aspect of Liszt's role in the film. This is strengthened by one spectator's whispered comment which compares Liszt's playing to the act of pulling a rabbit out of a hat – a typical magician's trope. Furthermore, the seductive overtones of the scene are given a particularly sexualized quality by Liszt's breaking of a piano string at a rising and climactic moment in the music. The virtuoso briefly acknowledges the audience's impressed murmurings, before springing across the room to a second piano and concluding the piece.

Liszt next plays a transcription of 'Widmung' (1840) by Schumann, and the concert atmosphere changes dramatically. Apart from the more subdued and melodic music, the tone of the film changes due to several formal alterations. The close-up shots of Liszt's hands are fewer, less energetic and less visually 'impressive'; the shots of the diegetic audience watching the performance are closer framed to accentuate their postures and eyes as they listen.

But Clara is unhappy with Liszt's interpretation, which she afterwards critiques for being too visual. When Clara plays the piece herself – attracting Liszt's audience back to their seats – it is represented as an authoritative usurpation of Liszt's musicianship. Clara's gentle chastising dialogue locates this alternative power in a feeling of 'love' (interior) rather than Liszt's visual 'storms' and 'glitter' (exterior). Close-up shots of Liszt, hunched over the piano and visibly affronted, and Brahms, standing upright and nearer to Clara on the opposite side of the piano, emphasize this musical victory of the conservatives' authenticity over Lisztian showmanship.

With an attitude of self-deprecating humour, Liszt rises above Clara's comment and recommends Schumann's music to Reinecke; this eventually leads to a performance of Schumann's orchestral music, which, according to the convention identified in *A Song to Remember*, marks his social ascent. His 'innate' musical genius is already implied, but what is attained during the narrative is social recognition of that fact.

In some biopics, character development inverts this logic. Instead of presenting an individual character arc that develops according to diegetic social and environmental structures, the biopic will sometimes represent that society itself developing around a more 'stable' biopic subject. It is perhaps a certain limited characteristic of this inversion which guarantees the worthiness of a historical figure to be the subject for a biopic at all. The genius' cultural importance is based upon their impact upon history, not history's impact upon them.

Changing contexts in Hollywood towards 1960

By 1960, composer biopics were shaped by different industrial, political and aesthetic contexts. The time between the productions of *Song of Love* and *Song Without End* covered nearly the entire dissolution of classical Hollywood cinema, and the extensive transformation of its methods. The role of the historical feature film exemplifies these changes by charting one of the key developments of the period: the rise of the blockbuster.

According to David Eldridge, between 1950 and 1959, Columbia made 174 historical films out of a total of 391, with 1951 being their peak year: twenty-nine historical features out of a total of fifty-eight.[18] After 1953 Columbia's historical output declined steadily, falling from twenty-six to sixteen the following year, then to an average of twelve per annum between 1955 and 1959.[19] This reflected a general trend during the 1950s, when most studios experienced a drop in production after 1953, although the overall proportion of historical features

---

[18] David Eldridge, *Hollywood's History Films* (London and New York: I.B. Tauris, 2006), 38.
[19] Eldridge, *Hollywood's History Films*, 38.

remained constant.[20] The reasons for, and impact of, these changes are obvious to all those familiar with the breakup of the Hollywood studio system: the changing laws over distribution, the end of block-booking, changing audience demographics in response to the post-War baby boom and the rise of television. Consequently, studios adopted new strategies to construct and market profitable films. The blockbuster model involved increased production costs on fewer films whose financial returns could be more certain. As mentioned earlier, by investing in star-vehicles, visual spectacle and pre-sold audiences, the biggest studios could offer audiences what television could not.

The lives of classical composers provided just such opportunities for lavish visual spectacle, historical exoticism and charismatic acting roles, and also attracting a pre-sold audience who were likely to be familiar with the composer's life and music. They were also a cheaper prospect than military or biblical subjects due to the interior locations and comparatively small scale of most dramatic set-pieces; musical performances are generally cheaper to stage than battles, for example. Classical music themes and content also provided the studios with greater symbolic capital, even as it attracted and repelled different segments of diversified 1950s audiences. Those audience groups not attracted to the life story of a Romantic composer might still be potentially attracted by the balancing of other elements, such as star casting or exoticism.

1950s studio productions often placed new emphasis on 'the picturesque and the touristic'.[21] Visual spectacle spanned the increasingly diversified audience categories, including 'road show' audiences – the big-budget epic or spectacle picture which attracted audiences desiring 'the very best and most lavish' visual and musical spectacles.[22] In 1959, the influential producer Jerry Wald expressed the need for 'superior film making' to attract younger and more educated audiences with youth-oriented narratives and controversial topics; this industrial need was compounded by an increasing domestic interest in European art cinema and foreign cultures.[23] Like other studios in the late 1950s, Columbia diversified both its output and methods of production and distribution by expanding into different markets, including television, teen audiences, distribution of international films and independent production

---

[20] Eldridge, *Hollywood's History Films*, 39.
[21] Lev, *The Fifties*, 218.
[22] Lev, *The Fifties*, 215.
[23] Lev, *The Fifties*, 215.

contracting.[24] These factors, when combined, might seem to explain a return to the composer biopic format as a part of this studio diversification.

Production and casting

The first director of *Song Without End*, Charles Vidor, died of a heart attack three weeks into filming, and was replaced by George Cukor, who considered the film an unwanted distraction from his own projects.[25] Cukor apparently found 'a troubled set, with a badly demoralised cast . . . dull sets, costumes and furniture'.[26] Armed with a copy of Sacheverell Sitwell's biography of Liszt, Cukor cooperated with new talent to reorient the film; Walter Bernstein helped to shape a workable script, Gene Allen improved the 'redesign and camera strategy', and Vidor's cameraman was replaced.[27] Typically for a classic composer biopic, a network of accurate historical detail was considered an important factual base upon which to build a semi-fictitious narrative. Cukor consulted Bernstein about Oscar Millard's script and found it 'terrible, like a parody . . . egregiously awful', and initially advised replacing Bogarde with Sid Caesar.[28] The rewriting sparked Cukor's perfectionism, and the pair spent several weeks improving the dialogue. Bernstein reported that '[Cukor] couldn't let it go. He was fascinated by it. It hurt him to let it go'.[29] The effort Cukor displayed in redrafting the script and in invigorating the cast and crew can in part be attributed to his personal discipline, his respect for Vidor, but also to the professional consideration to save a project which had entrusted to him by Columbia. Ultimately, Cukor insisted that Vidor get sole directorial credit.[30] This decision was possibly a show of respect for his late friend, but possibly an effort to distance himself from the film in anticipation of its tepid reception.

The starring role had been originally offered to the American pianist Van Cliburn, but English actor Dirk Bogarde, eager to make his mark in Hollywood,

---

[24] Lev, *The Fifties*, 205.
[25] Clarens, *Cukor*, 178–9; Emanuel Levi, *George Cukor, Master of Elegance: Hollywood's Legendary Director and His Stars* (New York: William Morrow and Company Inc., 1994), 253.
[26] Patrick McGilligan, *George Cukor: A Double Life* (London and Boston: Faber and Faber, 1991), 263; Levi, *George Cukor*, 253.
[27] Coldstream, *Dirk Bogarde*, 248; McGilligan, *George Cukor*, 263.
[28] McGilligan, *George Cukor*, 264.
[29] McGilligan, *George Cukor*, 264.
[30] Clarens, *Cukor*, 178–9; McGilligan, *George Cukor*, 265; Levi, *George Cukor*, 254.

accepted after Cliburn turned it down.[31] The casting of Bogarde, perhaps best known before 1960 for *Doctor in the House* (1954) and its sequels, was potentially another result of the diversification of Hollywood audience marketing. As Eldridge notes, the Hollywood trade press reports on audiences stressed the need for rebellious young stars to solidify an audience for historical features;[32] Bogarde neatly filled this role, with his early work as troubled criminal types in *The Blue Lamp* (1950) and *Cast a Dark Shadow* (1955), adding a rebellious quality to his matinée-idol image. *Song Without End* was a brief and unsatisfying career detour into the Hollywood mainstream, but one which held a degree of continuity with his star image, creating certain tensions in the ways previously described by Dyer and Ellis.

The personal tension between sexualized public adoration and growing artistic ambitions in Liszt's life may have struck a chord with Bogarde, who was experiencing a similar tension c1960. His matinée-idol years had left him uncomfortable with public attention, and recalling teenage girls screaming during theatre appearances, breaking into his home, claiming he was the father of their children – in Bogarde's own words, being 'tiresome generally'.[33] Bogarde's desire for challenging roles attracted him to self-consciously 'artistic' and frequently controversial projects.[34] The 1960s saw the ambitious actor consciously exchange his matinée-idol image for that of an unconventional, often sickly or sinister leading man in dramas with auteur directors and more 'intellectual' material. Films such as *Victim* (1961), *The Servant* (1963), *The Damned* (1969) and *Death in Venice* (1971) developed in Bogarde a capacity for playing a 'predator-interloper [type], the working class or bourgeois changeling who transforms himself to fit every eventuality or situation'.[35] Bogarde's characters are often isolated men who encounter social boundaries, or are confronted by expectations for acceptable sexual behaviour, and this continuity of star thematics extends back to *Song Without End*. Bogarde may also have been attracted to Liszt's 'flamboyant wickedness'.[36] The film's construction of Liszt created tensions with Bogarde's star image as it stood in 1960, functioning as a text which 'exceeds the circulated image' or presents a 'problematic fit'.[37] Seen in

---

[31] Coldstream, *Dirk Bogarde*, 244–5, 249.
[32] Eldridge, *Hollywood's History Films*, 52.
[33] *Desert Island Discs*, BBC Radio 4, 31 December 1989.
[34] Sheridan Morley, *Dirk Bogarde: Rank Outsider* (London: Bloomsbury Paperbacks, 1999), 10–11, 111.
[35] Colin Gardner, *Joseph Losey* (Manchester: Manchester University Press, 2004), 5.
[36] Coldstream, *Dirk Bogarde*, 245.
[37] Dyer, *Stars*, 146–9; Ellis, 'Stars as a Cinematic Phenomenon', 94.

retrospect, *Song Without End* marks an important moment for Bogarde; it was the Hollywood non-starter which prompted a turn towards his career-defining collaborations with Basil Dearden, Joseph Losey and Luchino Visconti. Bogarde's favourable reaction to Cukor may also have contributed to his favouring auteur directors in later projects.

It is worth noting here the one crucial respect in which Bogarde's Liszt is obviously different from dominant historical representations: the hairstyle. Although dialogue and performance behaviour are often vacuums into which biopics pour appropriate supposition, costume and visual appearance often serve as among the few representational fields where historical accuracy can be qualitatively assured due to existing pictorial records that authenticate cinematic/theatrical convention. Yet in *Song Without End*, Liszt's iconic hair – that long straight 'feminine' cut that has, in many respects, become a cliché in the iconography of Romantic virtuosity – was replaced by a kind of quiff, with short back and curly locks over the forehead. This 'makeover' brings the composer in-line with schemas of attractiveness, fashionableness and artistic types dominant in Hollywood around 1960, making Bogarde's Liszt reminiscent of Elvis or James Dean. A protagonist with long hair may have activated schemas that conflicted with the desired interpretation.

In a similar fashion, Bogarde's dignified and reserved, stereotypically English manners replace notions of French, German or Hungarian tropes of social conduct and behaviour. This cosmetic beautification at the expense of historical accuracy was by no means limited to Liszt. Carolyne zu Sayn-Wittgenstein's actual physical appearance and manners often created a less-than-favourable impression. George Elliot, for example, found her 'not pleasing . . . harsh and barbarian'.[38] By the casting of French model Capucine, history was beautified according to Hollywood's need to meet contemporary ideals of feminine attractiveness.

The opening scenes

The titles play over a background shot of a stage piano. The accompanying music functions as a kind of overture, with several key musical themes succeeding each other after a brief introduction. Several associative musical motifs recur throughout the film, the most significant being Liszt's 'Un sospiro' (1845–9),

---

[38] Cited in Walker, *Franz Liszt: The Weimar Years*, 247.

'A Sigh', a piece which accumulates broad associations with at least three ideas. The theme is used on several occasions when Carolyne appears on screen, and, as such, functions more directly as a character motif (1). Alternatively, Tibbetts states that 'Un sospiro' is 'assigned meanings of faith and love' (2), drawing an intertextual meaning from *Letter from an Unknown Woman*.[39] Columbia released a choral arrangement of 'Un sospiro' by Harry Sukman and Robert Wagner under the title 'Song Without End'. Ned Washington's lyrics emphasize romantic and religious registers:

> Eternal light shine unto me
> That it may guide me close to thee
> To gaze upon thy countenance
> Forever more

This suggests that there is, in addition to the character function and the association with 'faith and love', a sense of destiny or artistic ideal that drives the use of 'Un sospiro' (3). The music's prominence in the final scene of the film, when Liszt and Carolyne finally part ways, also suggests that 'Un Sospiro' is used as a means of calling out to the artistic ideals that Carolyne seemed to draw Liszt towards, and that now have his undivided attention at the end of the film. The 'eternal light' named in the lyrics can be read as a symbolization of Liszt's ever-sought-after Romantic artistic ideal, rather than Carolyne, who was, hypothetically, its vessel, although the 'sigh' alluded to in the title, considering its character function, also provides the heightened elegiac quality associated with the ending of the central romantic relationship. There is no need to reduce the meaning of 'Un Sospiro' to any one of these three 'most likely' possibilities.

Biopics often communicate historical information in economic and functional ways which do not impinge on narrative flow and a 'realistic' evocation of the past. Real events and people are sandwiched together for easy narrative digestion. This is apparent, for example, when Liszt meets Carolyne at the Thalberg concert; in reality, ten years and 1,200 miles separated the pianistic 'dual' with Thalberg (Paris, 1837) from the couple's first meeting (Kiev, 1847). Historical facts such as these become malleable in the service of the various requirements of the film as a narrative, ideological and commercial product, and the opening scenes establish this process of historical give and take. They likely present a loose dramatization of summer of 1836 in Switzerland, when Liszt, his first wife Marie d'Agoult and

---

[39] Tibbetts, *Composers in the Movies*, 76.

George Sand holidayed together following the composer's elopement, and their subsequent drunken carousals.[40] Into this historical space, the film squeezes Liszt's friendship with Chopin and the Thalberg duel.

The script is rich with contextual information, introducing the film's central themes in several ways. The conflict between domestic and artistic values is highlighted when Liszt's playing wakes his baby son; he changes to a gentler piece by Chopin, quieting the child. While Marie becomes associated here with serious composition, Sand is linked with virtuosity and pleasure, evoking the typical narrative formation of a male situated between two conflicting female influences: good woman/bad woman. This reading hypothesis is strengthened when the party of friends go drinking, and Marie stays at home with the children. Liszt only finally decides to publicly prove his superiority over Thalberg while intoxicated; in this way, the film devalues the desire for artistic superiority when primarily recognized as a social valuation.

The group passes a church, and the tolling bell prophetically interrupts their drunken song. Liszt enters, makes the sign of the cross and begins to play the organ. The other characters, suddenly sober and quiet, may match and validate the perspective of the film audience at this moment: puzzled as to the change in mood. The scene foregrounds Liszt's religiousness, linking this element to his valuation of the grand, discordant and voluminous musical style which Chopin, from the film's perspective, cannot provide, and that also inconveniently woke the baby. But now Liszt's music wakes the entire town, according to Marie, who enters the church angrily chastising Liszt while wearing a red coat. Elements of musical passion and social impact are displaced into costume; Marie's coat can be taken to symbolize the intrusion of some passionate and significant element of duty and impulse into the sanctuary of the church – the isolated artist has been awoken to the space outside (the Swiss townsfolk) by this intrusion. For the present, the place of 'duty' is taken by pride as Liszt returns to Paris, determined to oust his rival, Thalberg.

The first concert

The Parisian concert scene establishes a recurring visual motif. During the welcoming applause, Liszt theatrically removes a pair of white gloves before

---

[40] Walker, *Franz Liszt: The Virtuoso Years*, 220–4.

sitting at the piano and casually tossing them aside. This was one of the real Liszt's many ritualized theatrical affectations.[41] During the film, this motif appears to symbolize Liszt's changing attitude to performance, and the altering relationship between his persona, his public and his music. A female audience member will later take the gloves as a souvenir. The cultural significance of souvenirs taken by Liszt's audiences is well documented, serving as locations of personal contact between star and spectator.[42] According to Chris Rojek, such souvenirs serve a religious purpose, functioning as 'relics' that 'diminish the distance between the fan and the celebrity'; Rojek identifies a reliquary culture dating back to 'the earliest days of Hollywood', although we can see how Liszt was a significant early articulator of this threefold relationship between star, relic and fan.[43] As a metonymic embodiment of Liszt's being, or aura, the gloves are symbolically charged by their metaphoric relationship with his hands – the specific bodily location of Liszt's uniqueness. The gloves are endowed with a fetishistic quality, since they perform a visual and public game of concealment and revelation with his hands as objects of desire.

Lisztomania contains a playfully risqué version of this glove motif which also emphasizes its phallic interpretive potential. Before performing to an adoring audience of young girls, Liszt (Roger Daltrey) loosens the fingers of his garish green gloves one at a time; one finger becomes elongated with a playful and knowing gesture. As in *Song Without End*, several girls rush to secure the phallic memento.

Carolyne zu Sayn-Wittgenstein arrives late at the concert in company with her husband Prince Nicholas, and the couple sit on stage behind the curtain. Liszt makes eye contact with Carolyne and, without sheet music before him to dictate what he plays next, begins 'La Campanella' (1838–51). The choice of music is seemingly determined by Carolyne's presence, articulating a certain sexual dimension to the virtuoso performance. At the end of the music, Liszt and Carolyne's eyes meet significantly. Liszt's dark, slightly downturned and 'masterful' expression strongly suggests that the performance has been a method of proving his uniqueness or 'power', both musical and sexual. The intensity of emotion displayed by the characters; the power-play suggested by Liszt's momentary ignoring of the audience's applause; the orgasmic climax of

---

[41] Stasov, 'Liszt, Schumann and Berlioz in Russia', 121.
[42] See Kramer, *Musical Meaning*, 90; Loesser, *Men, Women and Pianos*, 370.
[43] Chris Rojek, 'Celebrity and Religion', in *Stardom and Celebrity: A Reader*, ed. Sean Redmond and Su Holmes, 171–80 (Los Angeles: Sage, 2007), 173.

Figure 8 *Song Without End* (1960)

the music specifically chosen to demonstrate the virtuoso's physical stamina and power; the proximity of her seemingly oblivious husband – all these points contribute to the symbolic construction of this moment as an illicit sexual encounter.

Ben Winters observes the potential for intimacy in such cinematic representations of classical concerts, whose dignified conventions place restrictions on audience behaviours which 'can result in particularly charged encounters'.[44] Encounters such as that between Liszt and Carolyne flirt with the taboos concerning types of social environment which, while typically containing great emotion, are constituted by many restrictions on interpersonal communication. Similarly, Lawrence Kramer notes that moments of stillness in virtuoso performance can, by their sheer absence of bodily activity, become 'an invitation to a still deeper intimacy' between performer and spectator.[45] This denial of bodily activity can form a moment of visual excess in itself through its very contrast to the expectations of virtuoso performance, fundamentally expressing bodily activity on emotional and eroticized terms.

The moment when Liszt and Carolyne's eye meet after 'La Campanella' is a moment charged with transgressive potential, and is made so specifically by the sudden absence of music. The embodied sensuality evoked by the virtuoso performance has, suddenly, nothing to be displaced into. The moment of meaningful eye contact between Liszt and Carolyne takes the full weight of that displaced sensuality.

---

[44] Winters, *Music, Performance and the Realities of Film*, 94.
[45] Kramer, *Musical Meaning*, 48.

The touring scenes

The first half of the film is punctuated by recurring travelling sequences. Liszt and his manager Portin are shown going from city to city in the back of a horse-drawn carriage. Each sequence is introduced by an establishing shot of the carriage in swift motion through countryside scenery, accompanied on the soundtrack by a brief musical 'travel' motif, from *Mephisto* Waltz No. 1. In the first carriage sequence, Liszt is shown dictating a letter to Marie while Portin suggests alterations. In the main, this creates a sense of distancing between Liszt and Marie that begins to justify their separation later in the film. In the second carriage sequence, Liszt is shown practising slowly on a dummy keyboard. This distinctly childish representation of practising colours the scene that immediately follows in an ambiguous way.

At the Russian royal palace, Liszt is forced to wait for the Tsar's arrival before playing Beethoven's Piano Sonata No. 14 'Moonlight' (1801) for the assembled nobility. Beginning in the Tsar's absence, Liszt is compelled to stop by his eventual arrival. The royal personage strides into the room, engaged in noisy conversation. Liszt slams the piano lid and chastises the Tsar for his disrespectful attitude. He speaks as a defender of the sanctity of mythologized musical values which supposedly transcend any social hierarchy. Although the event is only political artistically, this scene finds precedent in *A Song to Remember* when Chopin stormed out of a similar aristocratic recital declaring 'I do not play before Tsarist butchers!' In *Song Without End*, this event establishes Liszt as a musical populist, not only evoking certain anti-royalist audience sympathies but also, by 1960, even by a loose association with Russia, potential anti-communist sympathies as well. In addition, this outburst also extends that curious theme of childishness identified earlier. Liszt's impetuous anger throughout the film can potentially be read as superfluous, temperamental and 'feminine' in a misogynist sense – the sensitive Romantic artist 'showing his claws'. In *A Song to Remember*, Chopin is similarly credited with 'the emotion of a schoolboy'. Richard Dyer has noted how rebellious cultural types are sometimes ideologically disarmed, or rendered 'safe', by an association with youth.[46] In this respect, certain qualities of childishness become a way of explaining the represented rebel figure to be a victim of a temporary period of 'natural' social adjustment: 'Youth is the ideal material term on which to displace social discontent, since young people always

---

[46] Dyer, *Stars*, 60.

get older (and "grow up").[47] In Romantic composer biopics this ideologically negotiated adolescent contrarianism is often more directly associated with a willingness to 'give in' to passion and emotion in the defence of artistic ideals. As American films about European composers, this process also others the associated national type, contrasting a hypothetical 'stable' American ideal with 'emotional' foreign geniuses. These films thus ascribe a negotiated sense of value to composers in spite of their un-American emotionality. As we saw in Chapter 3, associations with femininity and madness, like childishness, are representational methods of rendering geniuses ideologically 'safe', or curbing the disruptive potential of their cultural transcendence.

After the following concert, a young and ambitious Richard Wagner introduces himself to Liszt backstage. Wagner says that he admires Liszt and presents him with a copy of *Rienzi* (1842), but Liszt displays no interest in the young man or his music. Both *Song Without End* and *Lisztomania* make a point of showing that the first meeting between Liszt and Wagner was a brief and unceremonious affair, with the enthusiastic Wagner being humoured and dismissed by a Liszt who is in too much of a hurry, or too socially conscious, to talk to his contemporary. Both films situate this historic meeting as an expression of Liszt's blindness to his true artistic calling as a 'serious' musician. By renouncing the virtuoso life and becoming a composer, these narrative developments are presented as an extension of Liszt becoming humbled to Wagner's 'genius' – a genius which he did not at first recognize.

When Liszt and his wife Marie meet again, their conversation communicates the unsatisfying aspect of Liszt's touring life. Liszt compares his audience to both a dragon and a woman: demanding and devouring. Dialogue also highlights Liszt's absence from his children and the permanent separation of the family unit. On the soundtrack, a non-diegetic orchestral version of Consolation No. 3 (1844–50) accentuates the scene's function as a tender interlude tinged with sadness. The subjectivity of the music is ill-defined, seemingly a commentary on the mood of the scene rather than either character's emotional point of view.

Liszt is angered at Marie's reminder of how much she has given up for him, sternly rebuking her for seeing their relationship in terms of give and take. Liszt's relationship with Marie is shown to be fundamentally unhappy and at odds with his artistic self, consistently defined in opposition to financial concerns. Liszt's

---

[47] Dyer, *Stars*, 60.

climactic outburst is couched in monetary language: 'Principle plus interest! . . . . My debt . . . . I'll pay it in guilt'.

Immediately after Marie slaps Liszt, a sudden musical accentuation of a physical action instigates a change in mood, and, in this sense, it functions as a stinger. However, for those with a greater awareness of the work of Liszt's Weimar period, the choice of music enables a more detailed thematic reading. The two themes that make a striking first appearance on the soundtrack at this moment are from Liszt's Piano Sonata in B minor and the *Faust* Symphony. Both themes are tonally ambiguous, tending towards the minor key, and are noticeably darker and more 'serious' in tone than the previously used extracts from the Consolation and 'Un Sospiro'. Consequently, this music also potentially functions as a thematic link to next narrative development: Liszt's introduction to Wagner's 'serious' music. It is perhaps significant – according to the Romantic valuation of suffering with regard to the achievement of artistic ideals – that the turning point marked by the introduction of 'serious' music in *Song Without End* arrives at the first significant moment of 'suffering' experienced by the protagonist.

The camera shows Liszt outside, walking along the pavement in a medium-close-up tracking shot of his lower half. The overture to Wagner's *Rienzi* rises in volume, and the camera pans-up to Liszt's face as he enters the door from which the music is implied to emanate. A rehearsal sign outside the door identifies the music, its composer, and the reason for its presence on the diegetic soundtrack. The upward camera movement might be read to indicate an 'awakening' on Liszt's part – from inert introversion to a kind of new 'awareness' – upon hearing Wagner's music. This awakening is accentuated in the dialogue which follows between Liszt and Wagner. Mirroring the earlier scene, the impatient Wagner is now the one who brushes-off Liszt. He dismisses Liszt's status as a virtuoso by regarding his instrumental ability as a mere functional capacity, and the piano as a lesser tool of musical expression: 'If I write some piano music requiring great technical skill', he says, 'I may send it to you'. This scene signposts a change in Liszt's character motivations and values.

The following dialogue between Liszt and his manager Portin creates a counterpoint between the virtuoso's irritation at persistent requests for command performances and Portin's contribution as an embodiment of the financial context of musical culture. Portin's obsession with financial opportunities serves to devalue the economic aspect of this culture in contrast to Liszt's more romantic and spiritual concerns. Public engagements, which are dependent upon prestige, and, by implication, profit, are now unsavoury to Liszt. Bogarde expresses this with temperamental flourishes and physical mannerisms which might evoke schemas of the sensitive Romantic artist. The thematic incompatibility between artistic ideals and commerce is given a Faustian significance by Liszt's comparison between Portin and the devil. Liszt is only finally persuaded to perform in Kiev after his manager's suggestion that doing so may bring Liszt and the unhappily married Carolyne together again.

The Kiev and Odessa sequences

As the audience applaud at the end of the Kiev concert, Liszt climbs an arched stairway at the back of the stage. He is distracted by the absence of Carolyne, who had departed before the performance ended. The diegetic space and mise-en-scène can be read to express the underlying themes and structures of the film at this point. The concert hall, decorated with gold embellishment and white panelling, is organized in right angles, squares and straight lines. The audience is similarly compartmentalized into clearly demarcated seating sections – the whole seemingly more spatially structured and organized than other concerts. As Liszt mounts the stairs and turns back to look for Carolyne, the camera shares his perspective of the hall below. Liszt's exit from the Kiev concert can function as a symbolic farewell from public performance, or a literal 'rising-above' of the socioeconomic categorical limitations of European public life by his upcoming retreat to Weimar.

Up until now, the world of Liszt's touring in *Song Without End* has been one defined by a combination of 'high' class environments, financial imperatives and the presentation of the performing musician as the focus of a unidirectional diegetic gaze. Liszt is now turning his back on this world. As the film processes, each of these elements will become devalued in comparison with alternatives: 'low' class environments, the spiritually-inflected imperative of 'duty' towards art, and the presentation of the performing musician as the focus of a more democratic multidirectional or 'reverse-panoptical' diegetic gaze. These last are ultimately assigned a higher value according to the film's attitude or explanatory metalanguage.

This transition, from 'bad' to 'good' elements of value, becomes apparent in the following scene as Liszt plays the organ at the cathedral. He is shown to have refused any fee, and the design of the performance space, as well as the representation of the process of looking, presents a marked contrast to the preceding concert. The choir sings a hymn praising God, while Liszt accompanies from the organ loft. A high-angle shot situates him at a considerable height above the people below, while Carolyne sits in a pew among the congregation; her black dress contrasts notably with the expensive-looking costumes of the previous concerts, suggesting that a kind of equality exists among this poorer crowd.

As in the previous performances, Liszt remains elevated above his public; but one crucial difference lies in the diegetic presentation of the act of looking. During the previous concerts all eyes were on Liszt, but in the cathedral the gaze of his audience is directed forward in prayer. Carolyne is the only one in the crowd who appears to notice Liszt, who sits high in the obscurity of the cathedral's ornate interior. In one particular shot, Carolyne in the foreground looks at Liszt, a tiny figure, barely noticeable high in the corner of the frame beyond the pulpit. His unassertive littleness, seeming to blend-in and merge with the 'eternal' ornaments of the church itself, is also validated and endowed with mythological significance by the gaze of 'the woman' – Carolyne as the object of the protagonist's own devotions.

At a climactic moment in the music, Liszt's gaze is lifted above the keys; he fixes his eyes on something 'higher'. It is the music itself, along with a 'spiritual' environment purged of the earlier arrangement of financial and visual performative elements, which seems to have elicited this 'vision'. Liszt sees something 'through' the music. (As we will see in Chapter 5, this sublime gaze is a recurring motif in Romantic Lisztian iconography.) When the music finishes,

Figure 9 *Song Without End* (1960)

the audience leave the cathedral quietly. The absence of applause is accentuated by the return of the glove motif, only this time the gloves are simply picked-up off the organ lid in silence by Liszt himself.

The scene changes to a private concert at Carolyne's residence, where Liszt is concluding a performance of Beethoven's Piano Sonata No. 8 (1798). He states that all of his previous musical endeavours had been guided by an ideal which he sees embodied in Carolyne herself. Liszt describes her in the third person as: 'A woman alone in a great hall. Every time I looked up from the keyboard all I could see was the light in her eyes'. This situates the object of Liszt's performing gaze as another typical Romantic trope: a feminine-sublime, functioning as antithesis of financial and social valuation.

Liszt informs Carolyne that his next concert will be in Odessa, adding: 'You'll see a performer, but if your faith is strong enough you might see something else'. This curious line communicates a sense of heightened value to the new performative mode Liszt has been employing. It is also evocative of several key concepts in Romantic aesthetics which we have already encountered in the previous chapters: (1) that artistic achievement is something through which a qualitatively different kind of truth ('something else') can be grasped, (2) but only by the spiritually developed or 'aesthetically educated' spectator ('if your faith is strong enough'), and (3) that music is an art form whose power resides elusive visual dimension ('*see* something else').

The following Odessa concert displays a representational actualization of each of these Romantic assumptions. Carolyne is shown in medium shot, sitting at the front of an audience who watch Liszt playing Mendelsohn's 'Rondo Capriccioso' (1830). A shot of Liszt, almost from Carolyne's point of view, is followed by one that provides a clearer perspective of Carolyne sitting at the very front of the audience, which is formed into a wedge shape. This accentuates Carolyne's special engagement with Liszt, and perhaps suggests a kind of 'community advancement', with Carolyne at its head. Another shot from a low angle shows Liszt's playing 'framed' by the hall's ceiling paintings, potentially accentuating Liszt's awareness of, or aspirations for, artistic ideals which are literally 'higher' than those offered by the crowd below. A meaningful chain of sorts has been established by scene construction and mise-en-scène: the vision of the crowd, shared by the camera, is directed towards the stage, where vision is then directed by the camera, only now *without* the crowd, towards what is, quite literally, 'high art'. This second vision is Liszt's alone, enabled by the upward 'pull' of the music (according to the formal articulation of the typical Goetheian

Romantic feminine-sublime: '*das Ewig-Weibliche ziet uns hinan*')[48] rather than by the gaze, and is therefore still the province of the artist as genius type inspired by his idealized feminine muse. Carolyne is also literally 'nearer' than anyone else in the audience. The tempo and registers of the Rondo compliment this theme of Romantic striving.

The imbalance established between Liszt, his audience and his guiding ideal is presented as a part of the motive for his retirement, which is announced to the crowd at the end of the performance.

Retirement to Weimar

This announcement discourages not only Portin but also Carolyne's husband Prince Nicholas, who accuses Liszt of dishonourable behaviour with his wife. At this stage in the narrative, the character of the Prince becomes a more explicitly defined antagonist, and when word reaches Liszt that Carolyne has sent for him, Portin warns his client against a possible trap. Yet Liszt rushes to meet Carolyne regardless, saying that he goes to a 'sublime fate', but whether to meet death or love is left uncertain. Liszt's 'Waldesrauschen' (1862–3) rises on the non-diegetic soundtrack, functioning as a bridge to the next scene; a musical quality reminiscent of *Tristan und Isolde* is highlighted by the association with *liebestod* in the dialogue. Liszt arrives by carriage at a darkened house, and musical extracts from Liszt's Sonata in B minor on the soundtrack recall their earlier use during an argument with the Prince. This adds to the uncertainty of who Liszt is meeting, and hint at a possibly violent outcome. The return of 'Un sospiro' a moment before Carolyne's appearance on screen – the moment when Liszt's fears are dismissed – creates a sense of a physical musical presence in the diegesis that extends beyond her represented body. It is as if Carolyne's music enters through the door before she does, emanating from herself, and announcing her arrival in a kind of aura that glows from her. Liszt learns of the potential for Carolyne to divorce the Prince, and the pair kiss in celebration; Carolyne then asks Liszt to go to Weimar at the invitation of the Grand Duchess Maria Pavlovna.

---

[48] Johann Wolfgang von Goethe, 'Faust', 1722–31, in *Selected Works*, 752–1049 (London: Everyman's Library, 1999), 1049. German original. This famous line featured prominently in Liszt's *Faust Symphony*.

Liszt's first meeting with the Duchess functions as a narrative recap clarifying the themes and issues in play at this point in the film. Liszt's temperamental side is twice roused by the Duchess' fear of scandal. With motherly mixture of firmness and kindness, she identifies a childish element in Liszt's character that needs to be controlled if he wishes to progress as an artist.

Typically for Hollywood films, the Duchess' authority as a powerful female presence is rendered unthreatening by the accentuation of a certain maternal quality. This is most clearly shown in later scenes, when her quiet and dignified poise while embroidering is combined with an apparent omnipotence of knowledge about Liszt's affairs. The Duchess is thus established as another guiding female presence for Liszt's spiritual/artistic development. This reading is accommodated by the dominant cultural schemas regarding the male Romantic artist, where the typical sublime feminine muse figure takes on a variety of idealized guises: both 'virgin' and 'mother' in addition to 'queen' and 'goddess'.[49]

At the end of Liszt's first scene with the Duchess, there is also an ambiguous moment of cultural transcendence which demonstrates a complex representation of the conflict between tradition and innovation, or structured social systems and individual genius. Liszt is introduced to an official, Chelard, and both men take leave of the Duchess. Where Chelard bows reverently and backs away slowly towards the door, Liszt simply turns and walks; this allows him to get to the door first and hold it open for Chelard, and the latter appears somewhat comically disarmed by Liszt's action. As a 'genius', Liszt's privileged independence from strict adherence to social convention has allowed him this mildly transgressive act of cultural transcendence. The effect is perhaps a humorous moment, when an antiquated tradition of reverence towards European royalty is deflated by an outsider. Yet despite this, Liszt also bows to the Duchess before leaving, resulting in what is potentially an ambiguous quality presiding over this threefold relationship between genius outsider (Liszt), conventional society (Chelard) and elite social authority (the Duchess), as well as the implied distribution between them of mythologized symbolic power.

In this way, the film represents the Romantic genius' potential for cultural transcendence to be, if not defined within strict borders of potential action, then at least without power to harm certain mythologized 'absolutes' of value, reinforced by aspects of both class and gender. As we will continue to observe throughout the remainder of the film, the notion of 'equality' that the film

---

[49] See Goethe, 'Faust', 1047.

appears to value is presented according to a certain limiting arrangement of explanatory features and ideologically charged conventions which limit the transgressive potential of the Romantic genius.

The love triangle breaks

Marie ultimately learns of Liszt's affair with Carolyne. The opening of *Tasso* accompanies her reaction and pleas against the couple's separation. The principal seven-note *Tasso* motif (a broken rhythm three-note decent, repeated, with a seventh lower note) accentuates the emotional 'descent' expressed through Marie's actions and dialogue. Another knock on the door silences Marie's pleas and Liszt's protests; the *Tasso* motif is then heard more clearly, as if to bracket the emotional scene between its first and last thematic statements. A summons from the Duchess calls Liszt away. A reprisal of the Consolation theme, in an unstable rhythm and minor key, recalls an earlier time of happiness, and suggests that the relationship between Liszt and Marie has now come, like the smaller-scale bracketing of *Tasso*, to its close.

Determined to secure his future with Carolyne, whose divorce has been denied by the Tsar, Liszt pursues her through revolutionary Vienna to a country lodge; 'Waldesrauschen' returns on the soundtrack to accompany the journey. The music builds to a climax as Liszt runs up a spiral staircase, with Carolyne waiting at the top. Their eyes meet and 'Un sospiro' returns in full orchestration and high volume as they embrace. The scene fades to black, transitioning to a shot of Liszt playing the piano. This is a convention of mise-en-temps suggestive not only of the passing of time, typically interpreted as 'the next morning' but also of a sexual encounter having taken place. The music Liszt now plays is 'Un sospiro', the theme that has been associated with their love and devotion, as well as the higher artistic calling which Carolyne embodies; here, it has emerged into the diegetic soundtrack, likely suggesting an equation between Liszt's renewed sexual and compositional energies.

Liszt next takes Carolyne to meet his mother, and the scene swiftly shifts focus through three clusters of narrative development. This scene initially serves to remind the audience of Liszt's humble class origins and the value the film attaches to the notion of a specific kind of equality. This is accomplished through Liszt's mother Anna calling Carolyne 'Madame'; Carolyne's dialogue both highlights this social formality and works to transcend it. However, they soon find that Marie is in the house as well, looking after the children, and the love triangle comes face-to-face for the first time. A third element is introduced when a cheering crowd of villagers appears outside the window, forestalling the need to resolve or develop the previous two elements.

Liszt is coaxed outside to play with a gypsy band, who serenade him with a folk tune. With their rustic costumes and flaming torches, the cheering, dancing and singing crowd present a spontaneous musical community; its 'authentic' quality appeals to Liszt, who goes outside to wander cheerfully among the villagers. The contrast with the glamorous yet static world of Liszt's concert touring is notable, and the mobile and energetic gypsy group is a more valued, a more 'desirable' kind of audience than the neatly ordered ranks of earlier concert halls, which were represented as simultaneously extravagant in decoration while remaining austere in human activity. Yet, as we will see, it is only by returning Liszt to these concert halls, and their 'non-gypsy' audiences, that the film's metalanguage will allow the protagonist's desire for serious artistic recognition to be fulfilled. The recognition of this gypsy community is not the *right kind of recognition* for Liszt as a Hollywood biopic subject.

The gypsy crowd falls silent, and in the centre of a ring of onlookers Liszt plays a piano that has presumably been taken from a nearby house. This impromptu concert shows significant differences and similarities with the previous concert scenes and their established social codes. Here the crowd stand close about Liszt, not separated by seating or stages; the surrounded Liszt is not elevated above the audience, nor subject to a one-directional gaze that is idealizing, upward and forward-directional, but central and lowered; Liszt is seated while his audience stand, becoming the centre, the 'heart', of a more democratic

Figure 10 *Song Without End* (1960)

'reverse-panoptical' gaze; the crowd remain respectfully silent during Liszt's performance, but at the end the applause and cheering is almost immediately joined by the gypsy band recommencing their rhapsody. It could be argued that, in this environment, it is the music's function within the community that is valued, not the isolation of the idol.

In the next scenes, Carolyne is shown speaking to the Duchess back in Weimar. Carolyne is willing to give up all she has, 'half the Ukraine', to win the Tsar's approval for divorce. This may develop audience sympathies for Carolyne by stressing her sincerity and devotion – qualities that are valued by the conventions of Hollywood romance. Carolyne and the Duchess go to see Liszt conducting a rehearsal of Wagner's *Rienzi*. In a representational sense, conducting is used here as a signifier of a kind of evolution to a 'higher' form of musical engagement. To evidence his new commitment to 'serious' music, Liszt angrily complains that the underperforming orchestra is 'betraying a man of genius!' Wagner's arrival at the rehearsal, seeking Liszt's assistance in escaping the authorities by fleeing to Switzerland, adds another point of biographical orientation for those who recognize it: the aftermath of the Dresden May Uprising of 1849, although the scene still functions for audiences without prior-knowledge of Wagner's revolutionary activities. His motives for fleeing the country are narratively unimportant and are blurred by comical references to 'bass clarinets' and obscure comments about 'exposure'. The scene ultimately establishes Liszt's willingness to help Wagner both musically and monetarily as an embodiment of higher artistic ideals. He gives Wagner some money and promises to produce *Lohengrin*, an opera 'no one else will touch', provided, Wagner stresses, that not a note is changed.

Wagner exits the scene, and the following exchange between Liszt and Carolyne brings the key thematic elements to the surface: Wagner is a 'monster', but one whose work 'enriches the human spirit'. Liszt feels he must put his 'vanity' aside and serve music as he would serve God. Carolyne, in turn, thinks Liszt should prioritize his own music. A public performance of *Tannhäuser* (1845) follows, dramatizing both visually and aurally the situation that is desired by Liszt: he can pursue his spiritual duty towards art, towards his ideal, by conducting a 'worthier' musical event. The religious content of the 'Pilgrim's Chorus' is accentuated for the film's audiences by the singers reciting an English translation of the libretto.

The romantic narrative then takes precedent again. Liszt and Carolyne plan to wed, necessitating a meeting with the archbishop, another privileged authority figure. The archbishop is first framed in long shot standing before an ornate wooden crucifix in (what is implied to be) his office. He says 'No' and turns around, advancing diagonally across the room, remaining near the centre of the frame as the camera follows. The seated figures of Liszt and Carolyne appear in the frame with their backs to the archbishop, who explains his objections to their marriage and his resolve to oppose them. He walks around the couple, and the camera follows his movements while Liszt and Carolyne remain static. Framed in this way, the archbishop's power is perhaps visually defined by combining his mastery over this location through mobility with an authority over the look of the camera. He also possesses linguistic capital, using complex terms like 'scandalous concubinage', 'licentious', 'profligate' and 'libertine' that may prompt the audiences' respect for the archbishop's command of language. He cuts-short Carolyne's objections by stressing the authority of 'God'. This motif returns in the later scene with the Pope's letter, when Latin serves as a confounding social divide between the film's audience and the film's privileged authority figures. The archbishop gives a lengthy chastisement of Liszt for his scandalous past and the neglect of his gifts; like the Duchess, this gives the archbishop an aura of omnipotent knowledge, despite the fact that Liszt's affairs are apparently known 'throughout the length and breadth of Europe'. Liszt never meets the archbishop's eye during the latter's objections, and his own eyes are downcast like a guilty child hearing corrective criticism.

It would be possible to interpret the archbishop as a character who embodies attitudes that conflict with the attitudes of the film itself – in other words, those attitudes and values that audiences might adopt and recognize as belonging to the film (according to judgements of appropriateness) in order to enact a sympathetic interpretation. The archbishop's criticism of Liszt and Carolyne might, in this case, appear unjust and without authority. But according to a 'dominant' interpretation of the film, the archbishop functions as a kind of built-in ethical film critic, ensuring that potential criticisms over the film's representation of Liszt as an egocentric adulterer are recognized and disarmed within the film itself.

In his summary of the Columbia production notes, John C. Tibbetts explained how official censorship significantly curbed the film for what were considered 'unsavoury' depictions of Liszt's marital infidelity.[50] As early as 1954, Joseph Breen and producer Harry Cohn were discussing certain issues which

---

[50] Tibbetts, *Composers in the Movies*, 76–7.

the Production Code Administration found troublesome in the proposed depiction of Liszt's affair with Carolyne. These problematic issues included the possible justification of adultery by reference to the privileges of genius, the balancing of audience sympathy against those who disapprove of Liszt's affair on screen and a more general need for 'clarification about the church's role in annulments'.[51]

On these grounds, the archbishop can be read to function as a pre-emptive defence against any potentially damaging claims that the film unethically glamorizes adultery. In doing so the archbishop becomes, like the Duchess, an element in the film's multifaceted construction of explanatory elements that effect an ideological valuation and limitation of certain concepts raised in the narrative. They are authority figures who are 'safeguarded' against the potentially transgressive effects of the Romantic genius' cultural transcendence. Against such mythologized authority, Liszt can make no scandal. He stands and makes a final plea, but the archbishop insists that he and Carolyne never meet again. There is a sense of summation and resigned finality to the result of the archbishop's imposition on their marriage plans, which is, through audio-visual explanation, made to seem 'right' and even 'beautiful' ('as it should be') by Liszt's respectful kissing of the archbishop's ring, and the bittersweet registers of the accompanying music.

Composing and performing 'serious' music

In the following scene, Carolyne collapses into Liszt's arms, asking him to 'take me away, anywhere'. Liszt's resigned response to the archbishop's judgement situates the lovers as perpetual outsiders: 'Society is the same everywhere. Its laws are rigid.' The pair is situated outside and, in a sense, 'above' society, but unable to receive its blessing. Carolyne resolves to send a petition to the Pope.

The scene fades through black to an image of Liszt writing at a desk; the inclusion of 'Liebesträume' No. 3 on the non-diegetic soundtrack suggests that he is writing music. A servant carrying a tray of food interrupts him, warning that Liszt is neglecting his health – a warning that Liszt dismisses, as did Chopin in *A Song to Remember*. Another fade, suggestive of time passing, returns us to the same room, where the non-diegetic sound of Hungarian Rhapsody

---

[51] Tibbetts, *Composers in the Movies*, 76.

No. 2 indicates that Liszt's struggle over the production of 'serious' music is still ongoing. In this way, Liszt is represented to be neglecting his health and 'suffering' in the process of committing himself to his ideal, pursuing his artistic 'duty' against all obstacles. These are qualities which are highly valued by both typical formulations of Romanticism and the ideological norms of Hollywood representation.

Yet there is an interesting slippage in value ascription apparent in this representation. K. J. Donnelly has noted that pre-existing pieces of 'art music' can sometimes become 'an "alien" in the system, a volatile element potentially damaging the seeming unity of a film'.[52] This might seem less of an issue in composer biopics, where authentic historical music is often contextually justified. It often appears in the 'right' place at the 'right' time. However, with the use of the Rhapsody and 'Liebesträume' in *Song Without End*, the choice of exactly *what* music to include – a choice determined by various considerations of audience recognition, sound and associated meaning – can still create conflicts. The fact that the Rhapsody and 'Liebesträume' are not considered among Liszt's most 'serious' compositions is arguably immaterial; they are the compositions most likely to be recognized by the film's prospective audiences as indicative of 'classical' music in a familiar and unthreatening sense. We might suggest that as far as a typical Hollywood biopic is concerned, it would have been unnecessary to attempt greater historical accuracy by presenting, for example, 'Après un lecture du Dante' (1837; 1849) or *Totentanz* (1849; 1865) on the soundtrack as an example of Liszt's 'serious' music. The Rhapsody and 'Liebesträume' are the pieces that prospective film audiences are most likely to recognize and enjoy as 'Liszt's music' – the music that is itself the reason he is a famous composer, and worthy of being the subject of a biopic in the first place.

Liszt's serious composition is interrupted again by a note pushed under his door. The low-pitched slow strings on the soundtrack give way to the 'Un sospiro' theme as Liszt reads the note and lifts his eyes upwards. Here the interpretation: 'the letter contains good news from Carolyne' is indicated almost exclusively by the musical motif. This interpretation is not refuted by the following scene between Liszt and the Duchess. The Pope has approved the annulment, and Carolyne is now free to marry Liszt. Once again, each line carries expositional significance in terms of characterization, historical realism, biographical detail,

---

[52] Donnelly, *The Spectre of Sound*, 41.

narrative orientation or thematic statement. Liszt appears to be finally capable of fully acknowledging and resolving his divided self in favour of his 'serious' side:

> My heart has never been on the concert stage. My tendency to vulgar exhibitionism . . . is misleading. I despise my career as a virtuoso.

An establishing shot of Rome sets the scene for the upcoming marriage. During the wedding preparations, Liszt suggests the bridal march from *Lohengrin* be played, keeping current the association between Liszt's ideals and Wagner's music. But Carolyne objects to this arrangement. The representation of Carolyne as Liszt's muse is reiterated as she insists that Liszt's music, and not Wagner's, be played at their wedding.

There then follows a climactic celebratory concert, the counterpart to Chopin's final European tour in *A Song to Remember*, where Liszt is shown to have won the right kind of public recognition for his compositions, that is, the recognition of the dominant social order: non-gypsy, wealthy, urban-centred and aristocratic. This final concert sequence is similar in construction to earlier concerts, but for a few key differences. First, the music presented in the earlier scenes was a mixture of various other composers, and now the film audience is primed to recognize the music played as Liszt's own – the 'Liebesträume' and Rhapsody. Consequently, the performance is suggested to function as a kind of narrative victory or self-actualization. Second, the difference is also secured by atypical camera techniques. A medium shot of Liszt from the side of the piano, unbroken for one minute twenty seconds, presents an unobstructed view of Bogarde's impressive mimed pianism. Another shot tracks slowly from left to right, beginning with Carolyne sitting in the first circle, across the audience, and then, with an accelerating burst of speed, to a medium shot of Liszt framed by the piano and lid. The motion corresponds with a musical crescendo, and the camera tracks-in on Liszt as he plays the last dramatic chords. A final crucial difference is that the scene ends immediately following the music's termination, with no fetishizing of the audience's applause. In this way, elements of the utopian gypsy performance have been introduced to this culturally 'legitimate' musical space.

Liszt is next accompanied by an orchestra in a performance of his Piano Concerto No. 1, with many audio-visually impressive trills, leaps and runs up and down the keyboard. The camera's reverse-panoptic perspective and mobility adds a utopian quality to the concert, with shots from the direction of the orchestra, the stalls and the circle emphasizing both a sense of united community and the centrality of Liszt's position in this space. The enthusiastic applause with which the sequence concludes is curtailed of fetishized qualities by three factors: (1) the establishing of the music as Liszt's own work locates the applause as appreciation of the music itself; (2) much attention is paid by the camera to Carolyne responding to the applause, looking around the hall satisfied at the public response, locating the applause within the broader narrative context of Liszt's struggle for recognition; and (3) Liszt is only seen responding to the applause at a distance, shaking hands with the conductor and quickly taking leave of the stage.

After the concert, Liszt and Carolyne arrive back at (what are possibly) their rooms to discover that the Pope has refused the grant the annulment. It is revealed that Carolyne had lied to the investigators in a way which now fatally undermines their case. There now appears to be no hope for a second marriage.

The figures are framed underneath a band of shadow which divides the image horizontally. This shadow might be interpreted to be symbolic of the overhanging oppression of the central love affair by Carolyne's husband Prince Nicholas and the Catholic Church, whose power is mythologized into the workings of 'fate' by the film's metalanguage. In this way, the melodramatic shadow could be read as the metaphorical presence of the antagonists – omnipresent and incontestable.

The slow minor-key strings on the soundtrack create a mood of seriousness and an atmosphere that is conductive of both fatalism and uncertainty depending on their ascription to narrative perspective. If they are read to be indicative of character point of view, Liszt's or Carolyne's, then the latter is a more likely interpretation; if an aspect of the film's metalanguage, then the former. At this emotional climax of the film the musical soundtrack displays increased visual-musical integration; the reprisal of the 'Un sospiro' theme is followed by a closer, moment-to-moment matching of dialogue. Liszt's outbursts against the couple's dashed hopes are accompanied by fortissimo accents, while Carolyne's idealizing of their love is accompanied by higher notes. As she says the words 'everything became clear to me', the music is similarly 'clarified' by being momentarily reduced to a single melodic line. A descending arpeggio scale then accompanies as Carolyne finally accepts the fact that she and Liszt are fated to never be together.

Carolyne's dialogue is ultimately brought in-line with the metalanguage of the expressive mise-en-scène, and the general attitude of acceptance which accompanies the film's narrative resolution here explicitly makes use of one particularly potent explanatory tool, one which Morse Peckham identified as the ultimate 'terminal explanation', or the ultimate instruction to ask no more questions and accept things the way they are: 'It is God's Will'.[53] Carolyne recognizes that it was her destiny to simply be the one who leads Liszt into the service of God. The strings play a melody displaying dynamics, harmonics and rhythmic figures reminiscent of religious registers, foreshadowing Liszt's subsequent entrance into the Catholic Church. The pair say goodbye, and Liszt leaves Carolyne silently praying before an icon. The band of shadow, which perhaps signifies the mythic oppression of the church, remains at the top of the frame.

The final scenes

Liszt's separation from Carolyne and entrance into Catholic orders was chosen as the end point for *Song Without End*. A likely reason was the institutional necessity for a Hollywood biopic to prioritize the romantic narrative. By beginning when it does and ending when it does, *Song Without End* presents a bracketing of Liszt's life to a certain configuration of potential 'Hollywood material' essentials: the Liszt/Marie/Carolyne love triangle and Liszt's evolution from concert pianist, through Weimar composer, to Abbé. The ending is therefore a moment chosen by the filmmakers to function as an appropriate conclusion to the film's prioritized events.

The final scene may, however, cast an ambiguous light over certain of these elements. For example, Liszt seemingly becomes a part of that very same institution that has been shown to be a 'shadow' over the protagonist's happiness. This tension can be resolved by recognizing that the film's attitude can appear to both valorize Liszt as the protagonist, worthy of the audience's sympathies and attentions, and also valorize his punishment and subjugation to Hollywood's ideological norms. The typical male Western hero type is obliged to live outside the confines of society, epitomized, for classical Hollywood cinema, by the stability of the heterosexual couple. By being a Romantic genius, Liszt, like the typical Western hero, is refused this kind of resolution. The film's final scene is, once again, concerned with a formal/diegetic communication between the public space of a church and the organ loft. Liszt plays 'Un sospiro' softly, complementing the modesty and spiritual authority implied by his change

---

[53] Peckham, *Explanation and Power*, 82–5.

in lifestyle upon taking holy orders. A shot panning-down from the church's decorated interior reveals the pews below, in which several female figures sit praying. One of the figures is Carolyne, who is shown to remain behind as the others leave; she makes the sign of the cross with eyes uplifted towards the impressive gold ornamentation of the church interior. As Ned Washington's choral version of 'Un sospiro' swells to accompany Liszt's playing, Carolyne turns and slowly exits. Liszt's expression appears to draw the camera upwards to a window over the organ, suggesting that Carolyne is no longer the object of Liszt's sublime gaze but rather some higher, Godlike ideal.

George Custen's Marxist structural analysis of the biopic genre suggests that suffering and salvation can function as a displacement of the institutional nature of traditional values; family and community may be rejected by outsiders such as Liszt, but the reassuring glow of comfort such institutions provide can remain for film audiences, who are reassured by being exposed to a dramatization of alternatives which are contained and diffused via a hegemonic resolution.[54] The sublime 'glow' created by the 'Un sospiro' choir, the visual splendour of the church interior, and the stoic and accepting demeanours of both Liszt and Carolyne may enable this kind of comfort. Spectators may feel confirmed as 'insiders' by the confirmation of Romantic biopic subjects as mythologized 'outsiders'. The film also presents two figures, the Duchess and the archbishop, as ideologically secure authority figures whom the potential rebelliousness of the artist-outsider has ultimately failed to harm.

Conclusion

Romantic cultural transcendence is a double-edged sword for Hollywood biopics. As prestige pictures that contribute to overall house styles, Hollywood historical biopics repay their large production costs not only in box office takings from prospective markets unfulfilled by television productions and smaller-scale features but also in symbolic capital. They must achieve all this while meeting both formal censorship and informal ideological expectations regarding their content. To achieve this balance, as Leo Braudy suggested, Hollywood biopics must present the stories of historical figures whose lives are interesting enough to attract audiences and bear narrativization as film entertainment, yet also

---

[54] Custen, *Bio/Pics*, 76.

not dynamic enough for their cultural transcendence to expose, question and endanger certain sustaining ideological imperatives.[55] One illustrative example of this process in *Song Without End*, as we have seen, is the resolution of Liszt's affair with Carolyne – a complex representational arrangement of attitude, explanation and evaluation across many different elements of form and content.

It might be objected at this point that concepts such as genius and cultural transcendence have been discussed so far as specifically Romantic ideas, and have been explored here in reference to a single biopic of a Romantic composer – what relevance do they have beyond these confines, as we have implied, in characterizing Hollywood historical biopics more generally? To answer this objection, we might credit an argument that recognizes the modern conception of 'genius' to be something that developed during nineteenth-century Romanticism. Contributory factors included the writings of Thomas Carlyle, the 'great man' approach to history; a revival of interest in the heroes of mythology; and the construction and reception of Beethoven's cultural image. The overarching Hollywood tendency for favouring charismatic male figures (although obviously not limited to Hollywood) might be rooted in this heightened Romantic valuation of the explanatory power of the 'great man' concept.

In summary, historical figures for classical Hollywood biopics had to be represented as Romantic geniuses in the right way. The cultural transcendence of their cultural image had to be malleable to various intuitional and ideological imperatives and expectations. Later developments in New Hollywood, beginning in the late 1960s, would redefine many of these expectations. As a cultural artefact forming part of Lisztian biographical discourse, *Song Without End* stands as an important explanatory contribution to the ways that Liszt, and Romanticism itself, is understood, or made sense of, in both informal and formal explanatory/ educational contexts.[56] It would be impossible to ascertain how much past or current public information about Liszt's cultural image results from this film, or how significant it may have been, or remains, in constructing, maintaining and altering that cultural image. To state the problem as a rhetorical question: Among people who know who Liszt was, and for whom Liszt is associated with certain

---

[55] Braudy, *The Frenzy of Renown*, 8.
[56] In terms of formal education, in the 1960s *Song Without End* was used as an official educational film for elementary to college level students in the United States by the Music Educators National Conference. Extracts from the film were assembled into shortened versions for use in schools. These educational versions sought to instruct American children in 'music appreciation', nineteenth-century European culture and history, and 'illustrate the virtuosity of Liszt'. MENC: The National Association for Music Education, 'Virtuoso Franz Liszt as Composer: A New Teaching Film from "Song without End"', *Music Educators Journal* 47, no. 2 (1960): 45–6.

Romantic ideas, images, works and other perhaps vaguer associations (a cultural image), what role did *Song Without End* play in forming that understanding? An impossible question to answer; but we can reasonably assume that the film's explanatory significance was, and remains, considerable.

The earlier analysis has advanced beyond the previous chapter and its methodological framework of cultural image and schematic types by addressing a single significant example from the Liszt filmography and analysing the explanatory processes that seek to direct audience responses by evoking a variety of representational conventions. Schematic types, star associations, biographical knowledge, the norms of Hollywood narrative and the demands of ideological censorship, all contribute to the shaping of the 'dominant' reading of the film. Guided by a concern for maintaining the three-dimensionality of the text in question, a combination of in-depth textual and contextual analysis guided our analysis of the dominant reading and its various contributory elements. In doing so, we demonstrated how filmic representations of Romantic historical figures, such as Liszt, construct, maintain and alter the cultural image of their subjects by selecting and employing various schematic types that function as explanatory tools, yet facilitate the acceptance of certain ideologically weighted explanans.

Expanding upon the need to address the representation of this Romantic figure from a variety of cinematic perspectives, the next chapter will present another textual and contextual analysis of another significant, yet very different, biopic of Franz Liszt.

5

'Piss off, Brahms!'

Lisztomania (1975) and Ken Russell in 1975

The sphere of popular music . . . mummifies the vulgarised and decaying remnants of romantic individualism.

—Theodor Adorno[1]

The only performance that makes it – that really makes it – that makes it all the way – is the one that achieves madness.

—Turner (Mick Jagger) in *Performance* (1970)

Introduction

Ken Russell's *Lisztomania* (1975) remains largely unexplored by Film Studies. Its infamous reputation rests upon a clash of 'high' subject and 'low' style, supposedly rendering it unsuitable for serious analysis.[2] To some, the film is simply a failed attempt to reproduce the success of Russell's previous film *Tommy* (1975), a rock-opera based upon the 1967 concept album of the same name by British rock group the Who. *Lisztomania*'s reputation has also foundered due to a consensus that the film is a 'failure', in both artistic and economic terms.[3] Beyond these points, the film also fell victim to the wholesale scholarly relegation of Russell and 1970s British cinema until comparatively

---

[1] Theodor Adorno, 'On the Fetish Character in Music and the Regression of Listening', 1938, in *The Culture Industry: Selected Essays on Mass Culture*, 29–60 (London and New York: Routledge, 2001), 55.
[2] See for example Cornelia Szabó-Knotik, 'From "Deutschösterreich" to Pop/ularity: Celebrating Liszt at his Birthplace (1936–2011)', in *Liszt's Legacies*, ed. Michael Saffle and James Deaville, 300–12 (Stuyvesant: Pendragon Press, 2014), 308. Charles Rosen is also content to dismiss Russell's films as 'trash'; Ro sen, *The Romantic Generation*, 604.
[3] See for example Gene D. Phillips, *Ken Russell* (Boston: Twayne Publishers, 1979), 167–9.

recently; calls for reappraisal have also gone unheeded.[4] In existing analysis, *Lisztomania* is often overshadowed by *Tommy*, a film with which it shares, as this chapter will explore, a close relationship.[5] Liszt's exclamation 'Piss off, Brahms' epitomizes the film's agenda to subvert cultural values and assert its subject's contemporaneousness; it also evokes the tone, methods and context of Russell's composer biopics in opposition to the Hollywood 'Song' films explored in the previous chapter.

Sue Harper, Justin Smith and Sian Barber's recent studies of 1970s British cinema highlight a need for researchers to explore a wide variety of production contexts and histories in order to make sense of its products.[6] To present an analysis of any film requires the selection of 'appropriate' categories or tools, which, in the case of *Lisztomania*, include the British pop music film genre, Russell as auteur, *Tommy*, Roger Daltrey, the Who and Liszt's relationship with schemas of Wagnerian proto-Nazism. These diverse interpretive categories not only offer fresh perspectives on *Lisztomania* as a key member of the Liszt filmography – allowing us to understand in greater detail its contribution to Liszt's cultural image – but also return us in various ways to those key Romantic themes we have pursued throughout this book, including virtuosity and genius, sublimity and ideology, art and society, and multimedia and explanation.

British cinema and music in the 1970s

Lisztomania was a product of a so-called decadent period for the British pop music film, a genre that peaked in the late 1960s, featuring an intersection of innovative film techniques and musical soundtracks that appealed to

---

[4] James Deaville, 'The Making of a Myth: Liszt, the Press, and Virtuosity', in *Analecta Lisztiana II: New Light on Liszt and His Music*, ed. Michael Saffle and James Deaville, 181–95 (Stuyvesant: Pendragon Press, 1997), 182; John C. Tibbetts cited in Ken Russell, 'Interviews with John C. Tibbetts', in *Liszt: A Chorus of Voices*, ed. Michael Saffle, John C. Tibbetts and Claire McKinney, 304–8 (Stuyvesant: Pendragon Press, 2012), 304–8.

[5] See Justin Smith, 'The "Lack" and How to Get It": Reading Male Anxiety in *A Clockwork Orange*, *Tommy* and *The Man Who Fell to Earth*', in *Don't Look Now: British Cinema in the 1970s*, ed. Paul Newland, 145–59 (Bristol and New York: Intellect, 2010), passim; Anna E. Claydon, 'Masculinity and Deviance in British Cinema of the 1970s: Sex, Drugs and Rock 'n Roll in *The Wicker Man*, *Tommy* and *The Rocky Horror Picture Show*', in *Don't Look Now: British Cinema in the 1970s*, ed. Paul Newland, 133–41 (Bristol and New York: Intellect, 2010), passim.

[6] Sue Harper and Justin Smith, *British Film Culture in the 1970s: The Boundaries of Pleasure* (Edinburgh: Edinburgh University Press, 2013), 227; Sian Barber, *The British Film Industry in the 1970s: Capital, Culture and Creativity* (London: Palgrave MacMillan, 2013), 182.

emerging youth markets.[7] Throughout the 1950s and the 1960s, music stars such as Cliff Richard and Tommy Steele became film stars, and directors such as Richard Lester experimented with techniques inspired by the contemporary avant-garde. By the mid-1970s, the British pop music film was characterized by irony, hybridized generic forms, cultural influences and intermedia collaborations.[8] Some considered the genre to have become moribund by end of the decade, and various attempts at reinvention, including *Quadrophenia* (1979) and *Pink Floyd – The Wall* (1982), were seen as evidence, by their very hybridity and diversity, of the genre's overall breakdown, despite remaining popular with audiences.[9]

Due to a newly significant desire for higher cultural status, some pop/rock musicians pursued various connections with the British film industry throughout the 1970s; many composed film soundtracks, adopted soundtrack aesthetics in their music and transferred their star personas into acting roles. Mick Jagger, David Essex and Roger Daltrey, for example, starred in *Performance* (1970), *Stardust* (1974) and *McVicar* (1980), making constructive use of their star personas.

A loosening of film censorship combined with rising foreign interest in British music, providing opportunities for music films to present sexually challenging content which sometimes bordered on the pornographic. Filmmakers such as

Figure 11 *Lisztomania* (1975)

---

[7] Stephen Glynn, 'Can't Buy Me Love?: Economic Imperatives and Artistic Achievements in the British Pop-Music Film', in *The Cambridge Companion to Film Music*, ed. Mervyn Cooke and Fiona Ford, 67–80 (Cambridge University Press, 2016), passim.
[8] Glynn, 'Can't Buy Me Love?', 68–78.
[9] Glynn, 'Can't Buy Me Love?', 78–9; Barber, *The British Film Industry in the 1970s*, 70.

Ken Russell thrived on the freedom over explicit material that could be passed by the BBFC, so long as 'serious artistic intent' was made manifest.[10] Sian Barber emphasizes a need to look beyond reductive explanations like 'crisis in masculinity' and cultural or economic 'stagnation', in order to understand British cinema in this period.[11] General tendencies of hybridity and recurring thematic interests in violence, excess, tastelessness and social anxieties typify interpretations of this 'baroque' era in pop culture; yet despite the currency of this label, the idea of Romanticism also looms large in characterizing at least a part of its output.

As Robert Pattison and Christopher Partridge suggested, certain Romantic themes can be read to characterize key aspects of 1970s rock; this includes an 'intense romantic yearning', sacred community experience, an emphasis on 'vulgarity' and a desire for 'authenticity'.[12] More specifically, 'the glorification of youth, its loathing of ennui, its celebration of energy, its hatred of formal education', an unquenchable 'desire to be moved' emotionally and a valuation of instinct over reason were among the many Romantic tropes indirectly appropriated by certain sectors of mid-century popular music culture.[13] A period of confrontational, self-conscious formal experimentation followed, in which various Romantic tropes and concepts were mobilized by musicians and filmmakers. Content and form were hybridized, and a developing interest in visual, sexual and behavioural excess was fuelled by an artistic drive for cultural transcendence, as the creators of cultural products explored the potential to transgress the sacred-profane dichotomy, along with other social norms. Liminal cultural spaces emerged in which contemporary taboos could be exposed and redefined.

In music, for example, the concept album was one tool for this redefinition, problematizing 'high' and 'low' cultural levels while looking to Romanticism for alternative models of artistic value. Groups such as the Beatles, the Who and Emerson, Lake and Palmer experimented with musical quotation and formal techniques taken from nineteenth-century models. They appropriated on behalf of 'low' music the 'high' values associated with opera, and specific composers such as Mussorgsky, Bartók and Liszt.[14] Such music sometimes encouraged contemplative listening rather than dancing, extending the

[10] Smith, 'The "Lack" and How to Get It', 146.
[11] Barber, *The British Film Industry in the 1970s*, 15–16.
[12] Robert Pattison, *The Triumph of Vulgarity: Rock Music in the Mirror of Romanticism* (Oxford: Oxford University Press, 1987); Christopher Partridge, *The Lyre of Orpheus: Popular Music, The Sacred and the Profane* (Oxford: Oxford University Press, 2014), 115–24.
[13] Pattison, *The Triumph of Vulgarity*, 87–8.
[14] K. J. Donnelly, *Magical Musical Tour: Rock and Pop in Film Soundtracks* (London: Bloomsbury, 2015), 97. One famous example is Queen's 'Bohemian Rhapsody' (1975), which suggestively evokes the Lisztian rhapsody form.

Romantic thematic concerns identified by Pattison and Partridge to include a range of complementary reception practices. As we will see, the Who and their lead singer Roger Daltrey, who would portray Liszt in *Lisztomania*, were, from early in their artistic development, heavily involved in this Romantic revaluation of contemporary youth music culture.

In addition, the iconic status afforded to musical personality and improvisation, which peaked in the mid-twentieth century, is historically related to the Lisztian culture of Romantic virtuosity. Certain contemporary perspectives on rock performance (such as: 'it doesn't matter who wrote it, so long as the right person is playing it')[15] recall the potentially subversive position of the virtuoso as a conflation of interpretation and originality, fabrication and authenticity, and the mythology of the artist and the financial success of the marketable star.

One of the most significant appropriations in this context was the suffix 'mania'. Heinrich Heine's term 'Lisztomania' is a direct etymological ancestor of the 'Beatlemania' that gripped pop culture in the 1960s. The latter's significant features include female 'hysteria', countercultural sexual liberation, collective identity and a celebration of the opportunity 'to abandon control'.[16] Perhaps more than anything else, this revival and redefinition of 'mania' establishes Liszt as a legitimate predecessor to twentieth-century stardom.

Liszt himself has long been associated with the modern star. In biographical discourse, he is commonly compared to famous musicians such as Michael Jackson, Mick Jagger, Robbie Williams and Justin Bieber.[17] A more general similarity between such popstars and classical composers continues to be widely disseminated, mostly between those associated with youth, sexual appeal and virtuoso performance, such as The Beatles and Elvis Presley. By 1975, Russell's *Lisztomania* was highlighting a well-established tendency, but one that was now augmented by new similarities, such as that between Liszt and Rick Wakeman, who both played multiple keyboards on stage.[18]

Both *Tommy* and *Lisztomania* are also associated with the term 'rock-opera', a concept which is supportive of numerous conflicting definitions. When

---

[15] Steve Howe cited in Derek Bailey, *Improvisation: Its Nature and Practice in Music* (New York: Da Capo Press, 1992), 39.

[16] John Muncie, 'The Beatles and the Spectacle of Youth', in *The Beatles, Popular Music and Society: A Thousand Voices*, ed. Ian Inglis, 35–52 (London: The MacMillan Press, 2000), passim.

[17] Szabó-Knotik, 'From "Deutschösterreich" to Pop/ularity', 309; Richard Taruskin, *The Oxford History of Western Music*, 6 vols (Oxford: Oxford University Press, 2005), 3: *Music in the Nineteenth Century*, 268; Oliver Hilmes, *Franz Liszt: Musician, Celebrity, Superstar* (New Haven: Yale University Press, 2016), passim.

[18] Taruskin, *Music in the Nineteenth Century*, 273. There is no evidence that Liszt ever played both at once, like Wakeman; Liszt's second piano was a backup in case the first one broke.

describing a film, it often expresses a sense of musical, narrative and conceptual ambition, and unity, or, more generally, identifies an 'adult' themed musical, such as *The Phantom of the Paradise* (1974) or *The Rocky Horror Picture Show* (1975). The rock-opera concept, while encouraging unconventional content and formal techniques, was tempered by the economic necessity that its products be accessible to mass audiences. Film such as *Rocky Horror* and *Tommy* combined generic hybridity, adult content and cult reception appeal, which allowed their market differentiation from more mainstream musicals. Yet the rock-opera was an uncertain prospect for film production, and its experimental nature and diversity of cultural impact was not only in accord with tendencies in British cinema circa 1975, but also with Ken Russell's own directorial output more generally.

Artists in Ken Russell's films

Although it may seem like a logical step when considering Ken Russell's overall filmmaking career, the marriage of composer biopic and 'rock-opera' was an obvious economic gamble. For some, the combination of Russell, Roger Daltrey and Liszt seemed 'a perfect match', but for others, it posed a significant financial and aesthetic risk.[19] As Daltrey himself was quick to foresee, 'It's so over the top it will either be incredibly successful or a terrible flop'.[20]

So, given the apparent incongruity of the film's main elements, why might *Lisztomania* have seemed a logical step for Russell to take at this point in his career? Along with Nicholas Roeg and Derek Jarman, Russell well represents that aforementioned resurgence of Romanticism in British cinema which blurred the boundaries between different genres, and fact and fiction, and that proclaimed anti-realism and creative intuition. In making his composer biopics, Russell worked from a position that considered the classical Hollywood tradition to have failed in exploring the spirituality or creativity of their subjects.[21] His own biopics were a radical attempt to find a balance between fact and truth. A kind of truth could be presented by taking liberties with, or sometimes creating extreme falsifications of, known historical facts. In a similar fashion to the Hollywood biopics, the known facts about a historical person's life become the raw materials for interpretation according to various industrial and cultural needs, only now, and in-line with Russell's auteur

[19] Tibbets cited in Russell, 'Interviews with John C. Tibbetts', 304.
[20] Cited in Tim Ewbank and Stafford Hildred, *Roger Daltrey* (London: Portrait, 2004), 142.
[21] Russell, 'Interviews with John C. Tibbetts', 306.

status, there is a brazen celebration of this historical brigandage. As Sue Harper put it: 'history for Ken Russell was a ship on the high seas... ripe for plunder.'[22]

Morse Peckham explained how Romantic music encouraged 'virtuoso listeners' who were no longer to be simply entertained, but expected to 'work' – to perceive and interpret abstract relationships between textual elements.[23] Russell's Romantic biopics appear to demand similar 'work' from their audiences in order to make sense of their content. For example, one of Russell's key recurring motifs is the sarcophagus: an upright male figure encased in a capsule, their face sometimes visible through a window. This motif appears most notably in *Tommy*, *Mahler* (1974) and *Altered States* (1980), variously suggestive of death, entrapment, castration, sexual control and submission, but most commonly as a Christ-like sacrifice, with an ambiguous quality of self-imposition. This motif can add sexual or religious significance to moments of its use, but, of course, only for those viewers who interpret it in this way. This culture of recognition and symbolic interpretation contributes to the popularity of the Romantic auteurist approach to Russell's work. His foregrounded displays of symbolism seek to convey as much meaning as possible: 'when every second counts, it is often necessary to do two things at once', he admits, resulting in films that are dense in detail and invitations for interpretation.[24]

Russell even expressed a desire for a 'quasi-musical' means of filmic expression – one which would supposedly enable cinema to profit from the richness, ineffability and intuitive clarity which the traditional interpretation of Romantic aesthetics ascribed to music:

> Musicians are trying to do what I'm trying to do: express the inexpressible ... discover the undiscoverable, plumb the unplumbable. If you're a musician, you do it in a musical way. If you're a filmmaker you do it in a filmic way, which is my craft. Musicians come nearest to plumbing this divine mystery.[25]

Russell would appear to share the Romantic belief that music's expressive indistinctness was a primary aesthetic virtue. This ineffability, paradoxically surrounded by potent and suggestive symbolism, is often anchored to the demands

---

[22] Sue Harper, 'History and Representation: The Case of 1970s British Cinema', in *The New Film History: Sources, Methods, Approaches*, ed. James Chapman, Mark Glancy and Sue Harper, 27–40 (London: Palgrave Macmillan, 2006), 33.
[23] Morse Peckham, *The Romantic Virtuoso* (Hanover and London: Wesleyan University Press, 1995), 38–9.
[24] Russell cited in Phillips, *Ken Russell*, 125.
[25] Cited in John Walker, *The Once and Future Film: British Cinema in the Seventies and Eighties* (London: Methuen, 1985), 99.

of narrative, as we will see, by the Romantic genius type. Russell further contributed to the revival of Romanticism in British culture by producing films which emphasize the subjective, 'inner' experience of characters whose spiritual struggles and adventures are explained to audiences through complex, innovative and varied formal techniques which playfully flaunt conventions of cinematic realism.

These choices, combined with the director's foregrounded authorial voice, provided an interesting and marketable contrast to the minimalist social realism of filmmakers such as Alan Clarke and Ken Loach. Rather than exploring the difficulties involved in articulating a sense of authentic and satisfying individual experience under the social pressures of a supposedly unjust and uncaring contemporary sociopolitical context, Russell, armed with a selection of Romantic schemas, themes and images, would more often choose to examine similar themes in hybridized realms of cinematic and historical allegory.

As several commentators have previously identified, one primary concern apparent in Russell's work is the 'search for a hero' – the consistent exploration of a certain uneasy heroic idealism.[26] It is in this context that Russell's frequent return to the relationship between genius and society is to be understood. The downfall of the artist, framed in messianic tones, is often brought about by a mismanagement of their relationship with a public – as Russell put it: 'the hero turning into mere celebrity'.[27] Chapter 1 introduced that typical Romantic figure of the striving, divided and suffering male genius who appears again and again throughout Russell's filmography. Many of his protagonists, including Tchaikovsky in *The Music Lovers* (1970), Father Grandier in *The Devils* (1971), Mahler in *Mahler*, Tommy in *Tommy* and Liszt in *Lisztomania*, have their artistic or religious fidelity challenged by circumstances. The great narrative threat is that they will make compromises and neglect their ideals, whatever they may be. The suffering characters experience may make them capable of not only recognizing their own capacity for heroism but also understanding its limitations. Russell's 'search for a hero' often finds only a martyr – a quasi-religious figure who, by means of cultural transcendence, is problematically differentiated from the public they seek to join and save, individualized only in order to be sacrificed in some sense, their attendant values negotiated.

A personal interest in Romantic music encouraged Russell to search for his hero among the ranks of nineteenth-century composers – a group that, as we saw in Chapter 3, can accommodate a high degree of schematic potential regarding typical Romantic tropes and ideas. Russell's own affinity with Romantic

---

[26] Phillips, *Ken Russell*, 91–3.
[27] Cited in Braudy, *The Frenzy of Renown*, 447.

composers ran deep. He apparently thought of his own films like a connected work of music: 'All my films have the same theme, but I don't tell anyone what it is. It's like Elgar's *Enigma Variations*'.[28] His directorial persona established musical composition as a primary frame of interpretation, sometimes citing classical musical works associated with excess and nature.[29]

It is revealing, therefore, that Russell adapted *Tommy* by incorporating many of these authorial preoccupations with Romanticism and classical music. He was attracted less to the sound of the Who's music than to its themes, and he saw the narrative as 'a kind of pilgrim's progress', redolent of adventure, suffering and transcendence.[30] It is also significant that both *Tommy* and *Lisztomania* contain ideas recycled from three unfinished scripts which Russell had been developing in 1975: *Gargantua*, *Music Music Music* and *The Angels*.[31] *Lisztomania*'s most notable extract is from *Gargantua*: a scene in which 'nursemaids decorate Gargantua's "codpiece" with flowers as his penis gradually "rises to the height of a maypole when they ... dance gaily around it, singing its praises"';[32] this became, as we will see, *Lisztomania*'s gleefully outrageous 'Orpheus' sequence. According to Joseph Gomez, *Music Music Music* and *The Angels* both have 'the role of the artist in the modern world' as a central theme.[33] This thematic consistency *across five scripts* in 1975 is highly suggestive. *Tommy* and *Lisztomania* may express a 'summing up' of what was important to Russell in 1975. As he himself stated, *Tommy* was 'a culmination of much of my work', although, as we will see, it was not a conclusion.[34]

As might be expected, the formal and thematic extravagances, and sometimes strikingly explicit content, of Russell's 1975 projects can be traced to a personal perspective on the value of art in general. Russell's comments on vulgarity express a sense of Romantic artistic idealism:

> Don't get vulgarity mixed up with commercialism. By vulgarity I mean over-the-top larger-than-life slightly bad taste red-blooded thing. And if that's not anything to do with art lets have nothing to do with art.[35]

---

[28] Cited in Walker, *The Once and Future Film*, 99.
[29] Russell once called Mahler's *Das Lied von der Erde* (1908–09) his 'bible'; *Desert Island Discs*, BBC Radio 4, 22 February 1987.
[30] Cited in Joseph Gomez, *Ken Russell: The Adaptor as Creator* (London: Frederick Muller Limited, 1976), 197.
[31] Gomez, *Ken Russell*, 194–203.
[32] Cited in Gomez, *Ken Russell*, 198.
[33] Gomez, *Ken Russell*, 196.
[34] Cited in Gomez, *Ken Russell*, 200.
[35] Cited in Walker, *The Once and Future Film*, 95.

Here, the concurrence between Romanticism and vulgarity might feasibly be located in their shared hostility to social norms. Russell's comment also betrays a certain distaste for commercialism, which appears as a key theme in both 1975 films. This engagement with commercialism finds expression in the films' visual excesses; oversized objects, props and costumes, in addition to their striking visual affect, are used to highlight thematic concerns.

Justin Smith terms this technique of mise-en-scène 'hypersignification'; it makes certain objects in Russell's films reminiscent of the sculptures of Claes Oldenburg, and gives them 'a greater, if less definable, power'.[36] The giant pinballs at Tommy's Holiday Camp, for example, become 'seductive and dangerous, promising plenitude yet proving to be hollow'.[37] Perhaps 'hyperobject' is a better term, since their sheer affective physicality often seems more important than any specific signifying function. Such oversized props and costumes add a gargantuan sense of vital identity to objects, bodies and characters – a kind of cartoon reality. In *Lisztomania*, this is most notable in the gargantuan maypole penis of the 'Orpheus' sequence. The commercial tone of Russell's hyperobjects may also have been inspired by the 1967 album *The Who Sell Out*, which was described in the press as a 'pop parallel to . . . Oldenberg's hamburgers or Andy Warhol's Campbell soup cans'.[38] In the publicity pictures, Roger Daltrey posed sitting in a bathtub of baked beans, and Russell may possibly have related this image to the 'Champagne' sequence in *Tommy*. Whatever commercially focused 'message' such objects may evoke is counterbalanced by their immediate impressiveness as objects of visual sensation. Their contemporary pseudo-political consistency becomes a motif – something befitting an 'auteur' like Russell who purports to be producing variations on the same theme.

In addition to Romanticism, the idea of the 'postmodern' appears to be another significant concept regarding these films. Very broadly speaking, postmodernism concerns a historical revaluation of concepts such as fragmentation, visuality, surface, technology and consumerism, and a blurring of the boundaries between real and fictional, local and global, self and other, and simultaneousness and sequence, all of which are connected to the rise of 'late capitalism' as an explanatory economic paradigm after the Second World War.[39] In this sense,

---

[36] Smith, 'The "lack" and How to Get It', 149.
[37] Smith, 'The "lack" and How to Get It', 149.
[38] Cited in Andrew Motion, *The Lamberts: George, Constant and Kit* (London: The Hogarth Press, 1987), 330.
[39] See Fredric Jameson, *Postmodernism: Or The Cultural Logic of Late Capitalism* (London and New York: Verso, 1991), ix–54; Ernest Mandel, *Late Capitalism*, 1972 (London: NLB, 1975), 8–12, 500–22.

Russell's Romanticism might be said to exist within a broader idea of artistic postmodernism, incorporating the resultant contradictions unproblematically.

The most obvious 'postmodern' qualities in *Lisztomania* are to be found in its playful (mis)treatment of history and in the consequent inaccuracies of fashion, language, decor and cultural/behavioural norms. The non-realist presentation of mid-nineteenth-century Europe is combined with specific references to mid-twentieth-century cultural artefacts. As commentators have pointed out, the visual style of *Lisztomania* and *Tommy* is reminiscent of not only Oldenburg but also the artwork of Roy Lichtenstein and the 1960s Batman comics.[40] Such intermedia references advertise *Lisztomania*'s contemporaneousness, and its affinity with the postmodern aesthetics of bricolage, pastiche and hybridization.

The Who and Romantic virtuosity

To understand the production, content and reception of *Lisztomania*, we must first address its relationship with *Tommy*. The two films, released the same year by the same production company and starring the same leading actor, were marketed and received as virtually a film and its sequel.

Despite containing what might seem, at first glance, to be dramatically incompatible subject matter, *Lisztomania* was marketed to the audience of its immediate predecessor. Advertising stressed the film's 'erotic' and 'electrifying' elements, stating: 'It out–*Tommy*'s *TOMMY*'.[41] Attempting to maximize public interest, US distributor Columbia stated that *Tommy* was, 'greater than any painting, opera, piece of music, ballet or dramatic work that this century has produced'.[42] So successful did *Tommy* prove both financially and, on the part of its cast, crew and critics, artistically, that to immediately set about realizing a sequel of sorts might have seemed an inevitable decision. Sian Barber reminds us that, in the British film industry at this time, a successful film was quickly followed by attempts at sequels and imitations, since producers had hoped to have found a reliable marker of public taste.[43]

---

[40] Smith, 'The "lack" and How to Get It', 149.
[41] See Ken Hanke, *Ken Russell's Films* (Metuchen and London: The Scarecrow Press, 1984), 293.
[42] Cited in R. Serge Denisoff and William Romanowski, *Risky Business: Rock on Film* (Piscataway: Transaction Publishers, 1991), 216–17.
[43] Barber, *The British Film Industry in the 1970s*, 70.

Not only do the two films share many stylistic similarities, cast and crew members and production contexts but the history and cultural image of the Who itself reveals a surprising confluence between the two projects on a thematic level – a confluence that Russell may have been cultivating during production of *Lisztomania*.

The Who's lead guitarist Pete Townshend spoke publicly about the band's credo of pop-art, which was founded on a mythologized valuation of youth, protest, and the maintenance of artistic principles in both public and private contexts: 'We stand for pop-art clothes, pop-art music and pop-art behaviour . . . we don't change off stage. We live pop-art'.[44] Townshend stated that the Who's music c1967 prioritized 'melody and humour. Pop music, we think, should be understandable and entertaining'.[45] Perhaps their most famous lyric, 'I hope I die before I get old' from 'My Generation' (1965), encapsulates the glorification of youth which forms a central tenant of both rock and Romanticism. The sentiment of this lyric was later given filmic expression at the climax of the Who's later film project *Quadrophenia*, when the adolescent protagonist Jimmy Copper drives his motor scooter off the cliffs at Beachy Head. Such glorification of life and death was not strictly nihilistic, but rather a potential celebration of feeling, 'newness' or authenticity. As we will see further, for Russell, these Romantic schemas enable an extraordinarily suggestive chain of signification extending from *Tommy* to Adolf Hitler and the Third Reich, by way of Liszt, Wagner and Frankenstein's monster.

In the late 1960s, the Who achieved a certain notoriety as a band for breaking their instruments on stage. The image of Pete Townshend smashing his guitar has become a widespread icon of rock culture. Keith Moon would kick over his drums, Roger Daltrey would break his microphone, and the band justified this 'sacrilege' against the technological apparatus of musical performance by claiming it was a method of achieving a desired aesthetic affect.[46]

As Townshend stated:

> It is very artistic. One gets a tremendous sound and the effect is great . . . but if the audience isn't right I don't smash guitars. They wouldn't appreciate the full visual effect.[47]

For Townshend, the act was one of audio-visual artistic authenticity – the right 'gig' deserved to be celebrated by a unique display of cultural transcendence.

---

[44] Nick Jones, 'Well, What is Pop Art?', in *The Faber Book of Pop*, ed. Hanif Kureishi and Jon Savage, 239–40 (London and Boston: Faber and Faber, 1995), 240.
[45] Cited in Motion, *The Lamberts*, 331.
[46] Jones, 'Well, What is Pop Art?', 239.
[47] Cited in Jones, 'Well, What is Pop Art?', 240.

What was desired was a 'great effect', audio-visual, visceral and unrepeatable, but with a distinct element of protest rooted in the ritualized destruction of expensive musical equipment.

This trope presents one obvious link between the Who and Franz Liszt, since the latter also broke his instruments on stage. One commentator called Liszt 'the greatest key-chopper, the most enraged piano-shatterer and string-breaker of our century'.[48] The virtuoso also exploited the theatrical quality of this display (another inheritance from Paganini, which was put to symbolic use, as we have seen, in *Song of Love*). But unlike Liszt, the audiences of the Who, according to the band's biographer John Atkins, saw instrument destruction as an aggressive and nihilistic statement of defiance, or a 'disturbing and radical form of performance art' with a specific social function.[49] This ritualistic scene was an 'anarchic trademark . . . encapsulating the frustrations and anger of the audience'.[50] In this sense, the Who's instrument destruction was profoundly different from Liszt's, which was typically viewed as an expression of the physical power of the virtuoso, or a sheer display of 'muscularity'.[51] The virtuoso gives a superhuman performance that exceeds the capacity of the instrument 'sacrificed' in the process of making music. Yet the destruction of instruments could mean different things to different observers. As one nineteenth-century reviewer stated, Liszt 'could have smashed ten pianos: it was heavenly, divine!'[52] The Who, as a cultural event, tapped into a vein of 'crude' popular discontent in a way that Liszt apparently did not. As we have seen in previous chapters, there are other, more significant, behaviours which render Liszt's performances potentially transgressive. The difference is that instrument destruction was not primarily presented by nineteenth-century virtuoso culture as a transgressive act in itself; Paganini or Liszt's ability to play music was something that triumphed *in spite of* instrument destruction. The 'crudeness' or 'vulgarity' of the Who's own similar actions were more potentially, depending upon critical perspective, moments of class-based celebration: a celebration of the performer's, and their audience's, Otherness, as defined by the perceived dominant ideology of 1960s British culture, achieving a kind of localized and contained 'quasi-cultural transcendence' around the subculture of rock fandom.

---

[48] Anon. cited in Gooley, *The Virtuoso Liszt*, 107.
[49] John Atkins, *The Who on Record: A Critical History, 1963–1998* (Jefferson: McFarland and Company, Inc., 2000), 19.
[50] Atkins, *The Who on Record*, 19.
[51] Loesser, *Men, Women and Pianos*, 411.
[52] Anon. cited in Gooley, *The Virtuoso Liszt*, 108.

As mentioned earlier, the Who took a key role in the legitimization of rock culture through the appropriation of Romantic tropes, techniques and terminology. They were encouraged in this respect by their producer Kit Lambert (son of the British composer, and Liszt enthusiast, Constant Lambert), who, by comparing the Who with Wagner, also set a precedent for similar future Romantic comparisons.[53] The Who consciously celebrated the culturally transformative functions of rock while seeking to increase the genre's symbolic capital; Liszt himself, as we have seen, was involved in a similar effort.

A number of other striking similarities can be found between the Who and Liszt, evidencing the very same connection implied by Russell's own pairing of the two seemingly incompatible musical subjects in his two 1975 projects. These comments from John Atkins' book *The Who on Record* (2000) might easily apply to Liszt as well:

> The Who was markedly different from all its contemporaries, seemingly being more detached and aloof and more willing to ignore the rules of exceed the limits ... [their music was] exploratory, disciplined, powerful, diffuse, and able to mix experimentation with mass appeal – but most important. They were not strictured by a category.[54]

Despite being a group, the Who can also evoke schemas of the individual genius and virtuoso. Townshend supposedly evoked 'the aura of the tortured creative genius', whose musical idealism was particularly remarkable because, giving credit to Atkins comments:

> Rock-and-roll musicians are (still) not expected to be thinking, caring, or intelligent people ... he [Townshend] also recognised (as few others did at this time) that rock had something vital of its own that the more respectable forms of music lacked.[55]

A similar position was occupied by Liszt nearly 150 years before, when he defended instrumental virtuosity against criticisms of aesthetic shallowness.

Physical displays during the Who concerts more obviously evoke the sexualized crowd-work of the Lisztian virtuoso. As one spectator described:

> Roger had acquired that magnificent male sexual image with his mane of curly hair .... His skill at swinging mikes ... was outstanding .... Keith was a show in

[53] Atkins, *The Who on Record*, 23; Ewbank and Hildred, *Roger Daltrey*, 37.
[54] Atkins, *The Who on Record*, 8, 9.
[55] Atkins, *The Who on Record*, 10.

himself... hurling drumsticks in the air and catching them and pulling the most incredible faces .... Pete was a powerhouse to listen to and watch. Jumping, leaping, twisting ... punishing his guitar and forcing everything he could out of it.[56]

The echoes of Liszt here are remarkable – echoes which Ken Russell, as a Romantic music enthusiast and film biographer, would have been likely to recognize when he was making the film adaptation of the Who's famous concept album *Tommy*. The story concerns a 'deaf, dumb and blind' young man who becomes a pinball virtuoso, only to be eventually rejected by his public. After he agreed to direct, Russell was given a 'crash course' in the Who's music and history, and would have been receptive to the points of contact between this subject and his previous work.[57]

Although we can only speculate as to how acutely Russell saw the parallels between his subjects, there is opportunity to suggest that much of *Lisztomania* can be productively understood in relation to *Tommy*. A brief textual analysis of *Tommy* will help not only to build understanding of the situation of the filmmakers immediately preceding production of *Lisztomania* but also to clarify several further Romantic thematic consistencies.

Tommy the artist-priest

As suggested earlier, one central Romantic theme shared by the cultural schemas of both Liszt and the Who's *Tommy* concerns the problematic relationship between the artist and their audience. The film adaptation accentuated several other Romantic tropes, including subjectivity, suffering, martyrdom and excess. These themes are underlined with the aforementioned array of striking audio-visual symbolism, much of it relating back to Russell's wider authorial preoccupations. Russell considered the recurrent use of silver balls and glowing spheres to be a 'leitmotif', a term here suggestive of a connecting theme which implies unity and deeper meaning.[58] The film also potentially evokes more specific nineteenth-century Romantic tropes, including virtuosity, the *Gesamtkunstwerk* and the paintings of C. D. Friedrich. The recurring image of a figure outlined against

---

[56] Cited in Motion, *The Lamberts*, 338–9.
[57] Atkins, *The Who on Record*, 211. By this time Kit Lambert was no longer involved with The Who; Atkins, *The Who on Record*, 211; Motion, *The Lamberts*, 343, 354–5.
[58] Ken Russell and Mark Kermode, *Tommy* DVD commentary.

Figure 12 *Tommy* (1975)

the sun, or at the summit of a mountain of giant pinballs, may be particularly reminiscent of Friedrich's iconic 'Wanderer Above the Sea of Fog' (1818).

Tommy (Roger Daltrey) can be interpreted as a typical Romantic hero: a young and isolated male genius driven by inner passions in a search for identity and purpose, displaying both charismatic abandon against social conventions and a paradoxical display of constitutional weaknesses and sexualized youth and virility. *Tommy* can also be read as a typical Romantic suffering-as-growth narrative. For example, following the abuse he endures during the Cousin Kevin and Uncle Ernie sequences, the 'deaf, dumb and blind' Tommy is shown looking at himself in a mirror. After each sequence of personal suffering, one more coloured copy appears next to him in the reflection. In the third mirror scene these reflected figures merge into one fully coloured Tommy dressed in white. It is this 'completed' Tommy, broken-down through suffering and then rebuilt, who he recognizes as his ideal self. The subsequent 'Sparks' sequence may evoke the idea of a Romantic hero 'finding his purpose' by being guided irresistibly towards a sublime ideal – as Liszt himself phrased it, the artist 'does not choose his vocation; it takes possession of him and drives him on'.[59] Tommy's ideal self leads him to the pinball machine which will become the vehicle for his 'art', and a means to societal advancement. His 'instrument' – the vessel of his virtuosity – will become the platform he will eventually use to lead humanity to a brighter future.

[59] Liszt, *An Artist's Journey*, 28.

On both formal and diegetic levels, the film *Tommy* is preoccupied with its protagonist's experience of subjectivity. His parents ask: 'What is happening in his head?' – an open question that the film attempts to augment, rather than explain in any totalizing way, by employing a visual aesthetic that often approaches the Romantic concept of the sublime. The 'Amazing Journey' sequence presents a pattern of alternative perceptual frameworks, combined abstract and representational images and evocative musical sounds, which evoke an idea of Tommy's unique sensory perspective as a kind of transcendental knowledge. This 'unique' knowledge, shared, in part, by the film audience, is also a condition of Tommy's disability. As he proclaims after regaining his senses: 'What I see now before me is . . . beyond your wildest dreams'. This representation of Tommy functioning on a different – 'higher' – field of perception or self-consciousness finds a curious parallel with the Romantic genius type.

But the connections with Liszt, specifically, are already mounting. By contrasting pinball-playing and piano performance, the famous 'Pinball Wizard' sequence directly equates pinball virtuosity and pianistic virtuosity, as well as evoking the 'dual' motif traceable to Liszt's 1837 competition with Thalberg. Tommy's incomparable ability at the pinball machine is confirmed through this affective musical sequence in which his virtuoso performance is accompanied by Elton John's singing and playing, and rapturous enthusiasm from an admiring audience. Tommy's wide-eyed, even 'vacant', gaze implies that his virtuosity makes no demands on physical effort, and it also divorces him from the public status of the performance and the commercial context of its reception. When combined with the emotional intensity of the soundtrack, Tommy's otherworldly gaze invites the audience, already primed by the sublime 'Amazing Journey' sequence, to attempt to understand Tommy's Othered state of awareness for themselves. It is precisely this mass identification with artistic genius which will be critiqued during the film's final sequence at Tommy's Holiday Camp.

Daltrey's Tommy displays what Leo Braudy called the 'gaze of destiny': a certain trope in the visual representations of, typically historical, figures who seem as if they are to looking 'toward a more perfect world' beyond the frame of the image.[60] Liszt himself recognized something similar in Raphael's *The Ecstasy of St. Cecelia* (c1516), and related it to the experience of the isolated, artistically inspired individual who is unable to communicate the 'celestial banquet' that

---

[60] Braudy, *The Frenzy of Renown*, 555.

Figure 13 *Tommy* (1975)

they alone perceive.[61] Diverse pictorial representations from the nineteenth century show Liszt himself looking at something above and beyond the frame, sometimes while performing at the piano. Such representations can be found in 'Franz Liszt Fantasising at the Piano' (1840) by Josef Danhauser, 'Franz Liszt' (c1869) by P. A. Healy and, as we have already seen, in the Hollywood 'Song' films.[62] Head uplifted, eyes fixed on an indeterminate point beyond what is visible to us, this sublime gaze provides visual proof of the genius' authority and separateness. As we saw in Chapter 3, Liszt's face was another site of visual excess serving to mythologize his performances even as it undermined their musical value. The 'gaze of destiny' displayed by Liszt and Tommy is the location of an impossible-to-bridge division between the uniqueness of the genius and their public. 'They see something we can't'.

Tommy's senses eventually return, and he is able to transform his star charisma and unique subjectivity into the locus of a quasi-religious humanitarian movement. His adoring audience become his followers; his erstwhile caretakers, mother and stepfather, his acolytes and administrators.

From a state of 'absolute inwardness', Tommy has 'become aware' and adopted a profound social imperative based upon a critique of established social conventions and traditions. He becomes an 'artist-priest', that figure we

---

[61] Liszt, *An Artist's Journey*, 164.
[62] These portraits, and several others featuring Liszt's sublime gaze, can be found in Ernst Burger, *Franz Liszt: Chronique Biographique en Images et en Documents* (Paris: Fayard, 1986), 126–7, 245.

encountered in Chapter 1 – a Romantic agent of cultural transcendence who supposedly acts as mediator between God and man. The artist-priest as a cultural type fights to better their community through aesthetic education while being doomed to be misunderstood, cast aside and martyred. As we have already noted, this is another a recurring theme in Russell's films. The Marilyn Monroe statue in *Tommy*'s earlier 'Eyesight to the Blind' sequence introduces the theme of celebrity worship as an ambiguous 'healing' process. Tommy gives hope to his public in believing that they can become like him – empowered through indefinite means. But as a Romantic hero, Tommy's profound awakening or alteration of the self is impossible to replicate – as demanded by the Romantic values placed on the genius myth and authenticity, and in accord with Russell's critique of commercialism – by means dependent on capital.

During the later holiday camp sequence, commercialization is shown to be akin with corruption, and the public's faith in their artist-priest is ultimately broken. The Uncle Ernie character (Keith Moon) – who, it is implied, had previously sexually molested the young deaf, dumb and blind Tommy – unites the themes of abuse, exploitation and profit by inviting Tommy's followers to 'Buy your way to heaven!' while driving a giant mobile organ that is a combination of instrument and cash register. This hybridized 'organ-register' enables the evocation and counterpoint of associations between 'high' religious spiritual authenticity and 'low' cinema-like entertainment and showmanship. The ultimately unreachable nature of the hero's subjectivity is accentuated by the representation of his physical height above his public. Tommy is frequently shown standing on rooftops, stages, towers, mountains of pinballs, or flying a glider; well out of reach of the crowds below whom he invites to join him. Tommy's efforts to raise his followers are shown to be absurd, counterproductive and eventually the cause of tragedy.

This comment on the martyrdom of the Romantic artist from Frank Kermode's *Romantic Image* (1957) might well apply to the film's conclusion:

> necessarily estranged ... his work may become increasingly unintelligible and offensive to all who cannot share his dream and his persecution, or believe that the grounds for joy are true.[63]

After a monumental public career, both Tommy and Liszt became artist-priests, redirecting their efforts from pursuing a 'shallow' kind of commercial virtuosity

---

[63] Kermode, *Romantic Image*, 14.

to a vague bettering of their public through 'art', but, ultimately, they both became martyred in the attempt. With a sympathetic interpretation, *Tommy* can be read to dramatize that great Romantic tragedy: the paradoxical political burden of the artist-priest, and the utopian impossibility of 'mass' cultural transcendence. Considering that one of Russell's favourite themes, in addition to Romanticism, concerns the corruption of social and artistic ideals and that the Liszt-Wagner relationship was of particular interest to him, it is feasible that in 1975, Russell might have made the connection between the downfall of Tommy and the obscuring of Liszt's socio-artistic ideals under Wagner's shadow.[64] Like Liszt the virtuoso, Tommy occupies a position where the elevated performance of miraculous feats leads to worship; it is the capacity for descent as well as elevation that leaves them both balanced on the knife-edge of celebrity – between a public's desire to worship a messiah and their passion to despise a treacherous Mephistopheles who betrayed a promise.

Russell's approach to *Lisztomania*

Russell's work with the Who on *Tommy* fired his imagination. Having just made what he considered to be one of his best films, he immediately set about organizing a second project for his new lead actor, Daltrey, and returning to the familiar composer biopic format.[65] The production of *Lisztomania* was a collaboration between Goodtimes Enterprises and the National Film Finance Corporation. During the 1970s, Russell specialized in securing one-off production contracts from distributing studios in order to negotiate the financial turbulence of the British film industry.[66] Illustrating this instability, *Mahler* was the first of six films Russell was contracted to make for Goodtimes Enterprises, a project that was interrupted by *Tommy*.[67] The second film *Lisztomania* ended the contract, mainly due to the film's poor financial takings, but also due to certain production and budgetary difficulties.

Russell recalls that *Lisztomania* was, in his opinion, heavily influenced by producer David Puttnam, whose many suggestions made the film run over

---

[64] Russell and Kermode, *Tommy* DVD commentary.
[65] Russell and Kermode, *Tommy* DVD commentary.
[66] Harper, 'History and Representation', 28.
[67] Gomez, *Ken Russell*, 194.

budget and five weeks over schedule.[68] Russell's recollection of pre-production also accentuates the role played by Puttnam in casting choices, script and music; Ringo Starr and Rick Wakeman appeared at Puttnam's request with 'the American market in mind', and the producer also persuaded Russell to rewrite the script to accentuate certain pop and rock elements.[69]

In addition to hybridized visuals and thematic elements, *Lisztomania* also mixes its musical styles. In biopics such as *Mahler*, the composer's music was presented without substantial acoustic alterations. In *Lisztomania*, however, Liszt's music was extensively reworked in instrumentation and tone by Daltrey and Wakeman, who also added lyrical accompaniments. According to Wakeman, these adaptations were made in the ways that they believed Liszt himself might have chosen if he had lived in 1975.[70] In this way, Daltrey and Wakeman's soundtrack relates to Liszt's music in a similar way that Liszt's own operatic fantasies relate to the work of Bellini, Donizetti and Meyerbeer. As Daltrey later recalled: 'We changed . . . [Liszt's] music a bit but basically it is still his music. I just sort of bluesed it up'.[71] Liszt's music, like his life, became the malleable raw material for a rock-styled Romantic fantasy.

The film's overarching principle of modernization was, in this sense, explained as remaining faithful to Lisztian Romantic aesthetics. Like Russell, Liszt also believed that 'important works of the past had to be adapted to more understandable . . . [more modern] practices'.[72] His operatic transcriptions and symphonic poems evidence this belief. Russell's own adaptations were similarly shaped by a desire to make his subjects seem contemporary. He was consciously exploring the historical shift from pianists to singers as objects of public sexual attention between the nineteenth and twentieth centuries; yet, surprisingly, this element was relegated to a secondary significance as the film developed. Russell became more interested in exploring the 'strange relationship' between Liszt and Wagner, an interest that, as we will see, is reflected in the film's narrative structure.[73]

---

[68] Ken Russell, *A British Picture: An Autobiography*, 1989 (London: Southbank Publishing, 2008), 143.
[69] Russell, *Lisztomania* DVD commentary; Russell, *A British Picture*, 143.
[70] Dan Wooding, *Rick Wakeman: The Caped Crusader* (London: Robert Hale Ltd., 1978), 140.
[71] Ewbank and Hildred, *Roger Daltrey*, 144, 146.
[72] Cornelia Szabó-Knotik, 'Franz Liszt's Historical Position', in *The Collected Writings of Franz Liszt, Volume 3, Part 1: Dramaturgical Leaves, Essays About Musical Works for the Stage and Queries About the Stage, its Composers and Performers*, ed. Janita R. Hall-Swadley, xv–xxi (Lanham: Rowman and Littlefield, 2014), xv.
[73] Russell, *A British Picture*, 143.

Roger Daltrey as Liszt

The suitability of casting Roger Daltrey, lead singer of the Who, as Franz Liszt was determined by several factors. By the early 1970s, the Who had reached a career-high in accolades and financial security, and its members began to explore solo projects. Daltrey in particular 'seemed to need The Who somewhat less than his compatriots', releasing solo albums and gaining acting experience.[74] Aside from his international fame, authoritative stage presence, virtuoso musical ability and physical resemblance to Liszt (long hair, prominent nose, cheekbones and jawline), Daltrey's previous experience in *Tommy* made the casting choice seem particularly appropriate. The decision also implied thematic continuity between the films.

As we have seen, such casting choices can mobilize a variety of schemas that encourage complex interpretive possibilities. For commentator James Deaville, the casting of Daltrey as the virtuoso Hungarian composer created a hybrid figure, 'Daltrey-Liszt', which encapsulated the complementary aspects of both persons' cultural images.[75] Russell and Daltrey recognized and explored the biographical similarities between Liszt and the rock singer, particularly regarding their relationship with women. Like Liszt, Daltrey had been married early in his career; they both, at one time, without actually 'hiding' it, carefully played down this fact in their public life, along with allegations of fathering illegitimate children.[76] The early concert scene in *Lisztomania* notably brings together these casting associations. Daltrey-Liszt is surprised on stage by a woman pushing a baby carriage and striving to attract his attention through the confusion of the screaming crowd. At this moment, the star on screen is both Liszt *and* Daltrey, since the allegorical actions apply with equal relevance to both character and actor.

Despite such familiarities, *Lisztomania* was a daunting experience for Daltrey, who approached the role without the confidence he had brought to *Tommy*. 'This Liszt lark!' Daltrey said, 'I thought . . . [Ken Russell] was kidding when he asked me. I still don't know if I'll be able to act. I still don't. I'll just do as I'm told'.[77] The singer newly-turned actor modestly admitted he felt possessed of too little acting experience: '*Tommy* . . . I could handle . . . . But when I

---

[74] Atkins, *The Who on Record*, 219; Ewbank and Hildred, *Roger Daltrey*, 121.
[75] Deaville, 'The Making of a Myth', 181.
[76] Ewbank and Hildred, *Roger Daltrey*, 43–7; Walker, *Franz Liszt: The Virtuoso Years*, 23–7.
[77] Cited in Ewbank and Hildred, *Roger Daltrey*, 141.

did *Lisztomania* I suddenly realised I was totally out of my depth'.[78] Daltrey admitted he was 'permanently bamboozled' during production, and trusted Russell to carry the film: 'Most of the time I hadn't a clue what was going on . . . . I just did what I was told'.[79] Interestingly, this sense of relinquishing authority articulates a significant issue connecting Daltrey's performances as Tommy and Liszt: the pop star, celebrity or artist-priest as a cultural agent unaware of their actions and the impact they make on the world. The freedom implied by the unique perspective of the Romantic artist is created from its apparent dissociation from the impact made on their audience; this extends a wider failure of effective communication between the genius and their public, creating tensions in the relationship between them. As we will see, it is possible to read *Lisztomania* as a dramatization of this dilemma over agency and communication, in which 'Daltrey-Liszt' achieves a degree of awareness and control of his (their) star persona(s). In this sense, the film can be read as a thematic continuation or resolution of the ideas extrapolated from *Tommy* earlier.

The opening scenes

The first two shots establish the playful and risqué tone of the film, introducing both sexual imagery and unconventional formal techniques. From a shot of a ticking metronome, Daltrey-Liszt is then shown in bed with Marie d'Agoult, and the ticking humorously accompanies his kissing of her breasts. When Marie reaches over and speeds-up the metronome, the virtuoso keeps-up with the rhythm at superhuman speed; to achieve this effect the film speed is momentarily increased. The cuckolded Count d'Agoult enters and confronts Daltrey-Liszt, and the pair engage in acrobatic sword fighting. The hero's attempt to defend himself with a candle, which is comically sliced short by the Count's sword, introduces an important castration motif. The soundtrack is dense with musical quotations and topical allusions which add to the scene's overall mood of spirited excess and bricolage.

These formally playful, performative and parodic elements draw a clear distinction between historical 'facts' and the film's overall biographical

---

[78] Cited in Ewbank and Hildred, *Roger Daltrey*, 158.
[79] Ewbank and Hildred, *Roger Daltrey*, 143–5.

approach. Allusion explicitly situates the film within a pre-existing history of cinematic representation; it announces itself to be primarily concerned with exploring certain 'themes' using the full resources of the cinema rather than with any attempt to be a 'conventional' biopic. Atypical post-production techniques, explicit sexual content, disregard for historical facts, a flaunting of many typical conventions of realism and a dense amalgamation of cultural references – all these elements, introduced during the opening moments, wrong-foot any potential audience expectations for a conventional treatment of its subject.

This swashbuckling adventure ends with another instance of Russell's sarcophagus motif, as the discovered lovers are nailed into a 'piano-coffin' hybrid and laid on railway lines. Reading symbolically, this might suggest Daltrey-Liszt's entrapment as a victim of conflicted artistic circumstances and sexual (non-artistic) desire, and also highlight such issues among those to be resolved as the film progresses. This 'damsel-in-distress' scene might also recall *The Perils of Pauline* (1914) – another part of the film's expansive canvas of cinematic allusion which celebrates both the text's anti-realist agenda and cultural heritage. Aside from the more extended references to Charlie Chaplin, Dracula and Frankenstein stories, other significant cinematic allusions include the baby carriage from *Battleship Potemkin* (1925) and the oversized phallic props of 'Lady in the Tutti Fruiti Hat' from *The Gang's All Here* (1943). These references comprise a film-literate mode of address which celebrates the film as a fiction while also announcing its malleable mode of historical representation. *Lisztomania* is presented as a cinematically, as well as historically, literate fantasy, one that is willing to break the 'rules' of the composer biopic genre in order to acknowledge and celebrate a Romantic relative in rock culture.

The concert sequence

Any remaining audience expectations that *Lisztomania* will show the customary reverence for classical composers are potentially extinguished by the following sequence. Daltrey-Liszt manoeuvres a backstage gathering where Brahms, Schumann, Berlioz, Rossini and others accost him with brief points of characterization. This scene offers a shorthand, caricature-like and anachronistic summary of European culture c. 1840. (Brahms was born in 1833.) Economic and weighted dialogue, such as Daltrey-Liszt's line 'Piss off, Brahms!', illustrates a disregard for realism on linguistic, as well as historical, levels. Sentence constructions serve a threefold purpose: (1) communicating historically pertinent information with efficiency, serving as shorthand for entire conceptual debates relevant to the characters and story; (2) achieving the stated effect without hampering narrative momentum through any lengthier exposition; and (3) matching the dialogue with a colourful and shorthand approach to visual symbolism. 'Piss off, Brahms' succinctly communicates the antagonism lying on the surface of the War of the Romantics. It might also be all that the audiences of *Tommy* would need in order to understand the charismatic and artistic 'something-extra' of Liszt compared to other, 'boring', composers such as Brahms.

Russell defended this scene by explaining that 'Liszt was prone to take the mickey' out of his fellow composers in his transcriptions and operatic fantasies.[80] In this way, Russell encourages a reading position that interprets *Lisztomania* as being analogous to certain of Liszt's own musical work – a free fantasy, with an entertaining mixture of urtext fidelity and light-hearted fun.

Daltrey-Liszt is amused by the interactions between Rossini and Wagner, and is situated in an observer's position; like the expectations placed on the audience of *Lisztomania* itself, the protagonist is observant, accepting of the depicted scene and able to find it all funny. This generates audience sympathy for Liszt as a protagonist and establishes him as an observer of diegetic events, small or large, which are beyond his control. This issue will resurface during the later scenes at Wagner's castle.

At his first appearance, Wagner accosts Daltrey-Liszt before his performance, desperate to get his work before the public. He calls the virtuoso's piano a 'harlot', evoking the schematic association between pianism and illicit sex. The casting of Paul Nicholas as Wagner provides another link with *Tommy*, in which Nicholas played the sadistic Cousin Kevin. The association may be, to those aware of the connection, that Wagner and Daltrey-Liszt will have an antagonistic yet intimate relationship, rather like two warring siblings.

At the following concert, Daltrey-Liszt improvises around themes from Wagner's *Rienzi* alongside the popular favourite 'Chopsticks'. In his address to the audience, he makes repeated reference to the Bonn Beethoven monument,

---

[80] Russell, *Lisztomania* DVD commentary.

establishing the presence of a sense of legitimate artistic responsibility alongside his self-awareness as a 'show business' performer. The scene is roughly reminiscent of a concert given on 3 April 1841, during which the audience reputedly interrupted Liszt's accompaniment of a Beethoven violin sonata to demand that the famous virtuoso play a more popular, 'less-serious', opera fantasy.[81] As in the Hollywood 'Song' biopics, *Lisztomania* is constructed from such scraps of history, changed, combined and altered to suit Russell's free fantasy on Lisztian themes.

This first concert scene notably presents *Lisztomania*'s central comparison of Romantic and rock stardom. As Kenneth Hamilton reminds us, the real Liszt would be accustomed to 'a much more relaxed nineteenth-century concert etiquette – radically different from the extreme formality' of the typical twentieth-century recital.[82] The idea of an instrumental concert being a solemn, almost ritualistic, event developed during the later generation of Brahms and Bülow. The virtuoso in the early nineteenth century would preside over an event which was often more akin to a modern pop concert:

> [Liszt] chatted to friends . . . even addressed the entire public . . . . Recitals were structured by improvisation and social activity, all bound together by the magnetism of the performer.[83]

It has been suggested that the culture of twentieth-century pop music inherited the image of the 'post-concert mobbing of the star' from Liszt in particular.[84] Typifying the discourse that mythologizes Liszt's more enthusiastic audiences, James Deaville continues:

> Insensate members of the audience . . . dragged out of the hall, crazed expressions of delight emanating from the lips of the audience, women losing their heads, deliria of jubilation.[85]

The similarities to concerts given by Elvis, the Beatles or the Who from such descriptions are noteworthy.

Daltrey's performance, the screaming extras; Russell and his production team use every opportunity to make the recital seem modern and familiar to *Tommy* audiences. The scene is also decorated with visual allusions to the

---

[81] Loesser, *Men, Women and Pianos*, 378.
[82] Hamilton, *After the Golden Age*, 88.
[83] Hamilton, *After the Golden Age*, 89, 261.
[84] Kramer, *Musical Meaning*, 91.
[85] Deaville, 'The Making of a Myth', 187.

Figure 14 *Tommy* (1975)

popular twentieth-century pianist Liberace, including a candelabra, tinsel curtains and the colourful, even gaudy, costume worn by Daltrey-Liszt. (The thematic significance of the value judgement implicit in the term 'gaudy' will resurface at the later scenes at Wagner's castle.) Russell would also seem to take as a visual model for this scene the famous 1842 caricature by Theodor Hosemann, with its representation of Liszt's female admirers as a raucous mass surging onto the stage. The sexual subtext of such performances, derived from a visual focus on the body of the virtuoso, the fingers in particular, is acknowledged and satirized by that comic variation on the glove motif we last saw in *Song Without End*.

The adulation of the crowd at this first concert is dulled, however, when the virtuoso's improvisation on Wagner's *Rienzi* appears not to be to their taste. Shouted requests for 'Chopsticks' eventually persuade Daltrey-Liszt to diplomatically conjure sections from the popular tune, interspersed periodically with bits and pieces of *Rienzi*. He buys the audience's patience with 'Chopsticks', then slips-in some Wagner, and in the process balances mass-appeal entertainment and progressive 'high' art. This affinity for compromise and negotiation with regard to audience expectations, tastes and sensibilities, combined with an implied desire to alter and supposedly 'improve' these qualities, succinctly establishes the protagonist of *Lisztomania* as another example of the Romantic artist-priest figure.

Again, the content of such scenes can be traced to certain historical accounts. Schumann's description of Liszt's playing, in addition to employing demonic and magical schemas, displays striking similarities to this scene:

He first played along . . . then gave them a taste of something more substantial until, with his magic, he had ensnared each and every one.[86]

However, Daltrey-Liszt's motivation for playing Wagner's music at all at this point in the scene might be unclear. The repeated mention of Beethoven strengthens the connections and associated valuations which contrast Wagner with the idea of 'popular' music. Daltrey-Liszt appears to play *Rienzi* to his crowd because he recognizes a shared value between Beethoven and Wagner – it is his artistic 'duty' to share such music with the audience. He marches up and down the stage and makes the audience repeat why they are there: To celebrate who? 'Beethoven', the audience reply, like a schoolroom to their teacher. In addition to charisma, masterfulness and an acknowledgement of his 'duty' towards the notions of art and social progress which are mobilized throughout the narrative, this cinematic depiction evokes two further qualities not commonly found in cultural representations of Liszt: diplomacy and patience.

Nevertheless, the visual splendour and sexualized pleasures of fame conclude the scene. Daltrey-Liszt dances on the piano lid and is swept-up by a surge of female admirers, like an extension of the Hosemann caricature. During the performance, he has also sent Hans von Bülow – who represented in *Lisztomania* as a kind of assistant – to scout for potential backstage guests, or, by implication, sexual 'conquests', from among the women in the audience who have caught the virtuoso's eye. One is Princess Carolyne, whom Daltrey-Liszt will meet in a future scene. But Wagner, who has listened with frustration to the compromises the adored virtuoso has made by pandering to his public, leaves the concert without acknowledging the polite applause which Daltrey-Liszt has solicited on his behalf. This scene re-establishes that familiar problem which can be found throughout Russell's work: the search for a hero, and the corruption of art by fame against a backdrop of sexualized, 'full-blooded', Romantic culture.

The Chaplin and Carolyne sequences

A short domestic scene establishes the protagonist's unhappy home life, introducing his wife Marie, his daughter Cosima and her paternal voodoo doll. A nostalgic flashback sequence in an idyllic cottage then provides a contrast to

---

[86] Schumann, 'Franz Liszt: Concerts in Dresden and Leipzig', 157.

Liszt's unsatisfying touring and domestic lives. (This was where *Song Without End*, and even *Lola Montès*, began – 'the good years' of carefree isolation and travel.) Love-heart shapes pervade the set, props and costume designs, all presented through formal elements reminiscent of silent comedy. Speeded-up film and hyper-expressive gestures compliment Daltrey-Liszt's Charlie Chaplin costume and mannerisms. The diegetic soundtrack is muted, and a vocal version of 'Liebesträume' No. 3 completes an overall effect of sentimental nostalgia. Shots of an increasing number of towels, suggestive of more children, are followed by a shot of blank music paper; this montage suggests that – consistent with certain conventions regarding creativity – the establishment of domesticity and family life causes the aspiring composer to lose creative inspiration. The narrative technique of accomplishing character development through audio-visual montage is another inheritance from *Tommy*.

After the flashback, Daltrey-Liszt goes to Russia and meets Princess Carolyne. He finds her standing in a dark chamber decorated with phallic pillars and religious icons. The mise-en-scène evokes a sense of sexual threat which stands over and against Daltrey-Liszt's soon to be established childlike innocence. The theme of antagonistic gender power between Liszt and women is not one original to *Lisztomania* – in *Song Without End*, his wife Marie asked: 'Are women dragons to you?' But the representation of Carolyne in *Lisztomania* is particularly multifaceted. The scene's playful manipulation of gender power is articulated through aspects of dialogue, set design, performance, narrative and costume. Daltrey-Liszt compares Carolyne to 'Ivan the Terrible', and she, in turn, makes him change into a dress – a visual metaphor corresponding to the insecure virtuoso's fears about prostituting his talent. (Incidentally, costume plays an important role in expressing changeable character interiority throughout *Lisztomania*. Daltrey-Liszt changes from womanizer to warrior to priest, and costumes function as the primary means of performing these changes with shorthand visual symbolism.)

Daltrey-Liszt's dialogue concerns his mother and father, his desire to write great music and his fear of prostituting his talent. Such exposition serves to contextualize the scene's figurative and symbolic articulation of sexual power while providing the audience with more historical background. Anticipating any potential psychoanalytic interpretations of Daltrey-Liszt's psychology, Russell will present Carolyne literally 'possessing the phallus' at the end of the following 'Orpheus' sequence.

Russell's films often appear to use sexual imagery for symbolism and visual affect rather than any explicitly voyeuristic pleasure. *Tommy* and *Lisztomania* are joined by *Mahler* and *Altered States* in containing musical montage sequences during which a male protagonist is encased helplessly in a coffin- or womb-like space while in the presence of an overwhelming, deathly and sometimes literally 'castrating' female figure. More specifically, *Lisztomania*'s 'Orpheus', along with the 'Cosima' sequence in *Mahler* and *Tommy*'s 'Acid Queen', appear to be very similar in content, address and function. Their formal arrangements are suggestive of ballet, and emotionally charged music accompanies visual fantasies of gendered anxiety and interior character development. During these scenes, an immobilized male protagonist is confronted by a 'threatening' female eroticism. The submissive figures' suffering becomes an implied means of transcending self-imposed limitations. By 1975, Russell has constructed a series of film representations sustaining certain interpretive readings; one such reading can identify a pattern in these musical scenes which presents female Otherness as seductive and dangerous, and male subjectivity as threatened and passive. It is through the articulation of this more specific authorial preoccupation that the Romantic themes of the 'Orpheus' sequence can be more richly understood.

The initial dance choreography can be read to symbolize a transition between the indulgencies of Liszt's youth and the loftier ambitions of the Weimar years – a transition made possible by Carolyne's intervention. Daltrey-Liszt is handed a lyre by Carolyne, and he uses the instrument to tame a group of dancing women. He plays the lyre like a modern rock guitar, employing expressive gestures and impassioned performativity.

Figure 15 *Lisztomania* (1975)

However, the idea of sexual power soon comes to dominate the scene. As the unreality of the 'Orpheus' sequence builds in intensity, Daltrey-Liszt is driven by a torrential wind into a giant vagina. Dominating female sexuality blends with the environment to become a dreamlike space of desire and entrapment. This hyperobjectification of sexual elements continues with the 'centrepiece' of the 'Orpheus' sequence: the infamous giant phallus, maypole dance and guillotine finale. Straddling a giant prosthetic erection, Daltrey-Liszt is led by the group of dancing women to an executioner's block, and, screaming for mercy, the music star's most prized possession is placed in jeopardy.

Most obviously this scene functions as a brazenly allegorical and celebratory moment of cultural sacrilege, yet its gargantuan explicitness can potentially obscure its rich interpretive potential. The 'Orpheus' sequence not only perhaps functions as an outrageous, entertaining and affective song-and-dance number but also potentially evokes several themes which are relevant to a biographical understanding of Liszt's life after c1847. It metaphorically represents the end of his performing career, articulating his retirement from the stage as a renunciation of sexual libido, once again equating virtuosity with sexuality; according to this reading, 'Orpheus' also dramatizes a kind of Faustian bargain in which Daltrey-Liszt's sexual freedom and identity is sacrificed in exchange for an ability to create 'great' music. The choice to represent this aspect of Daltrey-Liszt's individual 'creativity' as a deeply personal, albeit comically enlarged, element of his own sexual self also perhaps implies a deeper narrative significance. As we will see, this nightmare-fantasy of 'castration' potentially articulates a relevant issue regarding that 'strange relationship' which will develop between Daltrey-Liszt and Wagner in the latter half of the film. Perhaps the virtuoso-star's phallus symbolizes a kind of uncontrollable Wagnerian egoistic obsession, one which needs to be removed, or exorcised, in order to save the Romantic genius from certain darker potentialities.

The scene ends with a humorous transition edit: the climactic guillotine 'castration' is interrupted by a shot of Daltrey-Liszt reacting in pain after a piano lid shuts on his thumb. Perhaps it is obvious to state that this joke works because a pianist's fingers can be read as a site of creative production, and any threat to a male pianist's hands or fingers is therefore a potential threat to sexual identity.

But Russell's playful merging of the two serves a wider narrative function. By transitioning the scenes in this way, the film justifies the unreality and 'obscenity' of the previous sequence by situating it as a fantasy – possibly a daydream or reverie of Daltrey-Liszt himself – not part of the 'reality' of the film world.

A precedent for this technique has already been established in the opening scenes. When the piano-coffin was about to be hit by the train, the scene cut to Daltrey-Liszt being jolted to awareness at the start of the concert sequence. Following that moment, we can never be certain about the film's exact position on narrative diegesis; *Lisztomania* appears to be slipping between reality and fantasy. The cinematic events presented during the 'Orpheus' sequence, therefore, only partly correspond to their cinematic referent: the classical Busby Berkeley mode of the musical set-piece, with its privileged treatment of spatiotemporal unity and diegetic consistency and causation.

According to Ken Hanke's interpretation, Russell's mixture of reality and fantasy in *Lisztomania* is more integrated than in *Mahler* or *Tommy*, and the three films function as a trilogy in which the techniques for demarcating fantasy sequences become increasingly hard for audiences to read.[87] Moments of contrast such as the train and thumb scenes underline this disparity. Beginning with a 'real' situation, when Carolyne and Daltrey-Liszt meet, after the music begins, 'Orpheus' may become a fantasy on the interior psychological and social themes of their relationship. The retaining of characters, costumes, sets and locations from one moment to the other creates an uncertainty around the unreal or hyperreal effect that intensifies throughout the sequence. The terminating cut to Daltrey-Liszt nursing his thumb, therefore, seems like a cut from dream to reality, although we may be shocked at not realizing that the change had been made in the first place.

Wagner's black magic and Liszt's white magic

The allegorical castration, or the relinquishing of male agency to female power, becomes narratively 'justified' in the following scenes as Carolyne is shown to largely take charge of the composer's life. She makes his decisions, criticizes his work and forms his opinions by making statements such as: 'Art is so much greater than politics'. As the film progresses, it is the theme expressed by this last statement with which Daltrey-Liszt, as a Romantic genius, must come to terms. Accordingly, the second half of the film becomes increasingly dominated by the presence of Wagner.

---

[87] Hanke, *Ken Russell's Films*, 296.

Once again, after a character development montage featuring Liszt's 'Funérailles', several historical events are conflated for easy narrative digestion: Wagner's involvement in the Dresden May Uprising of 1849, his subsequent sanctuary with Liszt in Weimar, his affair with Cosima beginning in 1863, and Liszt's entrance into the priesthood in 1865. Wagner, appearing energized by the carnage of the revolution, visits his fellow composer, who now works atop an ivory tower. During the 'Funérailles' montage, he is shown to display a more serious commitment to artistic 'duty' through physical elevation, isolation and an anguished reaction to the conflict in the streets below. Key themes are, once again, underlined by costume. Daltrey-Liszt's cassock presents a sombre contrast to his former garish costumes, externalizing his partial change of character. According to Russell, the decision to dress Wagner in a sailor's uniform was another cinematic allusion, this time to the revolutionary iconography of *Battleship Potemkin*.[88] This may evoke analogies with the 'betrayal' of revolutionary feeling by the Bolsheviks during the Russian revolutions or, more broadly, early twentieth-century European history in general. This connection will soon become highly significant.

Feeling like an impotent observer, Daltrey-Liszt laments: 'Guilt is mine, for watching while my countrymen are dying', giving the audience an opportunity to sympathize with Wagner's activism. But, if so, this sympathy is complicated during the subsequent 'Man of Steel' speech, when Wagner's 'evilness' is plainly established. Wagner drugs Daltrey-Liszt and bites him with vampire fangs. The blood Wagner drinks is equated with music, since he sucks his victim's neck while pressing piano keys as if composing – a metaphor for the real Wagner 'stealing' musical ideas from Liszt.[89]

Lisztomania's Wagner is a schematically 'evil' character, becoming the prophet of a nightmarish 'Man of Steel' associated with Nazism, and confining Wagner to a monstrous caricature of anti-Semitic and nationalistic beliefs. (Arguably, Wagnerian musical culture itself can be interpreted as a kind of 'cult of darkness'; its entire cultural aura both constructs and upholds a more emotional, irrational, illicit, 'alternative' experience compared to the typically reserved, refined and intellectual schemas of classical musical reception which were developing in

---

[88] Russell, *Lisztomania* DVD commentary.
[89] The accusation that Wagner 'stole' musical ideas, common since at least 1859, has been contradicted by modern research; Walker, *Franz Liszt: The Weimar Years*, 545. The current understanding of the Liszt/Wagner musical relationship can be summarized more kindly as a reciprocal and ongoing 'cross-fertilisation of ideas'.

more conservative areas of contemporary European music.) We have already seen how Liszt evokes holy, diabolical and warrior schemas, although other factors combine to maintain a broad distinction between Wagner's 'black magic' as possession, and Liszt's 'white magic' as purification. In the second half of *Lisztomania*, Wagner becomes the antagonist against whom Daltrey-Liszt must prove himself the hero.

Peasants turn and run when Daltrey-Liszt asks directions to Wagner's castle – a cinematic cliché associated with Frankenstein and Dracula stories. The door is answered by Bülow, his former associate, who warns that Wagner's music is an 'evil drug'. In this way, the film announces its participation in a negative discursive theme mentioned in Chapter 2: the association between Wagnerian music and narcotics. Wagner's influence has often been conceptualized as a 'spell' that needs to be exorcised. The Adornian sense of mass regressive listening implied by the term 'drug' establishes credibility for the following allegorical ritual scene, in which audiences who are seduced or possessed by Wagner's music are equated with those seduced or possessed by Adolf Hitler and Nazism.

Daltrey-Liszt discovers that Wagner's castle has become the scene for a cult-like gathering of candle-bearing children dressed in superhero costumes; according to Russell, they represent a comic-book version of the Hitler Youth.[90] Nietzsche's concept of the 'Superman' is humorously taken literally, with the Wagnerian followers dressed in costumes which evoke the popular DC Comics character.

The children witness a ritualistic enactment of the opening of Wagner's *Das Rheingold* from *Der Ring des Nibelungen* (prem. 1876), when Albrecht steals the gold from the Rhinemaidens. The scene broadly functions as synecdoche for the mythic content and reception of the *Ring*. The Rhinemaidens sit around a phallic rock monolith capped with gold; the Albrecht character is a brutish man with a Star of David on his forehead, and the strong implication is that Wagner's *Ring* is related to anti-Semitic Nazi propaganda. The ritual is decorated with many elements of Nazi iconography:

> light and darkness, fire and smoke; a theatrical setting within seemingly monumental architecture; a solemn, almost religious worshiping of . . . [charismatic figures and symbols] military appearance and marching order.[91]

---

[90] Russell, *Lisztomania* DVD commentary.
[91] Reinhold Brinkmann, 'The Distorted Sublime: Music and National Socialist Ideology – A Sketch', in *Music and Ideology*, ed. Mark Carroll, 113–33 (London and New York: Routledge, 2016), 230; for a similar selection of Nazi cultural tropes see also Susan Sontag, 'Fascinating Fascism', 1975, in *Movies and Methods, Volume 1*, ed. Bill Nichols, 31–43 (Berkeley: University of California Press, 1976), passim.

Like a cruel parody of the climactic 'Listening to You' sequence from *Tommy*, the Jewish 'beast' Albrecht rapes the Rhinemaidens, climbs the monolith and raises the plundered gold above his head. Daltrey-Liszt watches helplessly through a castle window, and the child spectators run in confusion. Wagner now appears on the scene and declares himself harbinger of a 'new messiah' who will 'drive the beast from our land'; the context strongly implies that 'beast' means 'Jew'.

The initial placement of worshipping females around the giant monolith recalls the maypole penis of 'Orpheus'. The similarity with the earlier scene is available to those who recognize a connection between the monoliths (the maypole penis and the *Rheingold*-altar) and the circular audience of worshipping females. For Daltrey-Liszt, the giant phallus was a distinctly human element, sensual and interactive, something to be celebrated, but containing a certain element of selfish vulnerability that must be sacrificed for the greater good. But, for Wagner, the phallic symbol is inhuman, being made of stone and gold. According to this reading, the barbaric ritual is possibly what Daltrey-Liszt was saved from by Carolyne's castrating intervention. When Wagner professes the glory of Germany in song, his gaudy costume and long hair have also been appropriated from Daltrey-Liszt. The Nazi prophet is now potentially an evil reflection of the virtuoso's own self.

The Hitler Youth give Nazi salutes and march out of the hall behind Cosima to the sound of 'Ride of the Valkyries' – music whose cultural chain of signification, perhaps more than any other, is expressive of a kind of military aggression, where dignity, masculinism and glory disguise sadism and madness.

Figure 16 *Lisztomania* (1975)

Interestingly, this moment in *Lisztomania* re-enacts the primal scene of these very associations.

Daltrey-Liszt finally enters and confronts Wagner, who reveals to his visitor his sublime creation: the 'Man of Iron', Thor, played by Rick Wakeman, an unintentionally ludicrous combination of Nietzsche's 'Superman' concept, Siegfried from the *Ring*, and Frankenstein's monster. The grace Wagner sees in his creation is absurdly undercut by Thor's burping and sniggering, and Liszt comments that Wagner's mythic progeny looks like a character out of a comic book. With winged Teutonic helmet and warrior's dress reminiscent of a Norse or Arthurian figure, Thor parodies Wagner's ideal Aryan German hero, one rendered ludicrous by crude behaviour and silver body paint.

A typical formulation of the cultural associations embodied within, and parodied by, *Lisztomania*'s Thor was identified by Nietzsche in *The Case of Wagner*:

> 'Whence comes all the misfortune in the world?' Wagner asked himself . . . from customs, laws, moralities, institutions, from everything on which the old world, the old society rests. 'How can one rid the world of misfortune? . . . the old society?' Only by declaring war . . . *That is what Siegfried does* . . . he overthrows everything.[92]

This is a particularly pure expression of that Romantic drive for cultural transcendence, although one which clearly evokes its darker potential – the *Führer* as the doppelganger of the artist-priest.

In retrospect, such passages from Nietzsche's works often appear to prophesize the rise of Hitler. The association between the doomed mission of the Third Reich and the *Gotterdammerung* idea has been extensively explored in cultural products, *Lisztomania* being no exception. Throughout *The Case of Wagner* Nietzsche presents his former idol as some seductive sickness, the sign of 'some great creeping danger' which is overtaking Germany.[93] In the words 'overthrows everything', Nietzsche presents a revealing explanation of how Wagner's formulation of nationalistic heroism turns to self-destruction. The optimism inherent in the Siegfried myth was seen to be at odds with the pessimistic philosophy of Arthur Schopenhauer. According to Nietzsche's explanation, the fatal stumbling block this presented to Wagner meant that the philosophical dynamic of the *Ring* was to be recalibrated; the final objective was now no longer glorious victory, but rather

---

[92] Nietzsche, 'The Case of Wagner', 163.
[93] Nietzsche, 'The Case of Wagner', 181.

Figure 17 *Lisztomania* (1975)

glorious failure.[94] Like the martyrdom of the artist-priest, or any other agent of cultural transcendence, the threat of failure to accomplish the ideal in defiance of historical conditions can be reconciled as a kind of sublime victory in itself. From this perspective, it is easy to see how the supposedly self-destructive ideologies of Nazism can be traced back to, and explained by, Romantic philosophy and aesthetics. All this is mockingly evoked in *Lisztomania,* when Thor, instead of rekindling the fires of the German spirit, as Wagner intends, merely urinates into the fireplace. From the sublime to the ridiculous.

Having mobilized these schematic associations, *Lisztomania* then positions Daltrey-Liszt as an anti-Nazi hero figure who battles Wagner with his music, evoking, again, the warrior type introduced in Chapter 3. He mounts a nearby piano and plays *Totentanz*; the instrument begins to revolve, conjuring a cleansing wind that tosses Wagner about. Flamethrowers mounted under the piano create jets of fire, giving a visual and physical presence to Daltrey-Liszt's white magic – the music's purifying 'energy'.

Wagner is fatally wounded, but Bülow and Cosima incapacitate Daltrey-Liszt and ensure that Wagner can continue his work from beyond the grave. The defeated hero is locked up in a cell, once again helplessly witnessing the horrors of Wagner's plan through a window.

At a funeral scene styled after a Nuremberg rally, Wagner rises from his grave as a hybrid of Hitler and Frankenstein's monster. In a continued betrayal of musical values, Liszt's own Piano Concerto motif announces the monster's arrival in a Jewish street, where a cartoonish climactic allegory of the persecution

---

[94] Nietzsche, 'The Case of Wagner', 164.

of the Jews under the Third Reich plays out. This Frankenstein motif recalls *Tommy*'s 'Sally Simpson' sequence, when a young fan compromised her dream of being with Tommy and instead married a 'rock musician from California', a young boy who, like Wagner, is represented as an imitation of Boris Karloff's iconic monster from *Frankenstein* (1931). For Russell, the symbolic potential of Frankenstein's monster would seem to be decidedly negative, associated with compromise, immaturity, corruption and impurity – the other to Tommy and Daltrey-Liszt as figures of heroic identification.

Liszt, Wagner and Hitler

For commentator Luigi Verdi, the recurrence of the Concerto theme in *Lisztomania*'s soundtrack simply constructs a musical 'fate' motif to bind the film.[95] However, this reading ignores something that deepens the film's thematic content, and even works against motif reading. Wagner has here appropriated the musical syntax of Liszt's story to underscore his own work. We might go further and say that, in a very real sense, Wagner has stolen the film itself. *Lisztomania* has been appropriated by Wagner, whose influence is insidious and irresistible, but inevitably doomed. Ultimately, a genocidal Nazi monster is an unusual idea to bring to the foreground in a film about the life of Franz Liszt, and it is worth exploring the perspective Russell might have been employing when he chose to foreground this issue.

Figure 18 *Lisztomania* (1975)

[95] Verdi, *Franz Liszt e la sua Musica nel Cinema*, 63.

The three-way relationship between Liszt, Wagner and Nazism foregrounded in the last sections of *Lisztomania* can be approached in several ways.[96] Here we can explore two sets of relationships: (1) between Liszt and Wagner, and the latter's association with Nazism; and (2) between Liszt and Hitler, and their shared schemas of virtuosity.

i. Liszt and Wagner: The sins of the son

There is no shortage of connections to be found between Romanticism and Nazism.[97] The fascination with antiquated heroism, artistic idealism, nationalism and death are only a few of the Romantic tropes appropriated by the cultural iconographies of the Third Reich. Wagner and his music in particular have become highly problematic in relation to Nazism – an association which has the potential to contaminate Liszt. One significant concept is that of 'guilt by association': that Liszt shares guilt by being, in some sense, responsible for what Wagner came to potentially represent.

First, Liszt can be understood quite explicitly as Wagner's father figure. Despite becoming Wagner's father-in-law in 1870, when Wagner married his daughter Cosima, Liszt also provided financial and creative support to him throughout his artistic career. 'The sins of the son' is an inverted cultural paradigm that has curious consistency regarding Liszt and Wagner.,

Second, Wagner, Hitler and to a certain extent, Liszt can be seen to have similar views regarding the artist's duties, privileges and social function, and the language needed to express them. According to Hitler, 'art is a sublime mission that carries an obligation to fanaticism'.[98] As we have seen, Liszt was receptive to the Saint-Simonian view of the artist-priest as a mediator between God (ideals) and man (audiences) – the artist-priest 'must march' and his faithful public 'must follow'.[99] An ideologically-bound situation such as this is easily related to fascism.

Any 'guilt' to be found on the part of Wagner or Liszt concerning the Third Reich inevitably functions as part of *Sonderweg* theory, or the controversial

---

[96] Accusations that Liszt himself was an anti-Semite were clarified by Walker, who exposes this complex situation in Liszt scholarship; Walker, *Franz Liszt: The Final Years*, 405–11. Several of Liszt's closest acquaintances, including Wagner, Cosima, Bülow and Carolyne were anti-Semites, and Walker states that Liszt was a 'classic example of guilt by association'; Walker, *Franz Liszt: The Weimar Years*, 358.

[97] See for example Victor Klemperer, *The Language of the Third Reich*, 1957 (London: Bloomsbury, 2018), 2, 53, 60, 82, 133–51, 160; Sontag, 'Fascinating Fascism', 41; Rancière, *The Emancipated Spectator*, 64.

[98] Cited in Brinkmann, 'The Distorted Sublime', 215.

[99] Philippe Buchez cited in Locke, *Music, Musicians and the Saint-Simonians*, 44.

historicist conjecture that the Third Reich was an inevitable event – a crisis in a successive chain of historical developments innate to the unique national destiny of the German people. Despite the disputable validity of such ideas, they are central to the cultural discourse surrounding the relationship between Romanticism and fascism. As we will see, in addition to the retrospective reading of Nietzsche, historian William Shirer, director Han-Jűrgen Syberberg, novelist Thomas Mann and even Ken Russell himself, would all seem to share Hitler's assertion that 'to understand Nazism one must first know Wagner'.[100]

It is relatively common knowledge that 'Hitler worshiped Wagner', and that the content and iconography of Wagner's music dramas constituted a profound inspiration for Nazism.[101] Wagner's anti-Semitism has often led to him being termed a 'proto-Nazi', a branding that still remains on his cultural image.[102] Critics have suggested that it was not the specifics of Wagner's operas that were employed within so-called Nazi ideology, but rather the 'general "feel" of the *Ring*, with its atmosphere of destiny, blood-kinship and hysteria'.[103] Nazi culture appropriated piecemeal the *Ring*'s mythic panorama, its 'gods and heroes ... its blood feuds ... its sense of destiny'.[104] Wagner's philosophical writings themselves had comparatively little influence in this sense compared to the overriding dramaturgical determination that characters in his music dramas are either 'saved or damned', like Aryans and Jews.[105] The hypothetical 'causal' relationship between Wagner's *Gotterdammerung* and Hitler's self-destructive determination in the final weeks of the war is one that has often been explored and propagated by many prominent critical commentaries and cultural products.[106]

One such example is Syberberg's *Hitler: A Film from Germany* (1977), which explores the legacy of Hitler on Germany and the modern world, while being 'haunted', as Susan Sontag put it, by the figure of Wagner and his music.[107] The soundtrack includes work by Wagner, Liszt, Beethoven and Mahler, all

---

[100] Cited in William L. Shirer, *The Rise and Fall of the Third Reich: A History of Nazi Germany*, 1959 (Trowbridge: Redwood Press, 1973), 102.
[101] Shirer, *The Rise and Fall of the Third Reich*, 101.
[102] For a critical perspective on the discursive function of Wagner as a proto-Nazi figure, see Alain Badiou, *Five Lessons on Wagner* (London and New York: Verso, 2010), 11.
[103] Michael Tanner, 'The Total Work of Art', in *The Wagner Companion*, ed. Peter Burbidge and Richard Sutton, 140–224 (London and Boston: Faber and Faber, 1979), 145; Klemperer, *The Language of the Third Reich*, 53.
[104] Shirer, *The Rise and Fall of the Third Reich*, 101–2.
[105] Tanner, 'The Total Wok of Art', 156.
[106] Tanner, 'The Total Work of Art', 174.
[107] Susan Sontag, 'Syberberg's Hitler', 1979, in *Under the Sign of Saturn*, 137–65 (London: Penguin, 2009), 140.

conscripted into an audio-visual dialogue of guilt and victimhood over the cultural memory of the Third Reich.

In the context of *Lisztomania*, Syberberg's *Hitler* is notable for sharing a similar allegorical moment. Both films contain scenes in which Hitler rises from Wagner's grave. The titular *Hitler*, standing before a tombstone engraved with 'RW', states that *Rienzi* was 'the source of everything' (the Third Reich). Yet perhaps the most suggestive Lisztian motif in *Hitler* is introduced during the opening scenes. One character announces that the film is about, among other metaphors, 'Mephisto playing to a full house which is burning'. This motif is recalled later when Mephisto is replaced with 'Hitler', similarly 'playing to a full house' (Germany in the 1930s) 'which is burning' (the path to destruction in 1945). The association between 'Mephisto playing to a full house' and Liszt should, at this point, require no further explanation.

It can be argued that, despite how wildly divergent the truth may be from such associations, Liszt and Hitler, as represented in Syberberg's film, might appear to share similar views on nationalism, hero-worship and the possibility of realizing utopian aesthetic/political ideals. The more complex formulation of the Romantic virtuoso explored below is also articulated in *Hitler*, directly relating aspects of virtuoso performance with artistic idealism, artistic expressions of national 'spirit' and political charisma.

ii. Liszt and Hitler: Political virtuosity

> *The fascist ideal is to transform sexual energy into a 'spiritual' force, for the benefit of the community.*
>
> —Susan Sontag[108]

> *Not for nothing does the rule of the established conductor remind one of that of the totalitarian Führer ... he is the real modern type of the virtuoso.*
>
> —Theodor Adorno[109]

According to Leo Braudy, Hitler's understanding of himself as an 'artist' was cultivated from 'a collection of attitudes ... rooted in the nineteenth century artist's conflicts with the society around him'.[110] Hitler established his public oratory in relation to such changing attitudes towards cultural transcendence

---

[108] Sontag, 'Fascinating Fascism', 41.
[109] Adorno, 'On the Fetish Character in Music', 45.
[110] Braudy, *The Frenzy of Renown*, 565.

which were enacted and embodied, to different extents, by both Wagner and Liszt. Nietzsche himself saw Wagner and Liszt as equally responsible for what he called 'the emergence of the actor in music', which he equated with a loss of authenticity and the rise of an ideologically charged atmosphere of 'delivery', 'presentation' and 'virtuosity', which was also something to be feared.[111] The public personality of the artist was now as significant to society as those of political and military leaders. As we will see, there are notable schematic elements of the artistic celebrity in Hitler's own cultural image which are easier to associate with Liszt than with Wagner.

We can discover a similar suspicion of virtuosity, in comparable terms, by interpreting certain elements in the fiction of Thomas Mann. Lawrence Kramer cites a passage from Mann's *Buddenbrooks* (1901), in which one character's 'dead-on Liszt impersonation' is represented as empty, 'enthralling but destructive', like the ideal that fatally draws Aschenbach to Tadzio in *Death in Venice* (1912).[112] A similar tone pervades Mann's 'The Infant Prodigy' (1903), in which the performance trope of the Lisztian sublime gaze is represented as a pandering and vacuous social distraction; the titular character casts 'his eyes up prettily to the ceiling so that at least they [his audience] might have something to look at'.[113] One concern apparent throughout several of Mann's works, including 'Mario and the Magician' (1929), suggests that the enthralment and social disorientation associated with the charismatic performer deserves suspicion and mistrust, for they create social conditions which incubate fascism.[114]

Another potential link between Liszt and Hitler might be their respective eliciting of a certain mass enthusiasm among the people of Berlin. Liszt's most famous touring episode took place in Berlin in 1842, when Heinrich Heine coined the term 'Lisztomania' as a means of describing, in quasi-medical terms, a rampant, contagious 'sickness', an unhealthy level of unprecedented public enthusiasm, caused by Liszt's presence in the city.[115] For Heine, 'Lisztomania' was an 'unhealthy state of mind and spirit', a kind of madness suffered by groups of people infatuated with a charismatic figure.[116] What is more, 'Lisztomania'

---

[111] Nietzsche, 'The Case of Wagner', 178–9.
[112] Kramer, *Musical Meaning*, 80.
[113] Thomas Mann, 'The Infant Prodigy', 1903, in *Collected Stories*, 229–37 (London: Everyman's Library, 2001), 234; Thomas Mann, 'Death in Venice', 1911, in *Collected Stories*, 417–90 (London: Everyman's Library, 2001), passim.
[114] Thomas Mann, 'Mario and the Magician', 1929, in *Collected Stories*, 603–50 (London: Everyman's Library, 2001), passim.
[115] Gooley, *The Virtuoso Liszt*, 201–6.
[116] Gooley, *The Virtuoso Liszt*, 204.

was a concept supposedly relating to a specific capacity for hysteria in the German people themselves. That the behaviour of Liszt's audiences in Berlin in 1842 bordered on the 'hysterical', and that this interpretation by Heine has been preserved in the cultural history of the city as a famous episode in the German capital's identity, make this effect readily comparable with the rise of National Socialism in the 1930s.[117] Hitler becomes, by virtue of this reading, simply the latest object of 'Lisztomania'. Exactly how far Ken Russell was aware of this reading potential when he made his own *Lisztomania* is open to conjecture.

The various points of evidence presented here demonstrate that Hitler *can* be related to Liszt. It is a connection with potential to be recognized, and a cinematic example can demonstrate this by returning us to the concept of the 'sublime gaze' explored earlier.

In *Taking Sides* (2001), an American denazification officer investigates Wilhelm Furtwängler, openly comparing the famous conductor's charismatic leadership of an orchestra with the authoritarian allure of the former Führer. The key location of this shared power is identified as a specific masterful look in their eyes. The film implies (perhaps recalling the allegorical significance of the famous fictional hypnotist and criminal mastermind Dr Mabuse) that such looks are moments of personal 'virtuosity' which mythologize charismatic vision and validate blind obedience to such persons that display it. It is here, in the social function of the sublime gaze, that the connecting link between Romantic virtuosity and Hitler becomes most problematic. It is the combination of a display of exceptional personal power, fuelled by the sublime gaze that simultaneously validates and mystifies the motivation for such displays, combined with the eliciting of extreme emotion from their audience, which defines the Romantic virtuoso, and schematically binds Liszt, Wagner and Hitler together. If Wagner gave Hitler an array of mythic symbols and ideas, Liszt gave him a template for appealing to the emotions of his public through a display of the personal embodiment of power. Once again, this demonstrates the malleability and complexity of the Romantic genius figure as a cultural type, and the various functions that can be imposed upon it.

Accounting for such burdens, both *Lisztomania* and *Hitler* can be read to contain an element of forgiveness for Wagner as a kind of victim of history. The rhetoric of both films positions Wagner's artistic idealism as being betrayed by Hitler's perverse, destructive and self-destructive fanaticism. *Lisztomania*

---

[117] Gooley, *The Virtuoso Liszt*, 201–62.

conflates these ideas into a single, postmodern concoction of a character, as the Wagner-Hitler hybrid creature steps forth from the grave and begins destroying all in its path. Associations with egoism, crudeness and violence blend between the cultural images of both historical figures, splitting and displacing responsibility and victimhood in a similar fashion to the common cultural confusion between Frankenstein and Frankenstein's monster. Liszt, in the ways we have identified, becomes a third party in this process, taking part of Wagner's burden through a combination of paternal guilt and martyrdom.

The final scenes

Back in the castle cell, the imprisoned Daltrey-Liszt, helplessly witnessing the carnage outside, is killed by a final needle blow into Cosima's paternal voodoo doll. The scene transitions to a heavenly chamber group consisting of Daltrey-Liszt and the women he knew in life. Distanced from the destruction below, they play 'Liebesträume' No. 3 on harp and strings. The mood of the scene is plastic and insincere, yet poignant and consolatory. The pseudo-idyllic scene is undercut by elements of performance, narrative incongruity and the presence of the phallic pillars from Carolyne's rooms which serve to prop-up their platform. Budgetary constraints may account for the disguised presence of the phallic columns in this scene, yet they potentially undermine the scene's sincerity. But as Joseph Lanza noted, Russell allows his characters a chance at redemption even as he 'lampoons' them, and so returns Daltrey-Liszt to Earth for one last blow for good, and to put Wagner out of his misery.[118]

The hero returns to the fight in an organ-rocket hybrid. 'His women' are encased in the pipes, metaphorically 'preserved' in his music. The rocket dive-bombs the rampaging Hitler monster among urban ruins, and then flies away into space. This ending seems to symbolize Liszt's victory in the long term – a final fantasy on the ultimate survival of Liszt's cultural and historical value beyond the confines of Wagner's own, where the latter has been corrupted by an association with the Third Reich. Joseph Gomez subscribes to this reading (although he does not explain it in as much detail), ultimately concluding that *Lisztomania* presents 'one of Russell's most optimistic endings'.[119]

[118] Lanza, *Phallic Frenzy*, 191.
[119] Gomez, *Ken Russell*, 203.

Throughout *Lisztomania*, Wagner has been stealing things from Daltrey-Liszt, wielding them as instruments of destruction, leaving his victim lagging behind and impotently observing events over which he has little control. This final scene appears to break the pattern, leaving Wagner defeated and Daltrey-Liszt rocketing-off into space. Yet both hero and villain are equally removed from a functional relationship with the future, and both their endings might be interpreted as kinds of self-destruction. In this way, the finale of *Lisztomania* can be significantly compared with that of *Tommy*. Where the earlier film presented a cyclical return to origins when Tommy climbs the mountain – a moment liable to be read as narratively satisfying, primal and sincere, like the sublime yet potentially ideologically mystifying ending of a Romantic symphony – Daltrey-Liszt's flight into space is a potentially insufficient conclusion with delusional and escapist elements. Despite the fact that Daltrey-Liszt destroyed Wagner, and despite the fact that Tommy 'became aware' and climbed 'the mountain', in both cases, their final victories are perhaps somewhat hollow; an overall failure regarding the wider concerns of the narrative is overcome, and a sense of victory validated, by emotional displacement through musical affect.

So the impression of final 'victory' in *Lisztomania* is potentially less convincing than for its predecessor. Several factors might contribute to this reading. First, the song 'Peace at Last' may seem over-determined and negated when evaluated according to its lyrical content (when compared to the apotheosis offered by the less-definite lyrics of Tommy's 'Listening to You', already familiar to the Who fans), a content which explicitly underlines the narrative return to equilibrium and a 'happy ending'. In addition, the song's placement in the broader narrative of the Wagner situation, as we have seen, may suggest an ironic lack of authenticity. And finally, from a feminist perspective, the encasement and idealization of Daltrey-Liszt's women in his music may augment this final sense of uneasiness.

Yet despite such points, it is possible to find conflicting evidence in the soundtrack. During 'Peace at Last', Daltrey-Liszt turns-the-tables on Wagner's musical kleptomania, claiming Wagner's own themes from *Die Walkure* as a part of his final victory song. The ironic tone of the closing scene is perhaps tempered, therefore, by at least one tangible point of achievement for Daltrey-Liszt. For Wagner, the idea of appropriation is schematically identified with theft – literally vampirism – but for Liszt, according to the specific discourses mobilized alongside his own cultural image, as we explored in Chapter 3, appropriation is privilege, mastery and even duty.

Conclusion

In 1844, Liszt's wife Marie d'Agoult wrote a semiautobiographical novel called *Nélida*, a fictionalization of her troubled relationship with the famous virtuoso. This book has long been disdained by historians as a mere piece of scandal-fuelling self-serving historical revisionism.[120] Marie's famous book appears in *Lisztomania*, although its title is changed to 'Lisztomania' itself. This change may be read as a knowing reference to the possible reception by those audiences who approach the film with 'sufficient' historical knowledge – those who might conclude that Russell's film is similarly inaccurate, self-serving or obscene. Russell may be pre-empting such criticisms by displaying not only an awareness on the part of the film regarding obscure historical details but also a perspective that such 'scandalous', 'self-serving' retellings of Liszt's life have notable historical precedent and are, in fact, a significant part of Lisztian discourse. In his Liszt biography, Alan Walker justifies a lengthy analysis of *Nélida* on the grounds that, despite, in his opinion, lacking any historical or 'literary merit', d'Agoult's 'strange' book still made a significant contribution to what we have called Liszt's cultural image.[121] *Lisztomania* functions as a more recent successor to the kind of scandalous situation already occupied by *Nélida* in the discourse of music history.

As a part of this discourse, *Lisztomania* balances two kinds of accuracy. First, awareness of, and fidelity to, contemporary formations of historical facts and details judged correct by those able to recognize them; and second, the construction of a 'believable' sense of realism by cinematic means, determined by temporally transient, localized and individual standards. From a hypothetical purist perspective, the first demand is served by details such as the *Nélida* reference and Liszt's betrayal by Bülow (the real Hans von Bülow, who was Liszt's son-in-law following his marriage to Cosima, became a devout follower of Wagner, although the latter eventually had an affair with his wife); the second is 'undermined' by the fantasy sequences, songs, anachronistic cultural and historical allusions, and other anti-realist elements. Liszt's cultural image is drawn down one way to the level of microscopic biographical fact and up another to extra-factual metaphor and allegory. In retrospect, *Lisztomania* might appear to answer Susan Bernstein's observation: 'the greater the accuracy

---

[120] Walker, *Franz Liszt: The Virtuoso Years*, 396; Hilmes, *Franz Liszt*, 96.
[121] Walker, *Franz Liszt: The Virtuoso Years*, 395–401.

of the research, the greater, finally, the deviance from what is meant by "Liszt".[122] As with his other Romantic biopics, Russell appears to forge an entertaining pathway between the two distinct concerns – correspondence with the facts, and a more aesthetic sense of truth.

In his study of Russell's work, Joseph Gomez suggested that *Lisztomania* represented an experiment in bridging the gap between 'the popular and the classical' spheres of cultural value – a union which Russell believed was achieved by Shostakovich.[123] Typically for Russell, such authorial statements are balanced by admissions that *Lisztomania* was 'not an intellectual film'.[124] This sense of division is, as we have seen, central the film's contexts of production and reception. More specifically, a tension between Romantic historical subject and contemporary pop/rock-inflected rhetorical and visual style makes *Lisztomania* part of a wider trend for British cinema in 1975. *Lisztomania*'s fantastical historical revisionism was complemented by films such as *Monty Python and the Holy Grail* (1975), *Barry Lyndon* (1975), *The Man Who Would Be King* (1975) and *Royal Flash* (1975). Neil Sinyard describes such films as 'period romps', historical adventures which evidence a general mid-1970s retreat from contemporaneousness in the British film industry.[125]

In a broader sense, *Lisztomania* emerged at a turning point for the British film and music industries. According to Susan Harper and Justin Smith, the late 1970s witnessed a shift from experimental and fragmentary productions which appealed to niche audiences to a reassertion of the mainstream; this was due, in part, to increasing box office interest in Hollywood productions and a rising interest in themes exploring national identity.[126] Corresponding with this mid-decade shift, John Atkins states that '1975 marked a low ebb within the music industry . . . [a feeling of] lethargy, dearth of new ideas, and lack of imagination'.[127] Metaphorically, this general shift among musicians, filmmakers, audiences and critics may have come between the releases of *Tommy* and *Lisztomania*. *Tommy* can be considered the summation of a project, begun in the late 1960s, to reinvigorate rock, brought to the screen by an auteur on the tail-end of a period of critical and popular success, and successfully marketed to a pre-sold audience. On the other hand, *Lisztomania* might be considered an

---

[122] Bernstein, *Virtuosity of the Nineteenth Century*, 109.
[123] Gomez, *Ken Russell*, 200.
[124] Russell, *Lisztomania* DVD commentary.
[125] Sinyard, *Richard Lester*, 112.
[126] Harper and Smith, *British Film Culture in the 1970s*, 225, 232.
[127] Atkins, *The Who on Record*, 219.

attempt to cash-in on the former's success with an amalgam of disparate and conflicting elements, sold to a divided audience, and made by a film industry on the verge of economic and aesthetic transition.

Russell admitted that the film's 'relentless' symbolism was possibly 'above the heads of the Daltrey fans', a conclusion upheld by several commentators including Gomez and Phillips.[128] Where the positive judgements of appropriateness concerning the style of *Tommy* were bolstered by numerous textual and contextual elements, *Lisztomania*'s similar excesses did not wear as well with audiences, and, to some, their employment in the composer biopic format was simply 'oil and water'.[129] John Walker may not be alone in considering *Lisztomania* to be Russell's 'worst film', and contemporary public and critical reaction was not supportive.[130] Ross Care's useful summation of the film as one trapped in a 'limbo' between two audiences serves to explain the film's commercial failure.[131] *Tommy* audiences could not relate to the Liszt element; Lisztian audiences could not relate to the rock element. Perhaps both were alienated further by the explicit sexual content, cartoonish intertextual references and Nazi themes.

1975 was also the year in which Susan Sontag wrote her famous essay 'Fascinating Fascism', expressing a similar concern that pop culture was related to Nazism via their attendant Romanticism:

> The appeal of Nazi art may have been that it was simple, figurative, emotional; not intellectual; a relief from the demanding complexities of modern art. To a more sophisticated public now . . . precisely these qualities invite people to look at Nazi art with knowing and sniggering detachment, as a form of Pop art.[132]

By 1975, the Who's relationship with 'Pop art', as we have seen, was widely disseminated. Perhaps *Lisztomania*'s comparative position on Romantic iconography and Nazism can be read alongside Sontag's contemporary criticism of the whitewashing of Leni Riefenstahl, whose later projects, Sontag reports with significant emphasis, included 'photographing Mick Jagger'.[133]

In *Tommy* and *Lisztomania*, Russell presents both rock-star and fascistic others to Friedrich's fascinating figures who face the sublime. In this sense, the

---

[128] Russell, 'Interviews with John C. Tibbetts', 308; Gomez, *Ken Russell*, 200; Phillips, *Ken Russell*, 167–71.
[129] Gomez, *Ken Russell*, 199; Phillips, *Ken Russell*, 176.
[130] Walker, *The Once and Future Film*, 101.
[131] See Phillips, *Ken Russell*, 176.
[132] Sontag, 'Fascinating Fascism', 41–2.
[133] Sontag, 'Fascinating Fascism', 43.

film can also be read as an extension of the thematic concerns extrapolated from *Tommy* as given earlier, further exploring the social impact of an artist's work and the Romantic tension between artists as closeted/active social agents. The hybrid Daltrey-Liszt figure in *Lisztomania* undergoes a rebalancing of his personal connection with, and responsibility to, the world around him. He evolves from a typical rock-star figure through a period of familial relations, sexual experiences and renunciations, to a proactive engagement with a concrete antagonist who is represented as an evil reflection of his own self. The problematic cultural condition of Wagnerian Romanticism, represented as passionate, irrational and individualist to fault, becomes the defining issue of this diegetic world, one that is equal-parts artistic, political, spiritual and military. In Russell's own words: 'I took Liszt to task for pandering to his audiences . . . selling out . . . Art is always corrupted by show business'.[134] By representing Daltrey-Liszt dive-bombing the evil Wagner, Russell allowed his hero to transcend these failings, although in a way that (authorial intention aside, perhaps) self-critically refuses the sublime Romantic affirmation granted to Tommy when he climbed 'the mountain', saw 'the millions' and got 'the story'. The extension of the Who's Tommy into Franz Liszt comprises one of Russell's most interesting realizations of his search for a hero.

---

[134] Russell, 'Interviews with John C. Tibbetts', 308.

Conclusion

Summary of research interests, objectives and methods

Throughout this book, we have explored various connections between Romanticism and film by taking Franz Liszt as a guiding motif – that quintessential Romantic composer whose aesthetic philosophy centred upon a combination of sound and visual impression, artistic re-creation and social development. The relevance of Romanticism to film can be traced in many ways, but by focusing on the concept of audio-visual explanation, we have highlighted several interconnected strands of interest which, although far from exhausting this subject, each present their own methodological problems. An attempt to do justice to one results in new problems for the next:

(a) An interest in how and why the historical discourse of film and film music has engaged, or not engaged, with Romantic composers such as Wagner and Liszt. Extending a general conception of a multimedia trend in Romantic art, Jacques Rancière's concept of the aesthetic regime aids in developing an understanding of audio-visual aesthetics in nineteenth-century art and in tracing an alternative pre-history of cinema extending beyond reductive Wagnerian explanations. But beyond the specificities of these two prominent composers' works and cultural images, this connection highlights a second overarching interest:

(b) An interest in Romanticism as a concept, and in Liszt's role as a cultural embodiment of many significant ideas, tropes and types typically subsumed under that concept. Despite its continuing significance for Western culture and philosophy, Romanticism remains an under-theorized area of academic study. Perhaps there is a certain value in considering both 'modernism' and 'postmodernism' to be merely variations on a properly Romantic condition of Western subjectivity, which began around the time of the German Idealists and continues largely unimpeded through Nietzsche, Heidegger and the poststructuralists, and enjoys a special relationship with aesthetics and ideology. This fascinating argument, yet to be extensively developed, could even be extended to figures such as Rancière's contemporary Alain Badiou, and his work on the relations between film, subjectivity and politics.[1] Whatever the outcome, Film Studies and other academic disciplines may still have much to learn from a deeper theoretical engagement with Romanticism. The status of Romanticism as a discursive object, organized, in part, by filmic representations, also neatly relates to our third interest, which combines Liszt, as a representative Romantic figure, with film as a significant and ongoing cultural means by which Romanticism itself is explained and understood:

(c) An interest in how Liszt and his music have been represented in films. The various concepts which fall under this heading, including Romanticism, classical music, composers, the virtuoso and genius types, are among the most fascinating, multifaceted and under-examined elements in the field of cultural representation. Although concepts such as gender, race and nationality have been, and continue to be, extensively explored by academic studies of ideological representation, those we encounter when we examine Liszt's cultural image are not without considerable political significance. Although a selection of case studies provided opportunities for in-depth textual and contextual analysis of audio-visual explanations, exposing many of these ideological concerns, there was a perceived inadequacy in the existing or known methodological tools of representation studies to accommodate the kinds of analysis that this interest was deemed to require. This lack opened a fourth line of enquiry, one that relates back to, and also problematizes, all of the interests listed earlier:

(d) An interest in the various epistemological matters mobilized by Romanticism in the field of social explanation, as well as its relationship with the study of cultural representations. In order to ensure the theoretical soundness of the aforementioned analysis, it was judged necessary to construct an overarching methodological framework which was able to combine insights about perception, cognition and explanation provided by post-Kantian philosophy and cognitive psychology. Schema theory, rooted in Kantian transcendental idealism, and corresponding with certain concepts from twentieth-century philosophy, helped to frame an idea of risky archaeological analysis – a useful name for a commonly practised methodology which highlights the conjectural and criticizable character of statements made in the analysis of discourse and representation. Certain works by Kant, Gombrich, Popper, Bartlett and Peckham

---

[1] Alain Badiou, *Being and Event*, 1988 (London: Bloomsbury, 2017). See also Alain Badiou, '"Thinking the Emergence of the Event"', 1998, in *Cinema* (Cambridge: Polity Press, 2013), 105–28, 113–28; and Alain Badiou, 'On Cinema as a Democratic Emblem', 2005, in *Cinema* (Cambridge: Polity Press, 2013), 233–41.

aided in the construction of a more specific theoretical framework – consisting of the interaction between cultural image and schematic types – which aided in the textual analysis of filmic representations, and enabling a more rigorous exploration of interests a, b and c.

This book has far from exhausted these four interests, being merely concerned with a space where they all meet. To summarize this space, we can do no better than to repeat the statement with which we began: where Romantic music can encourage intuitive visual understanding of historical musical experience, and films can encourage intuitive musical understanding of visual historical experience, film music discourse, in turn, can encourage intuitive historical understanding of musical visual experience. With Franz Liszt providing our guiding thread, and inspired by the associated Romantic concepts his cultural image brings with him, we have examined the logic(s) of this overarching intuitive explanatory principle. In other words, we have examined a significant aspect of the audio-visual ways that things come to make sense, and the forces that guide that process.

Some methodological implications of studying Romanticism and film

When we turn our attention to the relationship between Romanticism and film in the broadest sense, some unexpected and fundamental methodological questions take centre stage. We have already seen that although the comparison between Wagnerian opera and cinema, the film theory of Jacques Rancière, and the relationship between sound and vision more generally each present promising potential bridges between cinema and the art and culture of nineteenth-century European Romanticism, a fuller understanding of what 'Romanticism' can mean raises far more significant issues. This occurs when we look back to the roots of Romanticism in German Idealist philosophy and consider what such developments meant to the history of aesthetics, politics and epistemology, and begin to consider the relationships between them.

The most pressing question concerns the problems involved in making any kind of analytical statement, or in making any kind of interpretation of available facts that retains an explanatory authority. What lurks underneath any attempt at academic analysis is the problematic conclusions which follow from the Kantian distinction between appearances and things in themselves:

the constructivist omnipresence of interpretive activity (Heidegger, Gadamer, Popper and Ricœur) and the prevalence, variety and authoritarian impetus of all explanations as interpersonal impositions upon making sense (Foucault, Bourdieu, Peckham and Rancière).

This is where the concept of risky archaeological analysis was deemed to be helpful. In order to talk about the concerns of each chapter – the content of Romanticism itself (Chapter 1); the role of Romantic aesthetics and of specific artists as functional constructs, in the discourse of film and film music (Chapter 2); how Liszt's cultural image, and the idea of Romanticism itself, has been represented in films according to schematic types (Chapter 3); and how individual film texts construct their representations according to broad and multifaceted production and reception contexts (Chapters 4 and 5) – we needed to establish an overall understanding of how we can best go about forming worthwhile and authoritative 'knowledge' about these topics in any respect at all.

To accomplish the task of enlightening the relationship between Romanticism and film, the central chapters took different kinds of archaeological risks in the process of studying different kinds of audio-visual explanations. Chapter 1 outlined a general introduction to Romanticism as a discursive construct, highlighting various points which helped to draw into focus the concept of audio-visual explanation as a Romantic phenomenon. By remaining alert to the pragmatic and functional imperatives behind the development and use of such explanations, Chapter 2 hypothesized an alternative path in the pre-history of film music by displacing Wagner's *Gesamtkunstwerk* in favour of Liszt's symphonic poems as an alternative Romantic prototype of the classical Hollywood film score. Chapter 3 suggested that the various audio-visual explanations provided by filmic texts might be illuminated by considering the relationships between the hypothetical notions of a cultural image and schematic types. By way of illustration, several Romantic schematic types associated with Liszt were identified and, along with various filmic examples, examined for their potential to contribute to the formation, maintenance and alternation of Liszt's cultural image. Chapters 4 and 5 then presented expansive and in-depth case studies of two Liszt biopics which were selected for their 'significance' to Liszt's cultural image; a combination of textual and contextual analysis sought to maintain the open-ended and irreducible three-dimensionality of the texts through a selection of a diverse range of appropriate interpretive frameworks. These various risks have been taken with the understanding that they will be, and have been, tested by the reader.

As Karl Popper helpfully suggests, the best we can hope for in the humanities as well as in the empirical sciences is not 'truth', but simply new and interesting conjectures which are 'better' to the extent that they take risks against falsification. By undertaking this multifaceted examination of the relationship between Liszt and the cinema, we have hopefully succeeded in presenting new and interesting interpretive statements about selected ideas, concepts and texts that bear upon the relationship between Romanticism and film. This relationship is one that, despite the efforts of Jacques Rancière, is still theoretically underdeveloped, and is certain to yield much that is new and interesting to future studies. To bring this book to a close, we can briefly outline some potential directions for future research.

Romanticism and film: Future research

Although Kant's writings form one of the most important foundations of Romanticism, he himself was no Romantic. Those who followed him, attempting to reconcile the subjective and objective that he had helped to split apart, have often been stigmatized with authoritarian legacies (Schelling, Hegel and Heidegger). Those later philosophers who, wounded by the spectacle of the Third Reich, rejected this temptation (Popper and the Frankfurt School, in particular) have apparently undervalued a nominally 'Romantic' pathway that lies between the two. It is here that post-Kantian aesthetics meets critical theory, critical rationalism and philosophical hermeneutics: in the Romantic concern with individual subjective agency and in its striving for cultural transcendence against 'the ways that things are', while acknowledging the very real risks involved in the absolute affirmation of the New in place of dogmatic tradition. In this book, we have explored one particular element of this immense programme which bears upon film specifically.

The approaches provided by Morse Peckham and Jacques Rancière suggest that the idea of Romanticism lies in a combination of cultural transcendence, as a critical imperative against traditions that determine appropriate action by explanation, and the erasure of the notion of appropriate form in aesthetics which makes the innovation of alternative audio-visual representations possible. In combining these ideas, we recognize what becomes significant to Film Studies: film's ambiguous potential to either select, order and direct audience responses, or leave its explicanda open to a freer kind of interpretative activity.

There is a genuine potential for filmic representations to free themselves from the sublime and mythologized explanatory authority of the filmmaker in the face of an honest and free profilmic reality. But hanging over this freedom, as with all formations of Romanticism, is the spectre of that schematic construct's darker legacies. Although all films claim to 'show' the world to us, real or fictional, with an immediate and intuitive audio-visual clarity, they do, in fact, explain it to us. Even what seems most free and unauthored in film is always selected, framed to include and exclude, becoming a raw interpersonal imposition upon making sense in a most 'innocent' and effective disguise. Perhaps explanations are nowhere less critically questioned than when we are in a position to say we are simply seeing and hearing what is immediately given to experience.

Yet there is a positive side to this idea as well. Intuitive audio-visual explanations have no imminence of meaning and, as both Rancière and Peckham recognize, this openness retains a precarious political dimension. Put simply, to understand the conflicts of freedom and power inherent to Romanticism means to understand the idea of intuitive audio-visual explanation. In other words, it is to understand film itself.

In the influential psychological study *Remembering* (1932), one of the foundational texts of cognitive psychology, F. C. Bartlett suggests that thinking itself 'is biologically subsequent to the image-forming process'.[2] As we saw in Chapter 3, this appeared to place Kantian schematic cognitive processes on a firmer scientific foundation, and gave legitimacy to what was called 'top-down' cognition. Ulrich Neisser's cyclical model then connected both ends of the process by suggesting that concepts such as 'top-down' or 'bottom-up' were not mutually exclusive but were, in fact, cooperative.

When Film Studies developed an attitude of 'piecemeal-theorizing' in the 1980s and the 1990s, this 'image-function' credited cognitive psychology with the potential to become a fruitful replacement for the problematic language-based Lacanian and structuralist theories which had dominated film theory in previous decades. It is interesting to note that the scholar who might be called the figurehead of this appropriation, David Bordwell, drew some of his theoretical framework from Gombrich, who, in turn, was appropriating from Popper. Looking back from this point over the ideas we have explored throughout this book, we can see the further connecting links between Popper, philosophical hermeneutics, schema theory, intuitive audio-visual explanation

[2] Bartlett, *Remembering*, 225.

and Romanticism as a development of German Idealism. We find that we have arrived back at Kant.

At this stage, we advance, as Kant himself did, from the question of epistemology to that of ethics, by asking: What are the fuller political implications of Romantic audio-visual explanation?

Throughout *Remembering* Bartlett treats schemas and images as concepts with similar although not identical functions:

> The image, to be communicated, has itself to be expressed in words, and . . . this can often be done only in a most halting and inadequate manner. Words . . . can indicate the qualitative and relational features of a situation in their general aspect . . . . This is, in fact, what gives to language its intimate relation to thought processes . . . . Used in this way, they succeed just where we have seen that images tend most conspicuously to break down: they can name the general as well as describe the particular.[3]

Having distinguished between these two levels of thinking, Bartlett then articulates the transformational potential of schematic cognition in a surprising way:

> The image method remains the method of brilliant discovery, whereby realms organised by interests usually kept apart are brought together; the thought-word method remains the way of rationalisation and inference, whereby this *connecting of the hitherto unconnected is made clear and possible for all* . . . lying in wait for both these processes is the common fate that may overtake all human effort: they may become mere habit . . . then they may take facility of images and variety of words to be satisfying things in themselves.[4]

These ideas mark out another potential path through the four interests listed earlier, between Romanticism, film, explanation and audio-visual aesthetics. This path also emphasizes the ideological implications of aesthetic representation as social explanation. As we mentioned at the end of Chapter 1, Rancière's film theory creates an opportunity to bring together a number of topics under a new kind of Romantic hermeneutics: German Idealist philosophy, the Romantic art of the aesthetic regime (including Liszt's poetic ideas), the politically transformative power of images in the modern world, and cinema. What is at stake here is what Rancière calls 'the distribution of the sensible', or the collapse

---

[3] Bartlett, *Remembering*, 225.
[4] Bartlett, *Remembering*, 226.

of the political and the aesthetic into a single determination of what is deemed visible or invisible, understandable and not understandable, and representable and unrepresentable.[5] It is a process whose historical and conceptual relationship with Romanticism is central to Rancière's film theory.

Here we can see how Bartlett's formulation of schematic cognition can become a supporting pillar for this 'method of brilliant discovery', one that must certainly have an aesthetic and a political dimension in bringing together the 'hitherto unconnected', making what is newly seen, heard and intuitively understood 'clear and possible for all'. With this point, we are also not far from the familiar concept of *Bildung*, and, as we saw in Chapter 1, perhaps also not far from something more problematic. Also lying at the heart of Romanticism is Peckham's concept of cultural transcendence, naming the same constant overturning of 'habit' that Bartlett mentions, or the constant striving to overturn the dominant distribution of the sensible: the mythologized and unquestioned way that things are as they are, sound as they sound, look as they look or mean what they mean. Rancière's work suggests that film and its power to connect the unconnected in new and unexpected ways ('aesthetic education') must be further addressed for its significant role in organizing the cultural imagination of alternative ways of living in the world, or alternative ways of explaining things.

Both Bartlett and Rancière agree that where words remain silent, images can speak; but to what extent does the Romantic poetics of film really make new ways of explaining things 'clear and possible for all'? The task of explaining how images speak, sometimes with the assistance of music, will remain a task for future words; words chosen by participants in discourse; words judged to be appropriate to the task; and words subjected to the best tests possible. This is the best chance we have of ensuring that our words do justice to our subjects. If we judge them to have failed, then we must, as the Romantics we still are, overthrow them and search for better explanations.

---

[5] Rancière, *The Politics of Aesthetics*, 7.

Appendix A

Music and language

The purpose of this appendix is to provide a thorough statement of the theoretical understanding of the relationship between music and language which is employed in this book. By adopting a historical approach, we will explain the more specific development of the relationship between Western classical music and the question concerning whether such music is capable of expressing a 'meaning' in a sense comparable to language.

Before the twentieth century

As Michael Long put it, it is not easy to discuss what music does without resorting to the idea of language.[1] The possibility that music possesses representational properties has attracted centuries of criticism. Philosophers like Diderot admitted that musical sounds 'do say *something*', but that the exact communicative possibilities of this potential 'language' were, like film, explored, contested and disputed over for many decades in both theory and practice.[2] In this sense, composers such as Franz Liszt, like Sergei Eisenstein, put theory into practice by creating works that explored the potential results of the communicative premise.

The specific belief that music could communicate somehow was, like Romanticism, a product of the late eighteenth century. At that time, certain composers sought methods of raising the status of music, contributing to a discourse that emphasized music's correspondence with the extra-musical, either (1) through mimesis – the direct imitation of certain sounds – or (2) by adopting a philosophical attitude that ascribed value to music's specific ability to exceed

---

[1] Long, *Beautiful Monsters*, 2.
[2] Cited in Mark Evan Bonds, *Wordless Rhetoric: Musical Form and the Metaphor of the Oration* (Cambridge: Harvard University Press, 1991), 63.

the supposed communicative limitations of language. These ideas, central to the tradition of programme music, excited heated debates over musical value which came to maturity in the Romantic period.

For some critics and philosophers, music was indeed 'a language, a much better one, the language *par excellence*';[3] while others declared that music gave pleasure, or should only give pleasure, on a purely abstract, non-representational level. A key turning point came with Haydn's *Seven Last Words* (1787), in which music appeared to assume communicative properties while making a serious claim for cultural legitimacy through a programmatic subject. Haydn used the 'low' method of 'characteristic music' to represent a 'high' subject which demanded the serious attention of its listeners.

As the decades progressed, musicologists refined the music/language problem. Music became increasingly viewed in rhetorical terms, or in terms analogous to thought processes, rather than in comparison with a strictly grammatical model of language. Charles Beauquier stated that 'it is a childish pursuit to wish to establish an other than metaphorical connection between music and language';[4] music does not 'create' emotions, 'nor express them by characterising them, but simply places the body in a certain situation the consequence of which is a general disposition of the soul'.[5] Friedrich Schlegel, in turn, commented:

> Is the theme [of an instrumental work] not developed, confirmed, varied and contrasted in the same manner as the object of meditation in a philosophical sequence of ideas?[6]

The Romantic prioritizing of music's indefiniteness – its ability to exceed language as a means of emotional, instinctual communication – meant that the concept of a musical language was partly replaced by a new species of 'music-idea' concepts. Liszt's formulation of the 'poetic idea', explored in Chapter 2, is a roundly developed example. As Mark Evan Bonds explains, it was during the mid-nineteenth century that the sequential concept of 'idea- and-elaboration', as identified by Schlegel, became entangled in notions of representational narrative, fostering a post-Beethoven interpretive reception culture that included the practice of mapping subjective plots onto non-programmatic works.[7] Beethoven,

---

[3] Charles Beauqier, '[from] *Philosophie de la musique*', 1865, in *Music in European Thought: 1851–1912*, ed. Bojan Bujić, 182–96 (Cambridge: Cambridge University Press, 1988), 188.
[4] Beauquier, '[from] *Philosophie de la musique*', 189–90.
[5] Beauquier, '[from] *Philosophie de la musique*', 184.
[6] Cited in Bonds, *Wordless Rhetoric*, 166.
[7] Bonds, *Wordless Rhetoric*, 68, 164, 187–90.

Mendelssohn and Berlioz, as well as Liszt, contributed various works that served as the raw material fuelling these debates.

The twentieth century

In his own writings on music, Theodor Adorno concluded that 'every musical phenomenon [potentially] points to something beyond itself by reminding us of something, contrasting itself with something or arousing our expectations'.[8] In this sense:

> Music *resembles a language* in the sense that it is a temporal sequence of articulated sounds. . . . They say something . . . . But what has been said cannot be detached from the music. . . . Music creates no semiotic system.[9]

Adorno's conclusions echo earlier comments, with a pertinent emphasis on the *resemblance* of music to language. Throughout the twentieth century, musicologists have supported such conclusions, assembling various explanations for music's potential expressive or communicative capacity.

Some argued that common aural phenomena have widely applicable non-aural associations existing across many cultural divides; they are based on 'synchronous relationships' – a sound's physical affect, its impact on the body – in addition to a possible significance to universal 'natural' experiences such as being in the womb.[10] Supposedly, the associations between, for example, the rise and fall of sound pitch and the rise and fall of an object in space, or the loudness and softness of a sound and the closeness or distance of an object in space, 'are all readily understood, and retain their associative potency to some degree however much abstracted'.[11] Many 'natural' sound-image relationships are therefore framed as the products of an association between kinds of physical movement and the aural consequences of that movement.

The bodily basis of these impressions has often given precedent to the 'gestural' quality of what they might appear to express. As early as 1865,

---

[8] Theodor Adorno, 'Music and Language: A Fragment', 1956, in *Quasi Una Fantasia: Essays on Modern Music*, 1–6 (London and New York: Verso, 2011), 1.
[9] Adorno, 'Music and Language', 6.
[10] David Kershaw, 'Music and Image on Film and Video: An Absolute Alternative', in *Companion to Contemporary Musical Thought, Volume 1*, ed. John Paynter, Tim Howell, Richard Orton and Peter Seymour, 466–99 (London and New York: Routledge, 1992), 470–7.
[11] Kershaw, 'Music and Image on Film and Video', 470–1.

Charles Beauquier recognized such relationships and sought to legitimize only those musical 'gestures' that had a perceived analogy in physical movements.[12] Beauquier makes the useful connection with anthropomorphism, which in this instance involves an individual listener seeking to impose existing schemas into abstract concepts and patterns in music; in Beauquier's words: 'man lends to everything he does not know his own form or his intimate nature, his ideas and emotions', and music is no exception to this process.[13] The resulting notion of 'musical-gestural wholes' continues to be studied and recognized across national and social boundaries, forming the semblance of a gestural, yet decidedly non-specific, 'language'.[14]

In the twentieth century, pursuing the opportunity afforded by a gestural attitude to musical communication, commentators such as Susanne Langer, Jean-Jacques Nattiez, Claude Lévi-Strauss and Morse Peckham variously explored music's potential to resemble emotional states, 'narrativize' in the abstract, and even become 'meaning' itself.[15] In a famous passage, Langer suggested that music was comprised of 'unconsummated symbols', being a means for 'expressiveness not expression' or 'significant form' removed from any stable anchoring in specific emotions.[16] Nattiez, in turn, concluded that music alone cannot 'link a subject with a predicate';[17] but with the integration of a specific non-musical element to form the illusion of a single multimedia utterance, changes things considerably. The idea that music is itself 'meaning' was upheld by Lévi-Strauss, who suggested that language, music and myth can all be seen to operate in relation to three levels of signification: phoneme, word and sentence.[18] Music, containing no equivalent for word, prioritizes the sound element, where myth prioritizes the meaning element, but only both are found in language. In this model, musical 'meaning' leaps over the grounding signifier from phoneme (note) to sentence (meaning) directly. Purely musical meaning is always only suggested, never grounded. But this grounding can be achieved by interaction with a non-musical element. As Nattiez noted, the listener is a

---

[12] Beauquier, '[from] *Philosophie de la musique*', 193.
[13] Beauquier, '[from] *Philosophie de la musique*', 194.
[14] See Patel, *Music, Language and the Brain*, 312–14.
[15] Susanne K. Langer, *Philosophy in a New Key: A Study in the Symbolism of Reason, Rite, and Art*, 1942 (Cambridge: Harvard University Press, 1957), 221; Jean-Jacques Nattiez, 'Can One Speak of Narrativity in Music?', *Journal of the Royal Musical Association* 115, no. 2 (1990): 240–57; Claude Lévi-Strauss, *Myth and Meaning*, 1978 (London and New York: Routledge, 2001), 46–7; Peckham, *The Romantic Virtuoso*, 160–1; Peckham, *Explanation and Power*, 127.
[16] Langer, *Philosophy in a New Key*, 240–1.
[17] Nattiez, 'Can One Speak of Narrativity in Music?', 244.
[18] Lévi-Strauss, *Myth and Meaning*, 46–7.

'gap-filler'. The narrative ... is not in the music, but in the plot imagined and constructed by the listeners from functional objects'.[19] These 'functional objects' can include a gesture, programme, topic or image, creating what Carolyn Abbate calls 'disruptive effects' that signpost a narrative reception of audible events.[20]

The Wagnerian leitmotif usefully illustrates Nattiez's notion of 'functional objects', operating, as it does, in relation to associative memory by establishing and recontextualizing extra-musical meanings. As Matthew Bribitzer-Stull notes, the leitmotif provides 'the possibility of accumulative association in which music, like language, becomes capable of modifiers – elements that qualify the meaning of an associative theme'.[21] Effectually, the leitmotif accrues a specific referential 'charge' through the initial establishment of an association with a visual or conceptual element. This charge is then potentially present in both elements, musical and non-musical, when each is encountered individually within the confines of the text or performance after the bonding relationship has been established. Functioning as an element of emotional memory, as Bribitzer-Stull describes the process, 'the dramatic portrayal of emotions' and the 'presentation of musical theme not only coincide but mesh semantically'.[22]

On a more fundamental level, the 1988 psychological studies by Marshall and Cohen suggested that 'music and image have a tendency to fuse together in meaning ... if element "a" of a film occurs during music "x", the two have a tendency to unite in perception and memory as "ax"'.[23] This effect, the basis of how film functions as an audio-visual experience, is also known as 'synchresis', a term popularized by Michel Chion.

Approaching the more specific issue of film music, Royal S. Brown noted that such binding of musical and visual elements accomplished the 'consummation' required for musical meaning, as suggested by Langer's idea of music as 'unconsummated symbol'.[24] Music alone can *appear* to signify in various ways, with varying degrees of rigour, but audio-visual combination allows for a far greater potential for meaning creation. As Noël Carroll put it, 'the movie elements', like almost all extra-musical elements, 'focus more precisely' the meaning of the music.[25] David Kershaw notes that 'so few are the equivalents in sound and visual

---

[19] Nattiez, 'Can One Speak of Narrativity in Music?', 249.
[20] Carolyn Abbate, *Unsung Voices: Opera and Musical Narrative in the Nineteenth Century* (Princeton: Princeton University Press, 1996), 29.
[21] Bribitzer-Stull, *Understanding the Leitmotif*, 4, 8.
[22] Bribitzer-Stull, *Understanding the Leitmotif*, 13.
[23] Summarized in Bribitzer-Stull, *Understanding the Leitmotif*, 276.
[24] Brown, *Overtones and Undertones*, 30.
[25] Carroll, 'Notes on Movie Music', 142.

image', based on these relations summarized earlier, 'that it becomes incumbent on the composer/film-maker to . . . make connections', to recognize and expand on this culturally determined vocabulary of musical gestures (subsuming topics, registers and mimesis).[26] Musical gestures were adopted by film music practices due, as we have seen in Chapter 2, to complex and multifaceted historical developments with industrial, aesthetic, economic and cultural dimensions. The establishment, conventionalization and development of a kind of sound-image vocabulary was undertaken, and continues to be expanded, by film music in relation to the history outlined earlier.

In summary, music *resembles* a language. Through a gestural capacity, it enacts a kind of 'pointing', although often in no particular direction. It can refer, however, by reference to something outside itself; it needs something else to determine the direction in which it points. This can be achieved by at least two means: (1) mimesis, auditory imitation dependent upon culturally and historically specific schemas of recognition, and (2) extra-musical reference, typically an audio-visual or audio-conceptual binding to functional objects as a result of synchresis.

---

[26] Kershaw, 'Music and Image on Film and Video', 477.

Appendix B

Wagnerian terminology and film

The purpose of this appendix is to explain in greater detail the relationship between film and three important Wagnerian aesthetic concepts: the leitmotif, 'unending melody' and the *Gesamtkunstwerk*. Each concept will be given a brief history concerning its origin and employment in discourses of film and film music.

Leitmotif

There has never been a unified theory or definition of the Wagnerian 'leitmotif'. A. W. Ambros coined the term in 1860, but it only gained widespread acceptance following the writings of Hans von Wolzogen in 1876.[1] Broadly speaking, a leitmotif is a recurring theme in a musical work that develops properties of associational memory. What might appear significant – particularly considering that this fact is apparently absent from film music history – is the acknowledgement that the term was originally used by Ambros to clarify an understanding of Wagner's operas as '"symphonic poems with a libretto" and Liszt's symphonic poems, in turn, as "Wagnerian operas without words"'.[2] Although subsequent developments in music criticism, not least by Wagner himself, have substantially altered the meaning of the term, it is revealing to note that the root of the concept be understood as a shared responsibility between Wagner and Liszt for the development of associative themes in the 1850s. As Ambros stated, 'Wagner's operas and Liszt's symphonic poems are essentially cut from the same cloth.'[3]

---

[1] Bribitzer-Stull, *Understanding the Leitmotif*, 22; Thomas Grey, '. . .wie ein rother Faden: On the Origins of "Leitmotif" as Critical Construct and Musical Practice', in *Music Theory in the Age of Romanticism*, ed. Ian Bent, 187–210 (Cambridge: Cambridge University Press, 1996), 189.
[2] Bribitzer-Stull, *Understanding the Leitmotif*, 22.
[3] Cited in Grey, '. . .wie ein rother Faden', 195.

Wagner's operas and Liszt's symphonic poems, despite the fact that they do not entirely dispense with traditional musical forms, seemingly consist of a mosaic or textured pattern that creates associations as it progresses in time. For Thomas Grey, this effect is analogous with a 'multicursal' maze, where the listener has freedom to take numerous paths through the text, perhaps encountering dead-ends, but a 'correct' path is marked by a musical thread, a thematic recurrence or leitmotif.[4]

It is well known that composers such as Gluck, Weber and Meyerbeer used various proto-leitmotif techniques to similar effect. Such 'reminiscence motifs', as Wagner used in his earlier works, are limited to the accentuation of key moments in the plot, and are defined by their perfunctory, non-developmental nature and lack of determination regarding the overall musical structure of the work.[5] They function as musical 'labels', rather than bearers of associative memory sensitive to narrative and emotional processes of the wider drama; the latter was a process Wagner began to explore following *Lohengrin* (1850).[6]

According to Carl Dahlhaus, in Wagner's later music dramas, leitmotifs 'form a dense web over the whole of the orchestral setting, determining its structure at any given moment'.[7] Joseph Kerman similarly uses the term 'web' to describe the resulting musical construction: 'Short suggestive motifs are the necessary material from which Wagner constructs his dense symphonic web'.[8] The use of the term 'web' endows the leitmotif with a certain organic quality – a sense that such musical-dramatic works are 'naturally' unified by this process, or are the result of a careful and balanced construction by a wise guiding hand. In large-scale musical works, the recurring motif creates a sense of unity within highly episodic or formally fragmented pieces. But this practice was not Wagner's legacy alone, nor was it confined to the leitmotif, but rather it was conspicuous in much of the orchestral, chamber and piano music of the nineteenth century.

What is important, in this context, was that the term 'leitmotif' was an attractive addition to the vocabulary of film music for its capacity to present a sense of unity across fragmentation, creating a musical structure of characterization and narrative, and capitalizing on the fluidity of temporal perspectives in a narrative context. The appropriation of the Wagnerian term

---

[4] Grey, '...wie ein rother Faden', 208–9.
[5] Dahlhaus, *Nineteenth Century Music*, 96; Bribitzer-Stull, *Understanding the Leitmotif*, 21.
[6] Dahlhaus, *Nineteenth Century Music*, 199.
[7] Dahlhaus, *Nineteenth Century Music*, 196–7.
[8] Joseph Kerman, *Opera as Drama*, 1956, 2nd edn (London and Boston: Faber and Faber, 1989), 172.

allows its subject to appropriate the 'high' value associations with organic, unified 'web' operatic construction while, in most cases, not straying far beyond the simpler reminiscence motif function that was practised before Wagner. Studies such as James Buhler's analysis of Wagnerian aesthetics in *Star Wars* (1977) demonstrate that what appears fundamental to 'Wagnerian' film scores, often actually stands at some distance from the 'true' Wagnerian method, however it might be defined.[9]

The sense of dissatisfaction with the leitmotif argument can also be felt when Claudia Gorbman asks if a particular theme from Steiner's score for *All About Eve* (1950), which is broadly associated with the titular character, denotes Eve, the impact Eve's presence makes on other characters, or is generally expressive of the film *All About Eve* itself.[10] For Gorbman, such thematic moments in classical Hollywood film music contradict definitions of Wagnerian leitmotif practice.

By linking an image to a specific musical idea in a way that appeared to unify the film, leitmotifs supposedly assign a more equal significance to disparate elements of the film experience; the result is a gesture towards the *Gesamtkunstwerk* existing as an evaluative principle. To return to a phrase used by Scott Paulin, the leitmotif remains a 'talisman', of sorts, for film discourse.

Unending melody

As we saw in Chapter 2, within a filmic context, 'unending melody' can be simply taken to mean the continuous musical accompaniment of a projected film to disguise the sounds of early cinema machinery. Obviously, this is another adaptational appropriation of a vague Wagnerian term.

According to Dahlhaus, in the context in which Wagner used the term, 'melody' was not employed for its traditional meaning, but rather meant 'expression'.[11] Instead of forming a musical narrative structure that followed what Eduard Hanslick called 'rhythm in the large' – the overall architecture of form, determined by balancing the content of sections, a kind of musical cause-and-effect – the leitmotif becomes a principal constitutive element of music

---

[9] James Buhler, '*Star Wars*, Music, and Myth', in *Music and Cinema*, ed. James Buhler, Caryl Flinn and David Neumeyer, 33–57 (Hanover: Wesleyan University Press, 2000), 42.
[10] Gorbman, *Unheard Melodies*, 29.
[11] Dahlhaus, *Nineteenth Century Music*, 199–200.

drama. Musical events are no longer subordinate to the demands of architectural balance, or 'rhythm in the large'.

Consequently, for Wagner, the requirement for 'unending melody' was the same as stating: 'the very notion of being consciously ... trivial – even in a single bar – was appalling to me'.[12] Every moment of the music becomes 'melodic', since it has an ever-refreshed relationship with the dramatic content now that it is divorced from 'rhythm in the large'. By the elimination of cadences, ornament, transitional or formulaic material – which for Wagner was the same as 'unmusical' material – 'endless melody' expands to include silences and percussive effects, since there is supposedly 'meaning' behind even that which is not strictly 'melodic'.[13]

This is an example of how Wagner's influence on film was felt through indirect currents of feelings attached to a radically affective reception culture rather than through set musical theories and concepts. Fanfares and ornamentation, or precisely what Wagnerian 'unending melody' sought to avoid, are common in many classical Hollywood scores.

Gesamtkunstwerk

The *Gesamtkunstwerk*, or 'total work of art', was an aesthetic ideal pursued by Wagner in his creation of operas such as *Tristan und Isolde* and the *Ring* cycle. These works present an amalgamation of music, drama, acting, stagecraft and poetry, all brought together in an environment that appears to foreshadow many of the conditions inherent to early and institutionalized notions of cinema.

In film and film music discourses, Wagner's *Gesamtkunstwerk* was recontextualized as a kind of precursor to cinema. It was easy to assume that cinema picked up where Wagner left off. André Bazin's essay 'The Myth of Total Cinema' (1946) quite explicitly mythologized a cosmetic similarity between film and the typically Romantic desire to integrate all the different forms of media into a unified and ultimate synthesis, and treated its emergence as an inevitable result of an evolution in art itself.[14] Yet, unlike Bazin, Wagner was not interested

---

[12] Richard Wagner, *Wagner on Music and Drama*, ed. Albert Goldman and Evert Sprinchorn (New York: Da Capo Press, 1964), 247.

[13] Understood in this way, 'unending melody' is something that even Brahms practised; Dahlhaus, *Between Romanticism and Modernism*, 55–7.

[14] André Bazin, 'The Myth of Total Cinema', 1946, in *What is Cinema? Volume 1*, 17–22 (Berkeley: University of California Press, 2005), 20–1.

in the potential for his operas to perfect the faithful reproduction of reality, but he rather attempted to reinvigorate a concept of a 'people's art', derived from the ideal of Greek drama, ideas associated with German Idealist and Romantic aesthetics, and the legacy of mid-century European nationalism.[15]

Studies in film and media have found much convincing evidence for the legitimacy of the *Gesamtkunstwerk* concept in relation to twentieth-century multimedia technologies, including the immersive, multisensory capacities of cinema, the internet and virtual reality. Several significant historical developments in the history of early cinema can be read as theoretical extensions of the *Gesamtkunstwerk*, including both the 1916 manifesto for Italian Futurist cinema and the Bauhaus School of abstract theatre, which integrated a Romantic desire for media unification with a modernist technological aesthetic. Crucially, as we have seen in Chapter 2, the Bayreuth *Festspielhaus* itself appeared to be a kind of 'proto-cinema auditorium', not only anticipating the darkened viewing space, invisible orchestra and front-facing seats of the modern cinema experience but also commercializing its suspicious ideological claim to present paying audiences with experiences of a vital cultural, and sometimes sublimely humanitarian, importance. Whatever the programme might contain, the *Gesamtkunstwerk*, for both Wagner and Hollywood cinema, sells itself as a show not to be missed.

---

[15] See Taruskin, *Music in the Nineteenth Century*, 487–90; Smith, *The Total Work of Art*, 8–21.

Bibliography

Abbate, Carolyn. *Unsung Voices: Opera and Musical Narrative in the Nineteenth Century*. Princeton: Princeton University Press, 1996.

Adorno, Theodor. *In Search of Wagner*. 1952. London and New York: Verso, 1991.

Adorno, Theodor. *Minima Moralia*. 1951. London and New York: Verso, 1987.

Adorno, Theodor. 'Music and Language: A Fragment'. 1956. In *Quasi Una Fantasia: Essays on Modern Music*, 1–6. London and New York: Verso, 2011.

Adorno, Theodor. 'The Natural History of the Theatre'. 1931–33. In *Quasi Una Fantasia: Essays on Modern Music*, 65–78. London and New York: Verso, 2011.

Adorno, Theodor. 'On the Fetish Character in Music and the Regression of Listening'. 1938. In *The Culture Industry: Selected Essays on Mass Culture*, 29–60. London and New York: Routledge, 2001.

Adorno, Theodor and Eisler, Hanns. *Composing for the Films*. 1947. London: The Athlone Press, 1994.

Adorno, Theodor and Horkheimer, Max. *Dialectic of Enlightenment*. 1944. London and New York: Verso, 1997.

Allen, Robert C. and Gomery, Douglas. *Film History: Theory and Practice*. New York: McGraw-Hill, 1985.

Altman, Rick. 'Early Film Themes: Roxy, Adorno and the Problem of Cultural Capital'. In *Beyond the Soundtrack: Representing Music in Cinema*, ed. Daniel Goldmark, Lawrence Kramer and Richard Leppert, 205–24. Berkeley: University of California Press, 2007.

Altman, Rick. *Silent Film Sound*. New York: Columbia University Press, 2004.

Atkins, John. *The Who on Record: A Critical History, 1963–1998*. Jefferson: McFarland and Company, Inc., 2000.

Badiou, Alain. *Being and Event*. 1988. London: Bloomsbury, 2017.

Badiou, Alain. *Five Lessons on Wagner*. London and New York: Verso, 2010.

Badiou, Alain. 'On Cinema as a Democratic Emblem'. 2005. In *Cinema*, 233–41. Cambridge: Polity Press, 2013.

Badiou, Alain. '"Thinking the Emergence of the Event"'. 1998. In *Cinema*, 105–28. Cambridge: Polity Press, 2013.

Bailey, Derek. *Improvisation: Its Nature and Practice in Music*. New York: Da Capo Press, 1992.

Balász, Béla. '[from] *Theory of the Film*'. 1945. In *Film Theory and Criticism: Introductory Readings*, ed. Leo Braudy and Marshall Cohen, 5th edn, 304–11. Oxford: Oxford University Press, 1999.

Banfield, Stephen. 'Music, Text and Stage: The Tradition of Bourgeois Tonality to the Second World War'. In *The Cambridge History of Twentieth-Century Music*, ed. Nicholas Cook and Anthony People, 90–122. Cambridge: Cambridge University Press, 2004.

Barber, Sian. *The British Film Industry in the 1970s: Capital, Culture and Creativity*. London: Palgrave MacMillan, 2013.

Barthes, Roland. 'The Death of the Author'. 1967. In *Image-Music-Text*, 142–8. London: Fontana Press, 1977.

Barthes, Roland. *Mythologies*. 1957. London: Vintage, 2009.

Barthes, Roland. 'The Rhetoric of the Image'. 1964. In *Image-Music-Text*, 32–51. London: Fontana Press, 1977.

Barthes, Roland. *S/Z*. 1973. Oxford: Basil Blackwell Ltd., 1990.

Bartlett, F. C. *Remembering: A Study in Experiential and Social Psychology*. 1932. Cambridge: Cambridge University Press, 1995.

Bazin, André. 'The Myth of Total Cinema'. 1946. In *What is Cinema? Volume 1*, 17–22. Berkeley: University of California Press, 2005.

Beauqier, Charles. '[from] *Philosophie de la musique*'. 1865. In *Music in European Thought: 1851–1912*, ed. Bojan Bujić, 182–96. Cambridge: Cambridge University Press, 1988.

Berlin, Isiah. *The Roots of Romanticism*. 1965. Ed. Henry Hardy. London: Pimlico, 2000.

Bernstein, Susan. *Virtuosity of the Nineteenth Century: Performing Music and Language in Heine, Liszt and Baudelaire*. Stanford: Stanford University Press, 1998.

Blanning, Tim. *The Romantic Revolution*. London: Phoenix, 2010.

Bloch, Ernst. 'On Music in the Cinema'. 1913. In *Literary Essays*, 156–9. Stanford: Stanford University Press, 1998.

Boime, Albert. 'An Interview with John C. Tibbetts'. In *Liszt: A Chorus of Voices*, ed. Michael Saffle, John C. Tibbetts and Claire McKinney, 31–7. Stuyvesant: Pendragon Press, 2012.

Bonds, Mark Evan. *Wordless Rhetoric: Musical Form and the Metaphor of the Oration*. Cambridge: Harvard University Press, 1991.

Bordwell, David. 'The Classical Hollywood Style, 1917–60'. In David Bordwell, Janet Staiger and Kristen Thompson. *The Classical Hollywood Cinema: Film Style and Mode of Production to 1960*, 3–84. London and New York: Routledge and Kegan Paul, 1985.

Bordwell, David. *Narration in the Fiction Film*. Madison: University of Wisconsin Press, 1985.

Botstein, Leon. 'Wagner and Our Century'. In *Music at the Turn of the Century: A 19th Century Music Reader*, ed. Joseph Kerman, 167–80. Berkeley: University of California Press, 1990.

Bourdieu, Pierre. *Distinction: A Social Critique of the Judgement of Taste*. 1979. New York and London: Routledge, 2003.

Bowie, Andrew. *From Romanticism to Critical Theory: The Philosophy of German Literary Theory*. London and New York: Routledge, 1997.

Braudy, Leo. *The Frenzy of Renown: Fame and Its History*. 1986. New York: Vintage, 1997.

Bribitzer-Stull, Matthew. *Understanding the Leitmotif: From Wagner to Hollywood Film Music*. Cambridge: Cambridge University Press, 2015.

Briggs, Asa. 'Manners Morals and Tastes: Changing Values in Art and Society'. In *The Nineteenth Century: The Contradictions of Progress*, ed. Asa Briggs, 291–326. London: Thames and Hudson, 1970.

Brinkmann, Reinhold. 'The Distorted Sublime: Music and National Socialist Ideology – A Sketch'. In *Music and Ideology*, ed. Mark Carroll, 213–33. London and New York: Routledge, 2016.

Brown, David. 'The B Minor Sonata Revisited: Deciphering Liszt'. *The Musical Times* 144 (2003): 6–15.

Brown, Royal S. *Overtones and Undertones: Reading Film Music*. Berkeley: University of California Press, 1994.

Buhler, James. 'Ontological, Formal and Critical Theories of Film Music and Sound'. In *The Oxford Handbook of Film Music Studies*, ed. David Neumeyer, 188–225. Oxford: Oxford University Press, 2014.

Buhler, James. 'Star Wars, Music, and Myth'. In *Music and Cinema*, ed. James Buhler, Caryl Flinn and David Neumeyer, 33–57. Hanover: Wesleyan University Press, 2000.

Buhler, James and Lewis, Hannah. 'Evolving Practices for Film Music and Sound: 1925-1935'. In *The Cambridge Companion to Film Music*, ed. Mervyn Cooke and Fiona Ford, 7–28. Cambridge: Cambridge University Press, 2016.

Bush, Richard H. 'The Music of Flash Gordon and Buck Rogers'. In *Film Music 1*, ed. Clifford McCarty, 143–65. New York: Garland Publishing Inc., 1989.

Caputo, John D. *Hermeneutics: Facts and Interpretation in the Age of Information*. London: Pelican Books, 2018.

Carroll, Noël. 'Film, Rhetoric and Ideology'. 1993. In *Theorising the Moving Image*, 275–89. Cambridge: Cambridge University Press, 1996.

Carroll, Noël. 'Notes on Movie Music'. 1986. In *Theorising the Moving Image*, 139–45. Cambridge: Cambridge University Press, 1996.

Casaliggi, Carmen and Fermanis, Porscha. *Romanticism: A Literary and Cultural History*. London and New York: Routledge, 2016.

Celenza, Anna Harwell. 'Liszt, Italy and the Republic of the Imagination'. In *Franz Liszt and his World*, ed. Christopher H. Gibbs and Dana Gooley, 3–38. Princeton: Princeton University Press, 2006.

Christensen, Thomas. 'Fétis and Emerging Tonal Consciousness'. In *Music Theory in the Age of Romanticism*, ed. Ian Bent, 37–56. Cambridge: Cambridge University Press, 1996.

Clarens, Carlos. *Cukor*. London: Martin Secker & Warburg Ltd, 1976.

Claydon, E. Anna. 'Masculinity and Deviance in British Cinema of the 1970s: Sex, Drugs and Rock 'n Roll in *The Wicker Man, Tommy* and *The Rocky Horror Picture Show*'. In *Don't Look Now: British Cinema in the 1970s*, ed. Paul Newland, 133–41. Bristol and New York: Intellect, 2010.

Coldstream, John. *Dirk Bogarde: The Authorised Biography*. London: Weidenfeld and Nicholson, 2004.

Copland, Aaron. *Copland on Music*. 1960. New York: Da Capo Press, 1976.

Cormac, Joanne. *Liszt and the Symphonic Poem*. Cambridge: Cambridge University Press, 2017.

Custen, George F. *Bio/Pics: How Hollywood Constructed Public History*. New Brunswick: Rutgers University Press, 1992.

Dahlhaus, Carl. *Between Romanticism and Modernism*. 1974. Berkeley: University of California Press, 1980.

Dahlhaus, Carl. *Esthetics of Music*. 1967. Cambridge: Cambridge University Press, 1982.

Dahlhaus, Carl. *Nineteenth Century Music*. 1980. Berkeley: University of California Press, 1989.

Darby, William and Du Bois, Jack. *American Film Music: Major Composers, Techniques, Trends, 1915–1990*. Jefferson: McFarland and Company Inc., 1990.

Davison, Alan. 'Liszt among the Degenerates: On the Vagaries of being a Musical Genius, c. 1890-c. 1935'. In *Liszt's Legacies*, ed. Michael Saffle and James Deaville, 236–58. Stuyvesant: Pendragon Press, 2014.

Davison, Alan. 'Liszt and Caricatures: The Clarity of Distortion'. In *Liszt: A Chorus of Voices*, ed. Michael Saffle, John C. Tibbetts and Claire McKinney, 68–75. Stuyvesant: Pendragon Press, 2012.

Deaville, James. 'The Controversy Surrounding Liszt's Conception of Programme Music'. In *Nineteenth Century Music: Selected Proceedings from the Tenth International Conference*, ed. Jim Samson and Bennett Zon, 98–124. Farnham: Ashgate, 2002.

Deaville, James. 'The Making of a Myth: Liszt, the Press, and Virtuosity'. In *Analecta Lisztiana II: New Light on Liszt and His Music*, ed. Michael Saffle and James Deaville, 181–95. Stuyvesant: Pendragon Press, 1997.

Del Mar, Norman. *Richard Strauss: A Critical Commentary on His Life and Works, Volume 1*. 1962. London and Boston: Faber and Faber, 1986.

Denisoff, R. Serge and Romanowski, William. *Risky Business: Rock on Film*. Piscataway: Transaction Publishers, 1991.

Donnelly, K. J. *Magical Musical Tour: Rock and Pop in Film Soundtracks*. London: Bloomsbury, 2015.

Donnelly, K. J. *The Spectre of Sound: Music in Film and Television*. London: BFI, 2005.

Dunsby, Johnathan. 'Chamber Music and Piano'. In *The Cambridge History of Nineteenth Century Music*, ed. Jim Samson, 500–19. Cambridge: Cambridge University Press, 2001.

Dyer, Richard. 'The Role of Stereotypes'. 1979. In *The Matter of Images: Essays on Representation*, 11–18. London and New York: Routledge, 1993.

Dyer, Richard. *Stars*. 1979. London: BFI Publishing, 1992.

Eisenstein, Sergei. 'Achievement'. 1939. In *Film Form: Essays in Film Theory*, 179–94. San Diego, New York and London: Harcourt, Inc., 1949.

Eldridge, David. *Hollywood's History Films*. London and New York: I.B. Tauris, 2006.

Ellis, John. 'Stars as a Cinematic Phenomenon'. In *Stardom and Celebrity: A Reader*, ed. Sean Redmond and Su Holmes, 90–7. Los Angeles: Sage, 2007.

Ewbank, Tim and Hildred, Stafford. *Roger Daltrey: The Biography*. London: Portrait, 2004.

Flinn, Caryl. *Strains of Utopia: Gender, Nostalgia, and Hollywood Film Music*. Princeton: Princeton University Press, 2006.

Foucault, Michel. *The Archaeology of Knowledge*. 1969. London and New York: Routledge, 2010.

Frank, Manfred. *The Philosophical Foundations of Early German Romanticism*. Albany: State University of New York Press, 2004.

Franklin, Peter. *Reclaiming Late-Romantic Music: Singing Devils and Distant Sounds*. Berkeley: University of California press, 2014.

Franklin, Peter. *Seeing Through Music: Gender and Modernism in Classic Hollywood Film Scores*. Oxford: Oxford University Press, 2011.

Gadamer, Hans-Georg. *Truth and Method*. 1960. London and New York: Continuum International Publishing Group, 2012.

Gamson, Joshua. 'The Assembly Line of Greatness: Celebrity in Twentieth-Century America'. In *Stardom and Celebrity: A Reader*, ed. Sean Redmond and Su Holmes, 141–55. Los Angeles: Sage, 2007.

Gardner, Colin. *Joseph Losey*. Manchester: Manchester University Press, 2004.

Gershwin, George. 'The Composer in the Machine Age'. 1933. In *Modernism and Music: An Anthology of Sources*, ed. Daniel Albright, 386–9. Chicago: University of Chicago Press, 2004.

Glynn, Stephen. 'Can't Buy Me Love?: Economic Imperatives and Artistic Achievements in the British Pop-Music Film'. In *The Cambridge Companion to Film Music*, ed. Mervyn Cooke and Fiona Ford, 67–80. Cambridge: Cambridge University Press, 2016.

Godøy, Rolf Inge. 'Postures and Motion Shaping Musical Experience'. In *The Routledge Companion to Embodied Music Interaction*, ed. Micheline Lesaffre, Pieter-Jan Maes and Marc Leman, 113–20. London and New York: Routledge, 2017.

Goehr, Lydia. 'Film as Visual Music: Duplication, Dissonance and Displacement'. In *Elective Affinities: Musical Essays on the History of Aesthetic Theory*, 204–56. New York: Columbia University Press, 2008.

Goethe, Johann Wolfgang von. 'Faust'. 1772–31. In *Selected Works*, 752–1049. London: Everyman's Library, 1999.

Goldmann, Lucien. *Immanuel Kant*. 1967. London: Verso, 2011.
Gombrich, E. H. *Art and Illusion: A Study in the Psychology of Pictorial Representation*. Oxford: Phaidon Press, 1959.
Gomez, Joseph. *Ken Russell: The Adaptor as Creator*. London: Frederick Muller Limited, 1976.
Gooley, Dana. 'Franz Liszt: The Virtuoso as Strategist'. In *The Musician as Entrepreneur, 1700-1914: Managers, Charlatans and Idealists*, ed. William Weber, 145-61. Bloomington and Indianapolis: Indiana University Press, 2004.
Gooley, Dana. *The Virtuoso Liszt*. Cambridge: Cambridge University Press, 2009.
Gorbman, Claudia. *Unheard Melodies: Narrative Film Music*. Bloomington and Indianapolis: Indiana University Press, 1987.
Grey, Thomas S. '...*wie ein rother Faden*: On the Origins of "Leitmotif" as Critical Construct and Musical Practice'. In *Music Theory in the Age of Romanticism*, ed. Ian Bent, 187-210. Cambridge: Cambridge University Press, 1996.
Gunning, Tom. 'The Cinema of Attraction: Early Film, Its Spectator and the Avant-Garde'. 1986. In *Early Cinema: Space, Frame, Narrative*, ed. Thomas Elsaesser, 56-62. London: BFI, 1990.
Gunning, Tom. 'Flickers: On Cinema's Power for Evil'. In *Bad: Infamy, Darkness, Evil, and Slime on Screen*, ed. Murray Pomerance, 21-37. Albany: State University of New York Press, 2004.
Habermas, Jűrgen. *The Philosophical Discourse of Modernity*. 1985. Cambridge: Polity Press, 1998.
Hall, Stuart. *Representation: Cultural Representations and Signifying Practices*. London: SAGE Publications, 1997.
Hamilton, Kenneth. *After the Golden Age: Romantic Pianism and Modern Performance*. Oxford: Oxford University Press, 2008.
Hanke, Ken. *Ken Russell's Films*. Metuchen and London: The Scarecrow Press, 1984.
Hanslick, Eduard. *On the Musically Beautiful*. 1854. Indianapolis: Hackett Publishing Co., 1986.
Haringer, Andrew. 'Liszt and the Legacy of Lamartine'. In *Liszt's Legacies*, ed. Michael Saffle and James Deaville, 72-91. Stuyvesant: Pendragon Press, 2014.
Harper, Sue. 'History and Representation: The Case of 1970s British Cinema'. In *The New Film History: Sources, Methods, Approaches*, ed. James Chapman, Mark Glancy and Sue Harper, 27-40. London: Palgrave Macmillan, 2006.
Harper, Sue and Smith, Justin. *British Film Culture in the 1970s: The Boundaries of Pleasure*. Edinburgh: Edinburgh University Press, 2013.
Hegel, Georg Wilhelm Friedrich. *Introductory Lectures on Aesthetics*. 1820-29. London: Penguin Books, 2004.
Hegel, Georg Wilhelm Friedrich. *Lectures on the Philosophy of History*. 1822-30. Aalten: Wordbridge, 2011.

Heine, Heinrich. 'Florentine Nights'. 1835. In *The Prose Writings of Heinrich Heine*, 179–242. London: Walter Scott, 1887.

Heldt, Guido. 'Film-Music Theory'. In *The Cambridge Companion to Film Music*, ed. Mervyn Cooke and Fiona Ford, 97–113. Cambridge: Cambridge University Press, 2016.

Heldt, Guido. 'Hardly Heroes: Composers as a Subject in National Socialist Cinema'. In *Music and Nazism: Art Under Tyranny, 1933–1945*, ed. Michael H. Kater and Albrecht Riethmuller, 114–35. Laaber: Laaber Verlag, 2003.

Hempel, Carl G. and Oppenheim, Paul. 'Studies in the Logic of Explanation'. 1948. In *Theories of Explanation*, ed. Joseph C. Pitt, 9–50. New York and Oxford: Oxford University Press, 1988.

Herbert, Stephen. *A History of Pre-Cinema*, 2 vols. London and New York: Routledge, 2000.

Herder, Johann Gottfried von. '[From] *Kalligone*'. 1800. In *Musical Aesthetics: A Historical Reader, Volume II – The Nineteenth Century*, ed. Edward A. Lippman, 33–43. Stuyvesant: Pendragon Press, 1988.

Hilmes, Oliver. *Franz Liszt: Musician, Celebrity, Superstar*. New Haven: Yale University Press, 2016.

Hindemith, Paul. 'From *A Composers World*'. 1950. In *Modernism and Music: An Anthology of Sources*, ed. Daniel Albright, 60–3. Chicago: University of Chicago Press, 2004.

Hindley, Geoffrey, et al. *The Larousse Encyclopaedia of Music*. 6th edn. London: The Hamlyn Publishing Group Limited, 1983.

Hölderlin, Friedrich, et al. 'The Oldest Program for a System of German Idealism'. c1795. In *Essays and Letters*, 341–2. London: Penguin, 2009.

Izod, John. *Hollywood and the Box Office 1895–1986*. London: The MacMillan Press, Ltd., 1988.

Jameson, Fredric. *Postmodernism, or The Cultural Logic of Late Capitalism*. London and New York: Verso, 1991.

Jarvie, Ian. *Philosophy of the Film: Epistemology, Ontology, Aesthetics*. New York and London: Routledge and Kegan Paul Inc., 1987.

Joe, Jeongwon. 'Introduction: Why Wagner and Cinema? Tolkien was Wrong'. In *Wagner and Cinema*, ed. Jeongwon Joe and Sander L. Gilman, 1–24. Bloomington and Indianapolis: Indiana University Press, 2010.

Johns, Keith T. *The Symphonic Poems of Franz Liszt*. Stuyvesant: Pendragon Press, 1997.

Jones, Nick. 'Well, What is Pop Art?'. In *The Faber Book of Pop*, ed. Hanif Kureishi and Jon Savage, 239–40. London and Boston: Faber and Faber, 1995.

Kant, Immanuel. *Critique of Judgement*. 1790. Indianapolis and Cambridge: Hackett Publishing Company, 1987.

Kant, Immanuel. *Critique of Pure Reason*. 1781. Indianapolis and Cambridge: Hackett Publishing Company, 1996.

Kerman, Joseph. *Opera as Drama*. 1956. 2nd edn. London and Boston: Faber and Faber, 1989.

Kermode, Frank. *Romantic Image*. 1957. London and New York: Routledge, 2002.

Kershaw, David. 'Music and Image on Film and Video: An Absolute Alternative'. In *Companion to Contemporary Musical Thought, Volume 1*, ed. John Paynter, Tim Howell, Richard Orton and Peter Seymour, 466-99. London and New York: Routledge, 1992.

Klemperer, Victor. *The Language of the Third Reich*. 1957. London: Bloomsbury, 2018.

Kracauer, Siegfried. 'The Cult of Distraction: On Berlin's Picture Palaces'. 1926. In *The Continental Philosophy of Film Reader*, ed. Joseph Westfall, 197-200. London: Bloomsbury, 2018.

Kracauer, Siegfried. *Theory of Film: The Redemption of Physical Reality*. 1960. Princeton: Princeton University Press, 1997.

Kramer, Lawrence. 'Classical Music, Virtual Bodies, Narrative Film'. In *The Oxford Handbook of Film Music Studies*, ed. David Neumeyer, 351-65. Oxford: Oxford University Press, 2014.

Kramer, Lawrence. *Musical Meaning: Toward a Critical History*. Berkeley: University of California Press, 2002.

Langer, Susanne K. *Philosophy in a New Key: A Study in the Symbolism of Reason, Rite, and Art*. 1942. Cambridge: Harvard University Press, 1957.

Lanza, Joseph. *Phallic Frenzy: Ken Russell and His Films*. Chicago: Chicago Review Press, 2007.

Lenz, Wilhelm von. *The Great Piano Virtuosos of Our Time: A Classic Account of Studies with Liszt, Chopin, Tausig and Henselt*. 1872. London: Kahn and Averill, 1995.

Leppert, Richard. *The Sight of Sound: Music, Representation, and the History of the Body*. Berkeley: University of California press, 1993.

Lev, Peter. *History of the American Cinema*, 9 vols. New York: Charles Scribner's Sons, 2003. 7: *The Fifties - Transforming the Screen: 1950-1959*.

Levi, Emanuel. *George Cukor, Master of Elegance: Hollywood's Legendary Director and His Stars*. New York: William Morrow and Company Inc., 1994.

Lévi-Strauss, Claude. *Myth and Meaning*. 1978. London and New York: Routledge, 2001.

Liszt, Franz. 'About Beethoven's Music to *Egmont*'. 1854. In *Dramaturgical Leaves, Essays About Musical Works for the Stage and Queries About the Stage, its Composers and Performers*, ed. Janita R. Hall-Swadley, 83-94. Lanham: Rowman and Littlefield, 2014.

Liszt, Franz. *An Artist's Journey: Lettres d'un Bachelier es Musique, 1835-41*. Chicago: University of Chicago Press, 1989.

Liszt, Franz. 'Berlioz and his Harold Symphony'. 1855. In *The Romantic Era: Source Readings in Music History*, ed. Oliver Strunk, 106-33. New York: W. W. Norton and Company, 1965.

Liszt, Franz. [Preface to] *Prometheus*. 1850–59. In *Liszt: Symphonic Poems*. 1.3, 1–2. Upper Saddle River: Gregg Press, 1966.

Locke, Ralph P. *Music, Musicians and the Saint-Simonians*. Chicago: University of Chicago Press, 1986.

Loesser, Arthur. *Men, Women and Pianos: A Social History*. New York: Simon and Schuster, 1954.

Long, Michael. *Beautiful Monsters: Imagining the Classic in Musical Media*. Berkeley: University of California Press, 2008.

Lowe, Donald M. *History of Bourgeois Perception*. Chicago: University of Chicago Press, 1982.

Mandel, Ernest. *Late Capitalism*. 1972. London: NLB, 1975.

Mann, Thomas. 'Death in Venice'. 1911. In *Collected Stories*, 417–90. London: Everyman's Library, 2001.

Mann, Thomas. 'The Infant Prodigy'. 1903. In *Collected Stories*, 229–37. London: Everyman's Library, 2001.

Mann, Thomas. 'Mario and the Magician'. 1929. In *Collected Stories*, 603–50. London: Everyman's Library, 2001.

McCarty, Clifford. *Film Composers in America: A Filmography, 1911–1970*. 2nd edn. Oxford: Oxford University Press, 2000.

McGilligan, Patrick. *George Cukor: A Double Life*. London and Boston: Faber and Faber, 1991.

MENC: The National Association for Music Education. 'Virtuoso Franz Liszt as Composer: A New Teaching Film from "Song without End"'. *Music Educators Journal* 47, no. 2 (1960): 45–6.

Mendl, R. W. S. 'The Art of the Symphonic Poem'. *The Musical Quarterly* 18 no. 3 (1932): 443–6.

Mies, Paul. '[From] *Über die Tonmalerei*'. 1912. In *Music in European Thought: 1851–1912*, ed. Bojan Bujić, 121–5. Cambridge: Cambridge University Press, 1988.

Millán-Zaibert, Elizabeth. 'Introduction: "What is Early German Romanticism?"'. In Manfred Frank, *The Philosophical Foundations of Early German Romanticism*, 1–21. Albany: State University of New York Press, 2004.

Moretti, Franco. *The Way of the World: The Bildungsroman in European Culture*. London and New York: Verso, 1987.

Morley, Sheridan. *Dirk Bogarde: Rank Outsider*. London: Bloomsbury Paperbacks, 1999.

Morton, Marsha L. '"From the Other Side": An Introduction'. In *The Arts Entwined: Music and Painting in the Nineteenth Century*, ed. Marsha L. Morton and Peter L. Schmunk, 1–21. London and New York: Routledge, 2000.

Motion, Andrew. *The Lamberts: George, Constant and Kit*. London: The Hogarth Press, 1987.

Mueller, Rena Charnin. 'From the Biographer's Workshop: Lina Ramann's Questionnaires to Liszt'. In *Franz Liszt and his World*, ed. Christopher H. Gibbs and Dana Gooley, 361–424. Princeton: Princeton University Press, 2006.

Muncie, John. 'The Beatles and the Spectacle of Youth'. In *The Beatles, Popular Music and Society: A Thousand Voices*, ed. Ian Inglis, 35–52. London: The MacMillan Press, 2000.

Nattiez, Jean-Jacques. 'Can One Speak of Narrativity in Music?'. *Journal of the Royal Musical Association* 115, no. 2 (1990): 240–57.

Neisser, Ulrich. *Cognition and Reality: Principles and Implications of Cognitive Psychology*. San Francisco: W.H. Freeman and Company, 1976.

Nelson, Robert U. 'Film Music: Color or Line?'. In *Hollywood Quarterly* 2 no. 1 (1946): 57–65.

Neumeyer, David. 'Film Theory and Music Theory: On the Intersection of Two Traditions'. In *Music in the Mirror: Reflections on the History of Music Theory and Literature for the 21st Century*, ed. Andreas Giger and Thomas J. Mathiesen, 275–94. Lincoln: University of Nebraska Press, 2002.

Nielsen, Carl. '[from] Words, Music and Program Music'. 1925. In *Modernism and Music: An Anthology of Sources*, ed. Daniel Albright, 55–60. Chicago: University of Chicago Press, 2004.

Nietzsche, Friedrich. 'The Birth of Tragedy'. 1872. In *The Birth of Tragedy and The Case of Wagner*, 17–151. New York: Vintage, 1967.

Nietzsche, Friedrich. 'The Case of Wagner: A Musicians Problem'. 1888. In *The Birth of Tragedy and The Case of Wagner*, 155–92. New York: Vintage, 1967.

Panofsky, Erwin. 'Style and Medium in the Motion Pictures'. 1934. In *Film Theory and Criticism: Introductory Readings*, ed. Gerald Mast, Marshal Cohen and Leo Braudy, 4th edn, 233–48. Oxford: Oxford University Press, 1992.

Partridge, Christopher. *The Lyre of Orpheus: Popular Music, The Sacred and the Profane*. Oxford: Oxford University Press, 2014.

Patel, Aniruddh D. *Music, Language and the Brain*. Oxford: Oxford University Press, 2008.

Pattison, Robert. *The Triumph of Vulgarity: Rock Music in the Mirror of Romanticism*. Oxford: Oxford University Press, 1987.

Paulin, Scott D. 'Richard Wagner and the Fantasy of Cinematic Unity: The Idea of the *Gesamstkunstwerk* and the History and Theory of Film Music'. In *Music and Cinema*, ed. James Buhler, Caryl Flinn and David Neumeyer, 58–84. Hanover: Wesleyan University Press, 2000.

Peckham, Morse. 'Cultural Transcendence: The Task of the Romantics'. 1981. In *Romanticism and Ideology*, 3–22. Hanover and London: Wesleyan University Press, 1995.

Peckham, Morse. *Explanation and Power: The Control of Human Behaviour*. New York: The Seabury Press, 1979.

Peckham, Morse. 'Introduction'. In *Romanticism and Ideology*, xiii–xx. Hanover and London: Wesleyan University Press, 1995.

Peckham, Morse. *The Romantic Virtuoso*. Hanover and London: Wesleyan University Press, 1995.

Phillips, Gene D. *Ken Russell*. Boston: Twayne Publishers, 1979.
Piaget, Jean. *The Psychology of Intelligence*. 1947. New York and London: Routledge, 2001.
Pisani, Michael V. 'When the Music Surges: Melodrama and the Nineteenth Century Theatrical Precedents for Film Music Style and Placement'. In *The Oxford Handbook of Film Music Studies*, ed. David Neumeyer, 559–82. Oxford: Oxford University Press, 2014.
Pocknell, Pauline. 'Clandestine Portraits: Liszt in the Art of His Age'. In *Analecta Lisztiana II: New Light on Liszt and His Music*, ed. Michael Saffle and James Deaville, 123–61. Stuyvesant: Pendragon Press, 1997.
Popper, Karl. *Conjectures and Refutations: The Growth of Scientific Knowledge*. 1963. London and New York: Routledge, 2002.
Preston, Katherine K. 'Introduction: From Nineteenth-Century Stage Melodrama to Twenty- First-Century Film Scoring'. In *Journal of Film Music* 5, nos. 1–2 (2012): 7–14.
Rancière, Jacques. *The Emancipated Spectator*. 2008. London and New York: Verso, 2011.
Rancière, Jacques. *Film Fables*. 2001. London: Bloomsbury, 2016.
Rancière, Jacques. *The Future of the Image*. 2003. London and New York: Verso, 2009.
Rancière, Jacques. *The Ignorant Schoolmaster: Five Lessons in Intellectual Emancipation*. Stanford: Stanford University Press, 1987.
Rancière, Jacques. *The Politics of Aesthetics*. 2000. ed. Gabriel Rockhill. London: Bloomsbury, 2017.
Ricœur, Paul. 'Phenomenology and Hermeneutics'. 1975. In *From Text to Action*, 25–50. London and New York: Continuum, 1992.
Rojek, Chris. 'Celebrity and Religion'. In *Stardom and Celebrity: A Reader*, ed. Sean Redmond and Su Holmes, 171–80. Los Angeles: Sage, 2007.
Rosen, Charles. *The Romantic Generation*. Cambridge: Harvard University Press, 1995.
Rosenstone, Robert A. 'In Praise of the Biopic'. In *Lights, Camera, History: Portraying the Past in Film*, ed. Richard Francaviglia and Jerry Rodnitzky, 11–29. College Station: Texas A&M University Press, 2007.
Russell, Ken. *A British Picture: An Autobiography*. 1989. London: Southbank Publishing, 2008.
Russell, Ken. 'Interviews with John C. Tibbetts'. In *Liszt: A Chorus of Voices*, ed. Michael Saffle, John C. Tibbetts and Claire McKinney, 304–8. Stuyvesant: Pendragon Press, 2012.
Said, Edward W. *Orientalism*. 1978. London: Penguin Books, 2003.
Saffle, Michael. *Franz Liszt: A Research and Information Guide*. 3rd edn. New York and London: Routledge, 2009.
Saffle, Michael. 'Orchestral Works'. In *The Liszt Companion*, ed. Ben Arnold, 235–79. Westport and London: Greenwood Press, 2002.

Samson, Jim. *Virtuosity and the Musical Work: The Transcendental Studies of Liszt*. Cambridge: Cambridge University Press, 2003.

Schelling, F. W. J. *System of Transcendental Idealism*. 1800. Charlottesville: The University Press of Virginia, 2001.

Schiller, Friedrich. *On the Aesthetic Education of Man*. 1795. London: Penguin, 2016.

Schmid, Mark-Daniel. 'The Early Reception of Richard Strauss' Tone Poems'. In *The Richard Strauss Companion*, ed. Mark-Daniel Schmid, 145–90. Westport: Praeger Publishers, 2003.

Schoenberg, Arnold. 'On Program Music, Tradition, and the Public - The First American Radio Broadcast: An Interview with William Lundell'. 1933. In *A Schoenberg Reader: Documents of a Life*, ed. Joseph Auner, 247–50. New Haven: Yale University Press, 2003.

Schumann, Robert. 'Franz Liszt: Concerts in Dresden and Leipzig'. 1940. In *Schumann on Music: A Selection from the Writings*, ed. Henry Pleasants, 157–61. Mineola: Dover Publications, 1965.

Shaw, George Bernard. *Shaw's Music: The Complete Musical Criticism of Bernard Shaw*, 3 vols, ed. Dan H. Laurence. 2nd edn. London: The Bodley Head, 1981.

Shirer, William L. *The Rise and Fall of the Third Reich: A History of Nazi Germany*. 1959. Trowbridge: Redwood Press, 1973.

Sinyard, Neil. *Richard Lester*. Manchester: Manchester University Press, 2010.

Smith, Jeff. 'Music'. In *The Routledge Companion to Philosophy and Film*, ed. Paisley Livingston and Carl Plantinga, 184–94. London and New York: Routledge, 2009.

Smith, Justin. 'The "Lack" and How to Get It": Reading Male Anxiety in *A Clockwork Orange*, *Tommy* and *The Man Who Fell to Earth*'. In *Don't Look Now: British Cinema in the 1970s*, ed. Paul Newland, 145–59. Bristol and New York: Intellect, 2010.

Smith, Matthew Wilson. *The Total Work of Art: From Bayreuth to Cyberspace*. London and New York: Routledge, 2007.

Sontag, Susan. 'Fascinating Fascism'. 1975. In *Movies and Methods, Volume 1*, ed. Bill Nichols, 31–43. Berkeley: University of California Press, 1976.

Sontag, Susan. 'Syberberg's Hitler'. 1979. In *Under the Sign of Saturn*, 137–65. London: Penguin, 2009.

Staiger, Janet. *Interpreting Films: Studies in the Historical Reception of American Cinema*. Princeton: Princeton University Press, 1992.

Stasov, Vladimir. 'Letters from Abroad'. 1869. In *Selected Essays on Music*, 38–51. New York: Da Capo Press, 1980.

Stasov, Vladimir. 'Liszt, Schumann and Berlioz in Russia'. 1889. In *Selected Essays on Music*, 117–94. New York: Da Capo Press, 1980.

Sturma, Dieter. 'Politics and the New Mythology: The Turn to Late Romanticism'. In *The Cambridge Companion to German Idealism*, ed. Karl Ameriks, 2nd edn, 314–35. Cambridge: Cambridge University Press, 2017.

Szabó-Knotik, Cornelia. 'Franz Liszt's Historical Position'. In Franz Liszt, *Dramaturgical Leaves, Essays About Musical Works for the Stage and Queries About the Stage, its Composers and Performers*, ed. Janita R. Hall-Swadley, xv–xxi. Lanham: Rowman and Littlefield, 2014.

Szabó-Knotik, Cornelia. 'From "Deutschösterreich" to Pop/ularity: Celebrating Liszt at his Birthplace (1936–2011)'. In *Liszt's Legacies*, ed. Michael Saffle and James Deaville, 300–12. Stuyvesant: Pendragon Press, 2014.

Tannen, Deborah and Wallat, Cynthia. 'Interactive Frames and Knowledge Schemas in Interaction: Examples from a Medical Examination/Interview'. 1987. In *The Discourse Reader*, ed. Adam Jaworski and Nikolas Coupland, 346–65. London and New York: Routledge, 1999.

Tanner, Michael. 'The Power of Performance as an Alternative Analytical Discourse: The Liszt Sonata in B Minor'. *19th-Century Music* 24, no. 2 (2000): 173–92.

Tanner, Michael. 'The Total Work of Art'. In *The Wagner Companion*, ed. Peter Burbidge and Richard Sutton, 140–224. London and Boston: Faber and Faber, 1979.

Taruskin, Richard. *The Oxford History of Western Music*, 6 vols. Oxford: Oxford University Press, 2005.

Thomas, Gary C. 'Men at the Keyboard: Liminal Spaces and the Heterotopian Function of Music'. In *Beyond the Soundtrack: Representing Music in Cinema*, ed. Daniel Goldmark, Lawrence Kramer and Richard Leppert, 277–91. Berkeley: University of California Press.

Tibbetts, John C. *Composers in the Movies*. New Haven: Yale University Press, 2005.

Tibbetts, John C. '"A Search Party of Orphans": Composers on Film'. In *Liszt: A Chorus of Voices*, ed. Michael Saffle, John C. Tibbetts and Claire McKinney, 334–45. Stuyvesant: Pendragon Press, 2012.

Toplin, Robert Brent. 'In Defence of the Filmmakers'. In *Lights, Camera, History: Portraying the Past in Film*, ed. Richard Francaviglia and Jerry Rodnitzky, 113–35. College Station: Texas A&M University Press, 2007.

Verdi, Luigi. *Franz Liszt e la sua musica nel cinema*. Lucca: Libreria Musicale Italiana, 2015.

Wagner, Richard. *Wagner on Music and Drama*, ed. Albert Goldman and Evert Sprinchorn. New York: Da Capo Press, 1964.

Walker, Alan. *Franz Liszt: The Virtuoso Years, 1811–1847*. London: Faber and Faber, 1983.

Walker, Alan. *Franz Liszt: The Weimar Years, 1848–1861*. London: Faber and Faber, 1989.

Walker, Alan. *Franz Liszt: The Final Years, 1861–1886*. London: Faber and Faber, 1997.

Walker, Alan. 'Liszt and the Twentieth Century'. In *Franz Liszt: The Man and His Music*, ed. Alan Walker, 350–64. London: Barrie and Jenkins, 1970.

Walker, Alan. *Reflections on Liszt*. Ithaca and London: Cornell University Press, 2005.

Walker, John. *The Once and Future Film: British Cinema in the Seventies and Eighties*. London: Methuen, 1985.
Wallace, F. C. *Culture and Personality*. 2nd edn. New York: Random House, 1970.
Weiskel, Thomas. *The Romantic Sublime: Studies in the Structure and Psychology of Transcendence*. Baltimore and London: The John Hopkins University Press, 1976.
Werbeck, Walter. 'Richard Strauss' Tone Poems'. In *The Richard Strauss Companion*, ed. Mark-Daniel Schmid, 103–44. Westport: Praeger Publishers, 2003.
White, Hayden. 'The Burden of History'. 1966. In *Tropics of Discourse: Essays in Cultural Criticism*, 27–50. Baltimore and London: The John Hopkins University Press, 1978.
Will, Richard. *The Characteristic Symphony in the Age of Haydn and Beethoven*. Cambridge: Cambridge University Press, 2002.
Williamson, John. *Strauss: Also Sprach Zarathustra*. Cambridge: Cambridge University Press, 1993.
Winters, Ben. *Music, Performance, and the Realities of Film: Shared Concert Experiences in Screen Fiction*. New York and London: Routledge, 2014.
Wolin, Sheldon S. *Politics and Vision: Continuity and Innovation in Western Political Thought*. 1960. 2nd edn. Princeton: Princeton University Press, 2016.
Wooding, Dan. *Rick Wakeman: The Caped Crusader*. London: Robert Hale Ltd., 1978.
Yerushalmi, Ophra. 'Benediction to Liszt in His Solitude'. In *Liszt: A Chorus of Voices*, ed. Michael Saffle, John C. Tibbetts and Claire McKinney, 370–75. Stuyvesant: Pendragon Press, 2012.

Index

Above Suspicion (1943) 42
Abschliedwaltzer (1934) 129
Adorno, Theodor 6, 11, 27, 28,
  35, 49–50, 72–4, 76, 120, 165,
  205, 225
  and Romanticism 6, 28, 35, 37, 49,
    120, 165
  and Wagner 6, 49–50, 72–3, 76
aesthetic ideas (Kant) 62, 77
aesthetic regime, the (Rancière) 22,
  27–30, 32, 37, 53, 57, 72, 76, 77,
  215, 221
d'Agoult, Marie 113, 124, 126, 140,
  141, 144–6, 152–3, 160, 187,
  192–3, 210
  in *Lisztomania* 113, 187, 192–3, 210
  in *Song Without End* 124, 126, 140,
    141, 144–6, 152–3, 160
All About Eve (1950) 231
Altered States (1980) 171, 194
Altman, Rick 46, 48, 53, 70
archaeology (Foucault) 12–13
artist-priest 32–3, 36, 59, 179–84, 187,
  191, 200–1, 203
  in *Lisztomania* 191, 200–1, 203
  in *Tommy* 179–84
audio-visual explanation 1–2, 7, 14,
  16–18, 23–7, 30, 36–9, 73, 79–80,
  86, 96, 99, 101, 109, 112, 121,
  126–7, 156, 215–22

Bach, J. S. 60, 94
  Toccata and Fugue in D minor
    (c1704–50) 94
Badiou, Alain 215–16
  and Romanticism 215–16
Balász, Béla 47, 110
Barry Lyndon (1975) 211
Barthes, Roland 11, 35, 73, 88–9, 128
Bartlett, F. C. 82, 88–9, 216, 220–2
Bartók, Bela 6, 111, 168

Battleship Potemkin (1925) 188, 197
Baudry, Jean-Louis 46
Bazin, André 232
Beatlemania 169
The Beatles 168–9, 190
Beethoven, Ludwig Van 22, 29, 34, 43,
  45, 53, 55, 56, 73, 93, 94, 97, 101,
  103, 104, 106, 130, 144, 149, 162,
  189, 192, 204, 224
  Ninth Symphony (1824) 45
  Piano Sonata No. 8 (1798) 149
  Piano Sonata No. 14 'Moonlight'
    (1801) 144
  Seventh Symphony (1813) 94
Berlioz, Hector 55, 59, 188, 225
Bernstein, Susan 90, 96, 98, 104, 108,
  111, 210
Bildung 33, 57, 64, 222
The Black Cat (1934) 93–8
Bloch, Ernst 44
The Blue Lamp (1950) 138
Bogarde, Dirk 124–5, 129, 137–9,
  147, 158
Bordwell, David 15–16, 46, 80, 220
Bourdieu, Pierre 8, 13, 18, 47, 218
Brahms, Johannes 69, 93, 110–11,
  133–5, 165, 166, 188–90
Braudy, Leo 127, 161, 181, 205
Breil, Jospeh Carl 45
Bribitzer-Stull, Matthew 50, 227
Brown, Royal S. 42, 227
Bülow, Hans von 111, 190, 192, 198,
  201, 210
  in *Lisztomania* 190, 192, 198,
    201, 210
Byron, George Gordon 23, 115

Carlyle, Thomas 162
Carroll, Noël 52, 67, 227
Cast a Dark Shadow (1955) 138
Chaplin, Charlie 113, 188, 192–3

Index

Chion, Michel 227
Chopin, Frédéric 60, 97, 103, 114, 117, 123, 129–33, 141, 144, 156, 158
  Polonaise in A flat, Op. 53 (1842) 130, 132
cognitive psychology 3, 15, 80, 83, 85, 216, 220
Coleridge, Samuel Taylor 21, 23
Copland, Aaron 6, 129
critical rationalism (Popper) 8, 12, 23, 25, 36, 38, 80, 83, 102, 219
  and Romanticism 23, 25, 36, 38, 102, 219
Cukor, George 137, 139
cultural image 2, 18, 24, 34, 72, 79, 80, 83, 86–122, 126–30, 131, 162, 163, 166, 176, 186, 204–10, 215–18
cultural transcendence (Peckham) 22, 24–9, 33–4, 64, 91–2, 98–101, 131–2, 145, 151, 156, 161–2, 168, 172, 176–7, 183–4, 200–1, 205, 219, 222

Dahlhaus, Carl 45, 61, 63, 66, 67, 230–1
Daltrey, Roger 126, 142, 166–70, 174, 176, 180–202, 208–13
The Damned (1969) 138
Dearden, Basil 97, 139
Death in Venice (1971) 138, 206
The Devils (1971) 172
Doctor in the House (1954) 138
Donnelly, K. J. 43, 50, 52, 92, 152
Dvořák, Antonín 70
Dyer, Richard 85, 87, 129, 138, 144

Eisenstein, Sergei 5, 223
Eisler, Hanns 49, 76
Elgar, Edward 70, 173
  Enigma Variations (1899) 173
Enlightenment, the 4, 22–3, 31–2, 38
explanandum, *see* explanation, theory of
explanans, *see* explanation, theory of
explanation, theory of 7–19
explicandum, *see* explanation, theory of

Fantasia (1940) 119
Fétis, François-Joseph 55–6, 59
Foucault, Michel 12–13, 21, 218

Frankenstein (1931) 176, 188, 198, 200–2, 208
Frankfurt School the 49, 50, 73, 219
Franklin, Peter 42, 43, 50, 51
French Revolution, the 22, 31, 66
Friedrich, C. D. 21, 24, 179, 180, 212

The Gang's All Here (1943) 188
Gaslight (1940) 102
genius 1, 2, 5, 17, 23–39, 59, 64, 92, 97–104, 107, 112, 118, 121, 127–8, 130–5, 145, 150–2, 154, 156, 160, 162, 166, 172, 178, 180–3, 187, 195–6, 207, 216
German Idealism 17, 22, 24, 25, 27, 30, 31, 32, 37, 38, 55, 102, 215, 217, 221, 233
Gershwin, George 66
Gesamtkunstwerk ('total work of art') 5, 28, 45, 47–9, 179, 218, 229, 232–3
Goethe, J. W. von 21, 24, 58, 62, 149, 150
Gombrich, E. H. 83–5, 91, 118, 216, 220
Gorbman, Claudia 44, 52, 53, 67, 231
Gunning, Tom 4–5

Hanke, Ken 196
Hans Christian Anderson (1952) 92–3
Hanslick, Eduard 60, 69, 72, 231
Hegel, G. W. F. 24, 31–2, 33, 36, 37, 55–9, 73, 219
Heine, Heinrich 1–2, 8, 10–11, 14, 34–5, 51, 169, 206–7
Herder, J. G. 24, 29, 55–9, 67
hermeneutic circle, the 8, 82, 85
Hitler, Adolf 36, 176, 198–208
Hitler: A Film from Germany (1977) 204–5
Hölderlin, Friedrich 21, 24
Holocaust, the, *see* Nazism
Horkheimer, Max 37, 49, 76

Impromptu (1991) 114

Kant, Immanuel 15, 22, 24, 26, 30–6, 56, 62, 77, 80–3, 216–21
Karloff, Boris 93–6, 202
Kermode, Frank 23, 100, 183
Korngold, Erich Wolfgang 48, 72, 76

Kracauer, Siegfried   4, 47, 49, 76

Lamartine, Alphonse   33, 59
Lambert, Kit   178
Leitmotif (Wagner)   45, 47–9, 52, 71, 76, 227, 229–31
Letter from an Unknown Woman (1948)   113, 140
Levi-Strauss, Claude   226
Liberace   191
Liszt, Franz   2, 3–7, 17–19, 22, 33, 42, 53–77, 79–122, 123–35, 137–63, 165–6, 168–213, 215–19, 221
  'Au bord d'une sourse' (1834–55)   93
  'La Campanella' (1838–51)   142–3
  Consolation No. 3 (1844–50)   145–6, 152
  Dante Sonata ('Après une lecture du Dante: Fantasia quasi Sonata') (1849)   118, 157
  Dante Symphony (1856)   73, 75, 118
  Faust Symphony (1854; 1857)   146
  'Funérailles' (1849)   132, 197
  'Gnomenreigen' (1862–63)   93
  Grande Galop chromatique (1838)   116
  Hungarian Rhapsody No. 2 (1847)   156–8
  Hunnenschlacht (1857)   60, 74
  'Liebesträume' No. 3 (1850)   96, 97, 116, 156–8, 193, 208
  Mazeppa (1826–54)   59, 72
  Mephisto Waltz No. 1 (1859–62)   93, 118–21, 134, 144
  Piano Concerto No. 1   42, 133, 158, 201–2
  Piano Sonata in B minor (1854)   93–5, 146, 150
  'Sonetto   123 del Petrarca' (1838–42)   102
  Tasso (1847–57)   59, 62, 94, 152
  Totentanz (1849; 1865)   157, 201
  'Un sospiro' (1845–49)   113, 139–40, 146, 150, 152, 157, 159–61
  'Waldesrauschen' (1862–63)   150, 152
Lisztomania (Heine)   1, 169, 206–7
Lisztomania (1975)   18, 107, 112, 113–16, 132, 142, 145, 165–213

Lola Montez (1955)   99, 193
Lugosi, Bela   93–4, 96, 116
  compared to Liszt   96

McVicar (1980)   167
Magic Fire (1955)   123
Mahler (1974)   171–2, 184–5, 194, 196
Mahler, Gustav   21, 43, 172, 204
Mann, Thomas   204, 206
  and virtuosity   206
The Man Who Would be King (1975)   211
Mendelssohn, Felix   112, 149, 225
  'Rondo Capriccioso' (1830)   149
The Mephisto Waltz (1971)   119–21
Metro-Goldwyn-Mayer (MGM)   123
Metz, Christian   46
Mies, Paul   69, 71
modernism   3, 22, 29, 43, 70, 121, 215
modernity   5, 26, 33, 37, 66
Monty Python and the Holy Grail (1975)   211
The Music Lovers (1970)   172
music of moments (Gershwin)   64, 66–7
myth (Barthes)   11, 35, 100, 106, 128, 151, 207, 220, 226

Napoleon Bonaparte   116
National Socialism, *see* Nazism
Nattiez, Jean-Jacques   226–7
Nazism   16, 24, 37, 166, 197–208, 212
Neisser, Ulrich   82, 89, 220
New Mythology, the   28, 32, 36, 64
New Viennese School, the   6, 43
Nietzsche, Friedrich   24, 50, 198, 200–1, 204, 206, 215
  and Wagner   50, 200–1, 204, 206
Novalis (Friedrich von Hardenberg)   21, 24, 27, 29, 37

Paganini, Niccolo   1, 2, 8, 11, 34–5, 105, 107, 117, 119, 177
Panofsky, Erwin   73
Peckham, Morse   7–8, 10–14, 21, 23–30, 93, 159, 171, 216–20, 222
Performance (1970)   165, 167
The Perils of Pauline (1914)   188
phantasmagoria (Adorno)   11, 35, 49, 73, 76

The Phantom of the Opera (1943)   118–19
The Phantom of the Paradise (1974)   170
philosophical hermeneutics   14–15, 23, 25, 36, 38, 80–1, 102, 121, 210, 219
Piaget, Jean   82
The Pianist (2002)   115
Pink Floyd – The Wall (1982)   167
poetic idea (Liszt)   17, 60–4, 66–7, 71, 73–5, 77
Popper, Karl   8, 12–13, 15, 38, 80, 83–6, 98, 102, 216, 218–20
postmodernism   23, 174–5, 208, 215
poststructuralism   3, 15, 215

Quadrophenia (1979)   167, 176

Rachmaninov, Sergei   70
Rancière, Jacques   5–6, 10, 19, 27–30, 32, 35, 37–8, 53, 57, 72, 76–7, 85, 121, 215–22
Rapée, Ernő   46
Raphael (painter)   56, 181
Ricœur, Paul   80–1
Riefenstahl, Leni   212
risky archaeology   12–18, 37, 88, 98, 216, 218
rock music   24, 167, 176, 178, 188
rock-opera   165, 169–70
The Rocky Horror Picture Show (1975)   170
Romanticism
    and audio-visual explanation   1–2, 7, 18, 23, 24, 25, 27–39, 80, 109, 121, 215–22
    and critical rationalism   23, 25, 36, 38, 80, 102, 219
    and critical theory   23, 36, 38, 102, 219
    and fascism   24, 203, 204, 206, 212
    and literature   23–4
    and philosophy   31, 55, 102, 201
    and rock culture   175–9
    and virtuosity   1–2, 7, 11, 34, 104–12, 205–8
Rothapfel, Samuel "Roxy"   6, 45
Rousseau, Jean-Jacques   22
Royal Flash (1975)   211
Russell, Ken   107, 112, 165–213

Saint-Simonism   33, 59, 203
Sand, George   131–2, 141
Sayn-Wittgenstein, Carolyne zu   124, 130, 139, 140, 142, 143, 147–51, 152, 154–62, 192–4, 196, 199, 208
Schelling, F. W. J.   24, 28, 31–2, 36, 56–9, 219
schema   1, 8, 12, 15–18, 77, 79–122, 216–18, 220–2
schema theory, *see* schema
schematic cognition, *see* Schema
schematic types   18, 35, 65, 79–122, 163, 217–18
Schiller, Friedrich   21, 24, 30–1, 33, 57, 58
Schlegel, Friedrich   24, 29, 37–8, 224
Schoenberg, Arnold   22, 43, 67
Schopenhauer, Arthur   200
Schubert, Franz   21, 93
Schumann, Clara   110, 133
Schumann, Robert   69, 93, 94, 97, 101–3, 107, 110, 117, 123, 129, 133–5, 188, 191
    Piano Quintet (1842)   94
    'Träumerei' (1838)   133
    'Widmung' (1840)   134
Second World War, the   22, 174
The Servant (1963)   138
Song of Love (1947)   102, 110–11, 123, 130, 133–5, 177
A Song to Remember (1945)   99, 123, 129–33, 135, 144, 156, 158
Song Without End (1960)   18, 99–100, 123–63, 191, 193
Sontag, Susan   204–5, 212
Stardust (1974)   167
Star Wars (1977)   231
Steiner, Max   6, 45, 48, 71–2, 76, 231
Strauss, Richard   21, 43, 68, 70–2
    Don Juan (1888)   71
    Ein Heldenlieben (1898)   71
    Till Eulenspiels lustige Streiche (1895)   71
    Tod und Verklarung (1889)   71
sublime, the   25, 30–6, 49, 62, 149–50, 161, 181, 212
Syberberg, Hans-Jürgen   204–5

Taking Sides (2001) 207
Tchaikovsky, Pyotr Ilyich 70, 93, 172
Thalberg, Sigismund 111, 124, 140–1, 181
Third Reich, *see* Nazism
Tibbetts, John C. 79, 123, 129, 140, 155
Tiomkin, Dmitri 45, 76
Tommy (1975) 165–7, 169–76, 179–84, 186–7, 189–90, 193–4, 196, 199, 202, 209, 211–13
'Total work of art', *see* Gesamtkunstwerk
Townshend, Pete 176, 178
Traumerei (1944) 129
20,000 Leagues Under the Sea (1954) 119

Victim (1961) 138
Vidor, Charles 137
Violent Playground (1958) 93, 96–8
virtuosity 1–2, 7, 11, 17, 34, 54, 73, 91, 99, 104–4, 116, 117–21, 128, 142–3, 169, 175–9, 181, 190–1, 193
  and fascism 203, 205–7
  and sexuality 112–14, 142–3, 195
  and vision 109–11
Visconti, Luchino 139

Wagner (1983) 115
Wagner, Richard 3, 5–7, 16–17, 24, 28–9, 34, 36, 41–57, 67–8, 71–6, 101, 103–4, 112, 115–16, 119, 123, 145–6, 154, 158, 166, 176, 178, 184–5, 189–92, 195–210, 213, 215, 217–18, 227, 229–33
  Der Ring des Nibelungen (prem. 1876) 198, 200, 232
  Lohengrin (1850) 158, 230
  Rienzi (1842) 145, 146, 154, 189, 191–2, 205
  Tannhäuser (1845) 154
  Tristan und Isolde (1965) 103, 150, 232
Wakeman, Rick 185
Walker, Alan 6, 54, 56, 75, 79, 116, 210
Weber, C. M. F. E. von 109, 230
  Konzertstück (1821) 109
White Zombie (1932) 116–17
the Who 165–9, 173–84, 186, 190, 209, 212, 213
Wordsworth, William 21, 23

CPSIA information can be obtained
at www.ICGtesting.com
Printed in the USA
LVHW051622220722
724181LV00022B/1291